MW01615794

PODHALE
A Companion Guide to the Polish Highlands

PODHALE

A Companion Guide to the Polish Highlands

Jan Gutt-Mostowy

Translated by

Maria Gieysztor De Gorgey

HIPPOCRENE BOOKS
New York

*To the Polish Highlanders in the United States of America.
When you had to leave Podhale, you took with you a great wealth of
spiritual heritage. Make sure that you do not diminish that heritage; as
you become Americans, you, your children, and grandchildren must
not cease to be "gorale."*
—*John Paul II*

Copyright© 1998 by Hippocrene Books.

For information, address:
HIPPOCRENE BOOKS, INC.
171 Madison Avenue
New York, NY 10016

Library of Congress Cataloging-in-Publication Data
Gutt-Mostowy, Jan.
Podhale : a companion guide to the Polish Highlands /
Jan Gutt-Mostowy.
p.   cm.
Includes index.
ISBN 0-7818-0522-8
1. Podhale (Poland)—Guidebooks.   I. Title.
DK4600.P6G88   1997
914.38'60456—dc20   97-42096
                                     CIP

Printed in the United States of America.

Contents

Foreword

Polish Highlanders Alliance is dedicated to preserving and celebrating the incomparably beautiful region of Podhale and the Tatra Mountains, and the world-famous culture and traditions of the highlanders who inhabit it. This heritage of ours, acclaimed as well by His Holiness John Paul II, a frequent visitor to the region, deserves to be presented to the English speaking world. *PODHALE A Companion Guide to the Polish Highlands* by native son Jan Gutt-Mostowy is the first comprehensive guide to the region in English and does a fine job of introducing Podhale to an American audience. I congratulate all concerned and wish them good climbing and hiking in the high Tatras.

—Edward Wilczek, president
Polish Highlanders Alliance of America

Author's Preface

This tourist guide is meant primarily for those Americans whose roots are in the Highlands, the Polish land nestled under the peaks of the Tatras. It is a peculiar place. The high elevation, the harsh climate and rocky terrain all demand from inhabitants an exceptional degree of stubborness and endurance in the struggle for survival. These characteristics, which also apply to the inhabitants of all mountainous regions of the world, were transported by the highlanders across the Atlantic Ocean, when they emigrated to the United States and Canada during the past 120 years. Today the descendants of those first emigrants from the Highlands are already third-generation Americans, but as Rudyard Kipling rightly wrote: "... even the smallest drop of high-lander blood draws a man sooner or later to the parts where he took his beginnings" (*The Second Jungle Book*). It is a must to visit the land of one's ancestors, the land where "one took his beginnings."

The Polish Highlands are lovely, closed off from the south by a chain of the Tatra Mountains (the tallest peak, Gerlach, at 2654 meters [8707feet] above sea level, lies on the Slovak side), and separated in the north from the Cracow region by the Gorce Range which merges into the Pieniny Mountains in the east. In the east and west the Bialka and Czarny Dunajec Rivers encircle the Highlands as they flow through the valleys amid glades and forests. Podhale itself is a south to north range of gentle elevations, covered by forests interspersed with arable fields furrowed by numerous streams. Beautifully situated settlements are built alongside the larger streams and picturesquely strewn over the mountainsides. Beyond the main arteries approaching the Highlands, there is peace, quiet, and an opportunity to get away from the hustle and bustle of the big cities.

The Tatras, the Pieniny and Gorce have wonderful terrain for hiking, trekking for beginners, as well as advanced climbing for those with the proper training. Even on rainy days, when visibility is somewhat limited, the air remains magnificent. The Highland peaks are also great for winter sports. There is an increasing number of trails with lifts for skiers. And the Dunajec River offers numerous possibilities for fishing. Although there are not too many trout, bulltrout, grayling or huchen (salmonoid fish), this only increases the satisfaction of a successful fishing expedition. For any recreation in the Highlands, it is a good idea to wear a windproof jacket and sturdy shoes.

Countrymen upon arrival in the Highlands will first want to find family members and friends, whom they already know or whom they have never met. Travelers who arrive by plane will probably find them waiting at the airport when they land in Warsaw. This is the nice custom here. But those who come by car through Germany and do not know how to find family members would do best to arrange through correspondence to meet them at the station of Automobile Communication in Nowy Targ.

The first days of a family visit are special, since visitors have to make the rounds of all the relatives and old friends, meet a horde of people, eat wherever they go, and drink as well, since this is the habit here. When these days of joyful reunion and indulgent hospitality along with the resultant headaches from consuming too much strong drink are over, and hosts finally return to their work, guests are left alone, or perhaps with the children of relatives. The question then is: What do we do with the time we still have? This guide will help you answer that question, presenting you with many possibilities for spending your time in pleasant and educational ways during your Highlands vacation.

—Jan Gutt-Mostowy

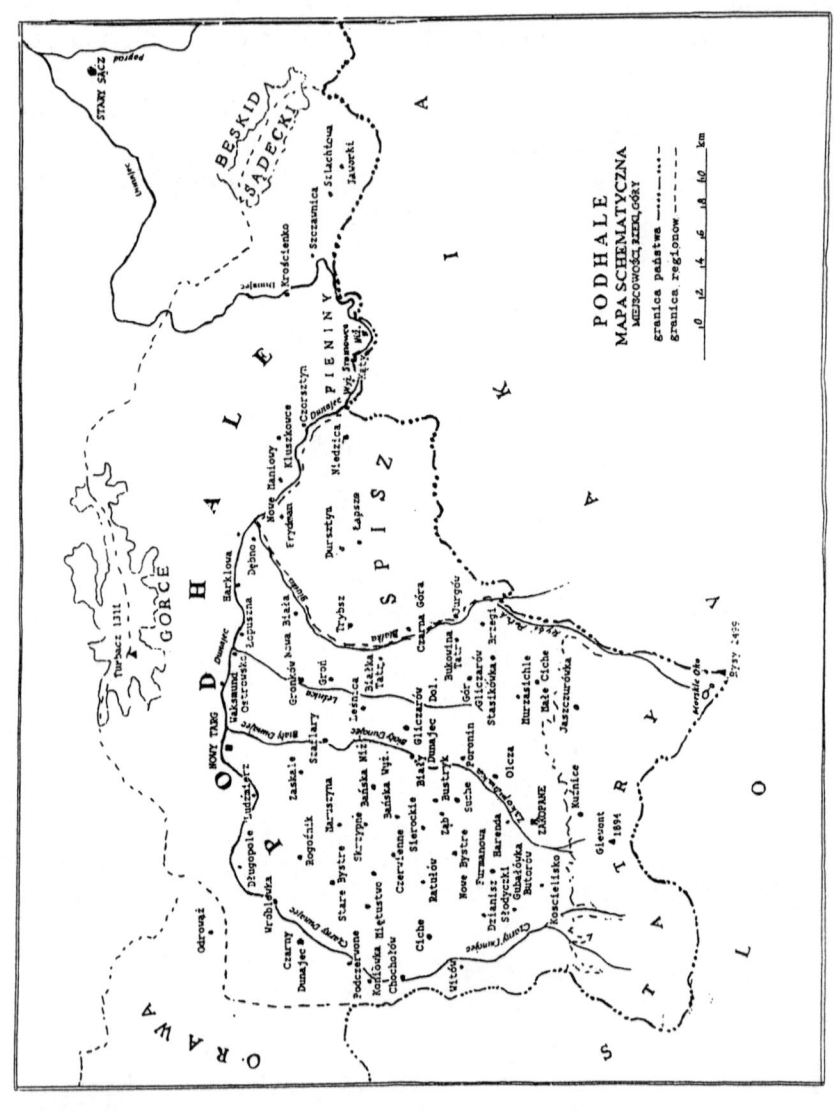

PODHALE
MAPA SCHEMATYCZNA
MIEJSCOWOŚCI, RZEKI, GÓRY
granica państwa ....
granica regionów ———

0 2 4 6 8 10 km

PART ONE

THE HIGHLANDS

CHAPTER I

Introduction to the Polish Highlands

The mountainous region of Podhale lies on the southern border of Poland under the highest elevation of the Sudeten-Carpathian Range. "Pod" means under, and the second part of the name, "hale," refers to the pasture fields and valleys between the upper border of the forest and the rocky mountaintops. The inhabitants of Podhale, the *gorale* (highlanders) consider "hale" the whole mountain massif. "*Going to the hale*" for them means going into the mountains.

The boundaries of the Highlands are also subject to various interpretation. For some, Podhale covers the territory between the Spisz Beskids on the east, the Zywiec Beskids on the west, the Tatras to the south and the Pieniny to the north, and includes these mountains. For others, Podhale means a smaller area, bordered by the Bialka River to the east and Czarny Dunajec River to the west (which, together with Bialy Dunajec lead eastward to the Pieniny under the Gorce massif which forms the northern border of Podhale, while the Tatras form the southern border). This limited area is called Rocky Podhale.

Spisz or Szepes, also a mountainous region, most of which is in Slovakia, lies to the east of the Rocky Podhale beyond the Bialka River. Orawa, partly belonging to Czech Moravia, is west of Rocky Podhale. The inhabitants of Szepes and Orawa are highlanders similar to the Tatra highlanders, differing little in language, customs and attire. The Zywiec Beskids further to the west are inhabited by highlanders "from Zywiec," who have their own peculiar folkle. The highland population of Rocky Podhale is the ethnic group which has been the least exposed to foreign influences over the centuries and thus is most representative of the Highlands. This is due to the geographic isolation of this land, closed off from the south by the Tatra peaks, and bypassed by the main merchant trails leading for centuries from southern Europe to Cracow and onward all the way to the Baltic (the amber trail).

The documented history of Podhale covers a period beginning in the XIII century. In 1234 Cracow Voivode Teodor received a privilege from Prince Henry the Bearded to bring settlers to Podhale. In the same year, Teodor was granted permission by Cracow Bishop Wislaw to build a church in the settlement of Ludzmierz on the Czarny Dunajec River, where the Cistertian monks began their missionary activities in 1239. A document from 1237 has been preserved indicating the existence of the settlement of Rogoznik. The settlement of Dunajec, also called Dlugie Pole (Long Field) and later Nova Civitas (New Town), first appeared in documents in 1327. It stood on the site of an even earlier settlement called Stare Clo (Old Customs Duty—Anticum Theloneum), where Czarny and Bialy Dunajec join into one river. This settlment, together with its town rights, was given the name Nowy Targ. For centuries this was the only town in Podhale and the seat of the office of the royal starost. A few kilometers to the south, on a limestone crag rising above the settlement of

Szaflary, stood a fortified castle, which was one of the border watchtowers. Further south, at the foot of the rocky Tatras, stretched the primeval wilderness interspersed by a myriad of streams. We can only guess what life was like in Podhale during the first centuries. The IV and V centuries were a time in Europe of migration of both large and small groups of people and the beginnings of the future nations of the European continent. Early in the V century, the areas of upper Laba, Odra and the Vistula Rivers, and the southern side of the Carpathians were occupied by tribes of West-German Longobards. At the beginning of the VI century, the Longobards moved south and in about 568 occupied Italy and conquered Rome. Their place on the northern side of the Carpathians was taken by Slavic tribes pushing down from the north, which populated the upper Vistula River basin and thus the valleys of the two Dunajec Rivers. These tribes, called the Vistula people, formed a strong territorial organization in the VIII and IX centuries, but in about 875 succumbed to the stronger Great Moravian State located on the southern side of the Carpathians. The invasion of the Great Moravian State by the Magyar tribes caused its downfall. At the end of the X century the Vistula people were dominated by the Polans, whose Prince Mieszko I was converted to Christianity about 960, laying the groundwork for the future Polish State.

All that remains of the period when the Vistula people ruled the southern part of the country, and thus also Podhale, are a few artifacts discovered by archeologists. But there is indirect proof of the Vistula tribe's penetration into Podhale. In documents from the beginning of the XII century, names of streams of a much earlier and Slavic origin appear, such as: Bialy Dunajec, Czarny Dunajec, Kasina, Kuna, Lesnica, Mszana, Niedzwiedz, Ponica, Poronin, Rogoznik and Slona. Settlements established in later centuries were named for the ancient streams.

Podhale's Old System

From the time of the Piast dynasty, Podhale was one of the crown lands, which means that it was the property of the ruling kings. A *voivode* gave dispositions on the king's behalf, while a starost administered it. The king granted *starostships* to people of noble birth for their services to the country, or sometimes leased them to people who had lent money to the king. The settlers who worked the land, forests and rivers in the the starostship were obliged to make specific contributions, first in goods and later in money. Those who owned the land outright were the exception. The *starost* kept a certain amount for the royal treasury, or else deducted it from the debts of the king.

Every ten years or so, the king sent out inspection commissions to test the honesty of the starosts. The commissions established on the spot the extent of cultivated lands of the villages and settlements, the size of the population and the resulting money due. Inspection documents preserved until today provide important information on the progressive course of the settlement of Podhale. Another source of information are the inventories taken when one starost replaced another.

Settlements and later villages in Podhale were created on the basis of location privileges (authorizations) granted by the starosts or else were formed spontaneously as a result of the individual occupation and settlement of territories suitable for cultivation. The location privilege was a document authorizing the settlement of a village, naming the starost and settlers, the place the village was located and the territory assigned to it, as well as the rights and privileges of the settler who was later referred to as *soltys*. The soltys received a large parcel of land, usually a whole fief (about 17 hectares), thus making that person a de facto suzerain of the inhabitants of the village where he collected funds for the starost. In later times the soltys was obliged to serve in the military, like the noble, and formed the so-called "field infantry."

Settlements which sprang up spontaneously were first recorded together with the closest village, and later, as the number of inhabitants grew, counted during the time of the census as separate villages. A village chief (*wojt*) and two aldermen were elected in such villages. In return for certain privileges, they answered to the starost for the villagers' dues to the crown.

The post of starost in Nowy Targ was not very attractive in the beginning because of the sparse settlement and cultivation of the land, the low or at most middling quality of the soil and the large tracts of land covered with forests. Also, there were spring floods which destroyed cultivated river banks. The people who came to this inhospitable land were those who could not find a place for themselves anywhere else, often fugitives from justice. At the end of the XV century, there were in Podhale, or strictly speaking in its northern part, only seven villages in the vicinity of Nowy Targ: Klikuszowa, Dlugopole, Krauszow, Waksmund, Ludzmierz, Rogoznik and Szaflary. In the beginning of the XVI century, there were already 26, and the 1767 census named one town and 40 villages.

As a result of the first partition of Poland, in 1772 Podhale became one of the cameral lands which were the private property of the Austro-Hungarian emperor in Vienna. The Cameral Office took up residence in Nowy Targ. This state of affairs lasted for 40 years. In 1811 the Austrian government decided to sell the Nowy Targ region at auction, as a property which failed to bring a decent return. For this purpose, the Nowy Targ starostship was divided into four domains: Bialka-Zakopane, Szaflary-Poronin, Witow and Czarny Dunajec, which were sold to private individuals. The year 1848 brought the enfranchisement of peasants in the Austro-Hungarian Empire on the lands where they had worked as tenants.

The Unique Characteristics of Podhale

People were always drawn to the mountains because of their inaccessibility and their shroud of mystery. It was imagined that the mountains or some particular peaks concealed a mythical world and untold treasures. Historians describing the various features of the Polish land had long known of the Tatras towering on its southern borders, dates of reliable written accounts of the Highlands and the Tatras are recent.

A book printed in Warsaw in 1815, authored by Stanislaw Staszic (1755-1826), was entitled *On the Natural Resources of the Carpathian Mountains and Other Mountains and Valleys of Poland*. This was the first scientific appraisal of the mines located in the Tatras, among other places. But mining began much earlier in the Tatras, probably on the southern side, where mining and metallurgy were practiced in Szepes in the XIV century. After 1410, Prokopowicz from Stara Lubowla and Kiszela, and Dempko from Kiptow, were mining in the Tatra valleys. When iron ores were discovered in the area, lack of roads made exploitation unprofitable. In the time of King Aleksander and Zygmunt the Old (1500-1550), mining efforts were undertaken several times on Ornak, without the expected results. But the conviction that riches were concealed in the Tatras lived on, inducing Poland's last king, Stanislaw August, to finance thorough professional mining surveys in the Tatras. Old mine adits were dug up, and new tunnels cut into the mountainsides. At the end of a valley later called Dolina Koscieliska (kosciol-church), because of the little church built there, was erected an installation for the treatment and exploitation of iron and copper ores. But this time again, despite initial success, the costs of exploitation proved to be greater than the profits. By 1768, mining endeavors in Dolina Koscieliska, on Ornak, Pyszna, in Banista and Stara Robota had come to a halt. However, the exploitation of iron ore at mines in Jaworzynka and Magura continued. Iron was smelted in the metallurgic-forging enterprise in Kuznice near Zakopane for more than one hundred years, and then iron ore deposits were exhausted.

Nevertheless, the decades of mining-metallurgic work in the Tatra region caused great damage to the standing timber, which had been one of the most important factors in the microclimate and ecological equilibrium. The healthy qualities of the Podhale climate were discovered relatively late, in the middle of the XIX century. About 1850, a well known Warsaw physician, Dr. Tytus Chalubinski (1820-1889), recognized the village of Zakopane as a place beneficial for people suffering from tuberculosis and other respiratory disorders. He also discovered in the same area a place that could be used for hydrotherapeutic treatment. Chalubinski maintained that Zakopane's climatic and geographic conditions were similar to those of the most renowned Austrian and Swiss health resorts in the foothills of the Alps. The enthusiasm of this well-known physician caused an increasing number of people to seek health and repose in the Tatras, despite the difficulties in getting there (the railway only reached Zakopane in 1911).

As Zakopane developed into a resort, hot mineral springs in its vicinity became popular both for health and recreation. Attempts to utilize the subterranean heat were begun in Podhale after the war. The presence of geothermal waters still provide an opportunity for development of present-day Podhale.

A special attraction of Podhale, particularly of Zakopane and the region of the Tatra Commune, is its tradition—a peculiar "genius loci"—more than a hundred years old. It has long been a meetingplace for writers, artists and scholars from the three sectors of partitioned Poland (the Russian, Prussian and Austrian); outstanding luminaries of the Polish nation have not had a fatherland since 1795. Some who customarily visited the Tatras include: Ignacy Paderewski,

Helena Modrzejewska, Henryk Sienkiewicz, Mieczyslaw Karlowicz, Stefan Zeromski, Jan Kasprowicz, Stanislaw Witkiewicz, Wojciech Kossak and many other famous Poles. Enchanted with the Tatras and the Highlands, as well as the traditions of the natives who have lived on this land for centuries—their speech, folk culture, beliefs—the visitors brought fame to this small corner of Poland, thus contributing to its progress. They discovered remnants of the Old Slavic language in the highlander dialect, and saw a source for national rebirth in the purity of the primitive traditions. Though this glorification, or perhaps even fashion for the highland ways, has diminished, the traditions have remained, as well as the "special something" the lowlanders see in the mountains and seek to find there. And this undoutedly still has merit for Podhale.

CHAPTER II

Settlement of the Highlands

When material evidence of historical events is lacking, people spin legends in the belief that everything can be explained with a little good will and imagination. Thus, with an enthusiasm worthy of a more noble cause, tour guides who lead excursions in the Tatras tell tall tales to the *cepzy* (non-highlander) of a time long ago when a man made his way from Cracow to the Tatras over primeval forests. He was dressed strangely in a striped tunic and trousers. Because those stripes made him look like a caterpillar or some insect, he was called Gasienica (The Caterpillar). This man was the progenitor of the most prolific clan of the Tatra region. What is more, he brought oat seeds in his pocket and planted those seeds in a meadow, thus establishing cultivation in the area. It is said that a settlement at the foot of the Giewont Mountain was named for this planting—Zakopane. A nice fairy tale, but only a fairy tale designed to replace the unknown.

Hypotheses based on widely known and documented

popular history are more useful. For instance, there are the suppositions made about the Vistula region tribes and their rule over the Vistula River Basin and thus over Podhale (The Tatra highlands). If we accept this theory, we can suppose that the Vistula tribes were the first settlers of the Tatra highlands—and those were undisputedly Slavic tribes. They left behind the names of rivers, mountain streams and large Tatra grasslands. Fixing the location of those names, mentioned in the first documents from the beginning of the XIII century, can provide indications of the extent of the settlement in the Tatra highlands region by the Vistula tribes.

But there is an indisputable historical fact that must have had a decisive impact on the fate of the Tatra highlands settlers. And this was the invasion by the Mongols (described as Tartars) from the northern side of the Carpathian Mountains at the beginning of the XIII century. Marching from the east, they got as far as lower Silesia, where they were stopped by the Polish knights in 1241 in the Battle of Legnica. It is hard to say what remained of the highlanders and their property after the invaders rolled over them. Certainly, only a few managed to survive. Did the Tartars reach the heart of the Tatra highlands? It was a terrain particularly difficult to conquer for the units of the Tartar cavalry. And yet ethnographers have found such historical names in Tatra highlands hamlets as "Tartars" and "At the Tartars." Some scholars see Mongol features in the highlanders' faces. If that is so, they could also be the descendants of Tartar prisoners who remained in magnate estates and crown lands.

Two old communication routes north to south and south to north ran near the Tatra highlands. The first, eastern route ran from Spisz to Czorsztyn, reaching Nowy Targ near Gorce (close to the crossing over the Dunajec River and the ancient settlement of Stare Clo). The second route from Twardoszyn on the Orawa ran to Jordanow and there joined the first route going from Nowy Targ through Gorce near the wooden castle of Obidowa. From Jordanow the way led to Myslenice, close to Cracow. Despite the existence of these routes,we should not assume that the settlement of the Tatra highlands occurred from the south, i.e. from Slovakia. Life on the southern side of the Tatras was very much easier, so that people's desires did not drive them to the north. Voivode Teodor received permission from his prince to bring German settlers into the Tatra highlands region but, probably for economic reasons, the settlement of the Saxons in the Tatra region never took place. The Saxons did populate rather large centers on the southern side of the Tatras (Spisz), mainly working in mining and metallurgy.

The earliest settlements in the Tatra highlands are Stare Clo and Nowy Targ (which was resettled in 1327), followed by Krausowa (1327), Ludzmierz (1333—its church one year later) and Szaflary (1338). The dates given in parentheses are documented. Meanwhile, the fact that Cisterian monks lived where the village of Ludzmierz was later established and that these monks were given Rogoznik attests to the existence of earlier settlements in these places, which were already there before the Tartar invasions.

The fertile lands of the Cracow and Sandomierz regions soon were insufficient for the expanding populations, and new terrain was sought for settlement. To the east lay the primeval forests of Red Ruthenia and to the south the wooded valleys of the rivers Raba, Dunajec and Poprad, virtually unexplored at that time. The banks of these rivers were first used for cattle and sheep grazing. Evidence from later times indicates the traditional sequence of the settlement process in the new territories: first, summer grazing for cattle and sheep, and then construction of sheds for protection from the rain, followed by the addition of simple dwellings to these sheds for winter use. Simultaneously, the fields were first used for agricultural purposes. Forests were cut down to enlarge these fields, and more substantial houses were built.

The settlement of the Tatra highlands took place spontaneously from two directions: from the Vistula through the valleys of the Raba and Skawa, whose sources are in Gorce near Nowy Targ, and from the Vistula through the valley of the Dunajec to the estuary of the Poprad near Stary Sacz and close to Pieniny into the Nowy Targ valley. The settlements spread out from Nowy Targ in four directions: the first connected to the Bialka River with the settlements of Bialka, Bukowina and Brzegi; the second based on the Lesnica River, with the settlements of Gronkow, Gron, Lesnica and Gliczarow; the third along the Bialy Dunajec, with settlements Szaflary, Bialy Dunajec, Poronin and Zakopane; and the fourth by the Czarny Dunajec, with the settlements of Ludzmierz, Krauszow, Dlugopole, Wroblowka, Czarny Dunajec, Podcerwone, Chocholow and Witow. Between these centers of population grew later communities on the banks of the lesser streams—tributaries of the rivers mentioned above—which drew on the streams for their names, such as: Rogoznik, Zaskale, Bystre, Maruszyna, Miedzyczerwienne, Skrzypne, Ciche, Ratulow, Dzianisz, Zab and Suche. Together with earlier settlements and villages such as: Obidowa, Pyzowka, Klikuszowa, Pieniazkowice, Morawszczyna, Lasek, Zaluczne, Odrowaz, Dzial, Krauszow, Niwa and Dlugopole, situated in the northern part of the Tatra highlands, the above-mentioned settlements, together with Nowy Targ, were listed and described in the Nowy Targ survey of the crown lands prepared in 1767, the last before the first partition of Poland.

No farming communities, such as in the plains, developed in the Tatra highlands. The hilly terrain and the relative shortage of level ground needed for extensive farming resulted in few large farms in the rocky Tatra highlands. There were actually only two: one in Szaflary and the other in Ustupie between Poronin and Zakopane. The Ustupie farm failed to survive for economic reasons and in 1765 was parcelled out to the peasants.

The settlement of the Tatra highlands brought with it, albeit slowly, the Catholic Church and religious architecture. After the first churches in Ludzmierz and Nowy Targ, built in the XIII century (naturally of wood), a chapel in Szaflary was built around 1350 as an outreach of the Nowy Targ church. In the year 1606 the Czarny Dunajec parish was designated, the Chocholow parish nearly one hundred years later, the Poronin parish in 1833 and Zakopanein 1848. According to church records, the residents of the Tatra highlands then numbered some 20,000.

PART TWO

THE HIGHLANDERS

*L*ife in the mountains has a special flavor because of its unique geographic and climatic conditions. This "difference" becomes apparent to the visitor, especially during his first encounter with the mountains—in some it elicits curiosity, in some pity for the natives, and in others utter delight. The end of the XIX century was an era of particular affection of the Polish intelligentsia for the Polish Tatras and the highlands. "How beautiful the mountains are, how lucky the highlanders are"—ran a song popular at that time. Many faulty judgments were formed in this period distorting highlander reality in the eyes of the inhabitants of the lowlands. But what was this reality in the middle of the XIX century when Tytus Chalubinski, and before him Stanislaw Staszic, Ludwik Zajszner and Seweryn Goszczynski published their first accounts of the land at the foot of the Tatras?

First of all, it was not a uniform reality. There are sizable differences in altitude within an area of less than 30 kilometers—the Gorce range and the foothills of the Tatras to the south—which greatly affect the economy of the region. For instance, in the Nowy Targ area, rye is cultivated, while near Zakopane this would be so risky that it is not even attempted. Also, the growing season, from the melting of the previous year's snow to the first snowfall of the new year, varies between Bukowina or Witow, and is longer in the vicinity of Ludzmierz or Waksmund. In view of the unification of the economy, these differences do not matter today, but 150 or 200 years ago they were immensely important to the inhabitants of the highlands.

During the early period of the settlement of the highlands, the highlander lived on what he produced on his land. There was not much to go around, and it was not rare to experience hunger before the new harvest. There was a high degree of infant mortality, and no one was troubled by the verse: "The Lord giveth, and the Lord taketh away, glory be to His name"—such was the highlanders' philosophy for long decades. The strongest survived. They learned to make do in harsh conditions, learned to cope. This produced the type of highlander admired by visitors to the Tatras.

The highlanders tend to be tall, slender, well-formed and display their good figures in clinging cloth trousers. They are also very agile, used to working hard with their hands under difficult conditions. According to highlanders of the old school, some of the hardest work was with the scythe, cutting heavy grasses, and the pickaxe, clearing tree stumps and large rocks from the fields. The most strenuous task of all was sawing the massive tree trunks lengthwise to provide beams for their houses and sheds. But of their hard manual labor, the highlander said optimistically: "It is nothing at all when you get used to it."

The highlanders were very well disposed toward visitors. The "gents" made it posible for them to earn extra cash. But they were in constant revolt against all authority that limited their freedom. The government official who demanded taxes and services in various forms, the landowner who curtailed their God-given right to the fruits of the field and woods, forest rangers who watched over game in the wooded areas and mountains—they were all the natural enemies of the highlanders.

The highlanders had a simple outlook and understanding of things. For instance, since they never saw the visiting guests working, they assumed that the "gents" never worked and had lots of money, so they charged as much as possible for rooms and meals, and when they served as guides. Consequently, many visitors spoke of the highlanders' greed and dishonesty when they told others about their stays in the Tatra highlands. But this is a great over-simplification.

The brigandage born in the shadow of the Tatras was not caused by a desire to get money at any cost. The area worked by the highland robbers was mostly the richer southern highland villages, as well as the mansions, castles and inns in Slovakia. Highland robbery was less extensive on the Polish side of the Tatras. The highlanders managed to justify this, claiming that "the highland robber equalizes the world—taking from the rich and giving to the poor." And although there were not many who profited from the robbers' largesse, the legend persisted and remains to this day.

Women in the highlands were of average height, shorter than the men, well turned out, their looks bursting with physical strength. The song went: "I like those girls with a nice wide back ..." The role of the woman in a highlander family was primarily to run the house. A proverb proclaimed: "The gal holds up three corners of the cottage,and the fellow only one." She also brought up and nurtured the children, took care of the household and of her husband. Family relations were characterized by practicality. Women gave birth every two years on the average, so despite the relatively high mortality rate, families consisting of ten or more children were not uncommon. It was generally accepted that when the oldest child was three years old, it would begin to take care of its younger siblings, and this care passed down the line from the older to the younger. This was a great help to the mother, who bore the burden of the whole household on her shoulders. Very young children also carried out many household chores. It began with minding the geese in the courtyard, carrying firewood, with an "advancement" to rounding up the cows; a few years later, at 10 or 12, a boy led the horse while his father plowed. From a very early age, girls were trained in stripping feathers, working linen and wool, and pitching in with the tending of the flocks as well. Thus the children in the highlands represented a sizable—and free—work force, since "the highlander did not count his own work or his own food," as he did not spend cash for it.

This highlander practicality condoned a peculiar custom different from what was generally accepted. It was not considered sinful for a suitor to "try out the goods" before marriage. The reason for this "test" was to see whether the girl would be able to bear children, since a barren woman was held to be a cripple and a burden. The parents of a girl of marriageable age allowed her to sleep in a separate (white) room or, during the summer, on the hay in the barn, so that she could let her beloved in at night. If the result of this "trial" was a baby and the marriage did not take place for one reason or another, the "single girl with a baby" did not cease to be attractive. Just the opposite, she could enter into marriage with a dowry in the form of her own free work force. The clergy naturally tried to discourage this custom with varying degrees of success. One form of discrimination the priests applied to illegitimate children was to give them names not popular among the highlanders.

When tourists began to visit the Tatras, the highlanders were their natural guides over the mountain trails and peaks. The visitors were impressed with their courage, lack of fear of heights, great sense of direction and the solicitude they lavished on their tourists. The highlanders' ingenuity allowed them to get out of the most difficult situations, often connected with the rapidly changing weather in the mountains. During these treks over the mountains the highlanders—born story-tellers—amused guests with tales in which native wisdom and the experience of generations blended with highlander humor. The best known Tatra story-tellers found their place in anthologies of folk literature. When the tourists were accompanied by a larger group of highlanders, there were sure to be musicians among them, and then sounds of highlander singing and music could be heard from the overnight camps, while young highlanders entertained the tourists with their dances.

The guests were impressed with the fact that almost everything needed for a highlander's life was produced either by him or by the common work of the village. Almost every highlander was skilled in carpentry and many could produce wonderful items for everyday use. They also knew how to cut down trees in the forest and to transport them from the mountains—sometimes trees of imposing size. The women made everything their families needed to clothe themselves out of linen and wool.

The primitive highlander dwelling, in which one living space was shared by people and livestock, became a rarity as time went on, but did not disappear altogether. Thus the stories spun about the standard of living in the Tatra highlands of the XVII and XVIII centuries vary greatly. Some writers cited examples of this primitive state as proof of the misery of the highlanders, while others saw the life of these people as superior to life in other regions. The number of two-room dwellings with a vestibule and a main room, with free-standing farm buildings, continued to grow in the Tatras. As the years went by, the sight of cottages without a chimney, where smoke escaped through the attic and the roof, began to disappear from the landscape.

It was a highlands custom to "ennoble" a man when he built a house for himself and later one for his children. Thus the building of houses for future generations was the goal of the hard work many families did on their own land or outside the home, even sometimes beyond the Tatra highlands (from the end of the XIX century in America). These aspirations sometimes drew the highlanders into risky enterprises, not always quite within the law.

In olden times there was a strong tribal solidarity among highlanders with regard to the outside world. One highlander could always speak freely with another about his business dealings, with certainty that the authorities—such as they were—would never learn of them. It was an internal matter of the community.

When people from the plains began to move to the Tatra highlands, bringing their capital and their different customs, there evolved a slow but sure erosion of the "old ways." Times changed, and the highlanders changed with them. Not physically; living conditions improved, medical care became more available, and highlander youth turned en masse to secondary and higher education, and highlanders learned that hard and determined work by the whole family and years of self-denial and toil were not the only way to achieve one's goal. The highlanders' mentality came to accept that it was not important how someone made his money; the important thing was that he made it. One old highlander principle remains unchanged: "You only count for something after you build your house." And this is undoubtedly a positive trait in today's highlanders.

CHAPTER III

Early Agriculture

Those who settled on the clearings (*polany*) in the primeval forests on the banks of the Vistula were called *Polanie,* and the first settlers in the Tatra highlands were referred to as *Polaniorze.* The clearings in the forests, as well as areas adjacent to streams, were places where men put down their roots. Because the streams, which often changed course during the springtime floods, created a potential danger to construction, the first huts and cabins were not built right on the rivers.

On a level stretch of land cleared of rocks, the primitive settler cultivated the ground with a hoe and planted seeds. In the highlands, this was usually oats and barley. Potatoes appeared in the highlands only at the end of the XVII century. If the year was good, that is if there was an early spring and a long, warm summer, the highlander could expect three seeds from every one sown. Then one third of the harvest remained for the new sowing, and two thirds were expected to feed the family until the next harvest. When it was a bad year, "a brother could not give birth to a brother," and destitution followed. The introduction of potatoes eased the situation somewhat, since in lean years potatoes (in highlander language *grule* or *rzepa*) could save the situation.

To increase the area of arable land, the forests were cut down. This provided wood for building and for heating, while the ashes from the branches served to enrich the soil in the first year. A larger plot of land called for other farming techniques; the hoe was not sufficient. Wooden ploughs with metal fittings pulled by oxen were needed.

If they were accessible, clearings deep in the woods were used to store hay for the livestock for the winter months. Natural grazing terrains for the summer were areas on the banks of the streams. As the population grew and the settlements became more crowded, the custom of row housing continued in the highlands. In later years, beginning with the XV century, legal permission was necessary to settle on a piece of land. Homesteaders received a strip of land 30 to 50 hectares in size, mostly tree-covered, which they cleared for fields, grazing pastures and meadows.

One of the dilemmas of early highland farming was finding a way to maintain proper proportions between land cultivation and animal husbandry (especially of sheep). Although less risky and more profitable, stock farming required pasture land and fields for keeping hay. And this limited the cultivation of oats, barley and potatoes. Thus terrain in higher elevations were increasingly utilized. These were not fit for settlement because of their severe climatic conditions, but could be used for pasture. The Valachians, a sheep-herding tribe who, at the time of the Turkish invasions, retreated to the territory of present-day Romania, appeared in the Tatra highlands in the XV century. In 1416 King Wladyslaw Jagiello allowed the leader of this tribe to settle west of Nowy Targ in the region of present-day Waksmund. Since the time of the Valachians, the era of shepherding blossomed, along with the utilization of the riches of the Tatra mountain pastures. Tending of flocks became the second component of the primitive highland economy.

The third element of this economy was gathering. The forest provided various items useful to man, at first in unlimited quantities. Undergrowth (mushrooms, berries, edible plants) and game played an important role in keeping the early settler alive in the difficult conditions he found upon his arrival. Since the highlanders did not invest anything in this branch of their economy, and the area of the forests progressively decreased, gathering gradually began to lose its earlier importance.

Since the highland valleys are post-glacial in nature, the terrain is naturally rocky. For long centuries of farming in the Tatra highlands, man had to remove rocks from the ground, where they seemed to sprout up after each winter's frotst. These stones were piled up at the boundary edges; there were so many added to the heaps every year that stone ramparts seemed to rise up between the fields. They became part of the highland landscape, but were never used for fencing as they are in some other parts of Europe. After World War II, when there was an increased need for stones for road building, what had been gathered for centuries disappeared within a dozen years.

After the land in the valleys and lesser elevations had been cultivated for several generations, highlanders began clearing of the mountainsides. This disturbed the natural soil conditions, and called for special measures. Where it was feasible, terraces were cut into the mountainsides, or rather half-terraces designed to slow the flow of water from the slopes and thus prevent soil erosion.

The highlanders early on discovered that the spreading of animal manure helped to increase yields. They also learned to improve soil structure by adding moss and forest plants mixed with natural manure. However, the stripping of the bedding or forest litter gathered in the fall impoverished forest undergrowth. The cultivation of fields high up the mountainsides made it necessary to bring fertilizer there. This was a particularly difficult endeavor, since it had to be done in the wintertime, as it was even more difficult to bring heavy loads up in the summer.

The period of primitive farming ended in the Tatra highlands with the introduction of modern farm implements, especially steel plows and harrows, along with artificial fertilizers, after World War I. Following World War II, mechanization came to the Tatra highlands, first on a small scale, when motorcycle engines were used to run grass-cutters; later old trucks were converted into small tractors in so-called "homespun industries," where the highlanders' ingenuity and manual talents were fully utilized.

CHAPTER IV

Highland Housing

The natural conditions of the Tatra highlands determined the form of housing in this region. In the beginning, all the buildings were wooden, since the primeval forests supplied trees in unlimited quantities. Stone was also available, although it was not much used in construction. The traditional belief persisted that wooden structures were warmer and more healthy for man.

The harsh mountain climate, where the temperature could plunge to 20C below in winter, imposed special thermal specifications for buildings, and the heavy rain and snowfall dictated the shape of the pitched roofs. Intense southern winds from the mountains in the spring and summer made construction capable of withstanding hurricane forces necessary. In time of strong winds, the highlander houses were said to "walk," that is sway as if on springs, bending to the wind and then coming back to their original positions.

The first houses in the highlands were located strictly on the banks of the streams. Since the river banks were free of trees, the roads ran alongside these rivers, with bridges or fording places for crossings. The houses were built along this only communication route. The closeness of the water—essential for both home and farm—was a vital factor in determining the location of the houses but, on the other hand, there existed great danger of flood both for the houses and cultivated fields. Later, when woods were cleared to extend the area of cultivated land, individual houses were situated further from the rivers and even on mountain ridges stripped of trees by the wind. Water for household use came from cisterns filled by barrels from the streams and brooks in the winter.

During the fall and winter the prevailing winds and blizzards blew from the north and west. That is why it is a characteristic of highland architecture to place windows facing the south. There was only one opening on the north side—the entrance door. The courtyard on the north side could be viewed through a peep hole—a small slit between the beams which was stuffed up for warmth during the cold months. The course of the road had no effect on the placement of the houses. The windows only faced the road when it ran on the southern side of the house.

The original highland homes, or rather cottages, were composed of one room, something in the nature of a shepherd's shack adapted for permanent living. During the winter, people stayed in this one space together with all their livestock, while from spring to fall the livestock was kept under a *pajta* (roofing attached to the house or the farm enclosure). Sometimes this pajta was walled in, and thus a barn appeared next to the house. But even so, young sheep and calves were taken into the living quarters during periods of great cold.

The next phase in the development of highland housing involved separating the living quarters from the stable by a barn—*bojsko*—(threshing floor in a barn). It had a roof, a dirt floor and large gates on either side. This made it possible to drive through the bojsko to unload the feed into the attic. The convenience of this form of building was that the whole farm was under one roof. Further experience dictated the advisability of situating farm buildings at a straight angle to the residence to protect it from the western winds which blew in the winter. The area between the bojsko and the living quarters was usually roofed to keep the convenience of one roof for the whole farm. This area was put to use as a coach-house and wood shed. The living quarters were often enlarged by another room and a vestibule that led to the front door. Extra rooms were added on the side or rear of the house to hold home supplies.

Initially, living quarters and farm buildings were constructed from newly cut logs, cut to size and peeled of their bark. Usually the trees that were the most prolific in the region were used, a variety of conifers officially referred to as spruce. The highlanders called them *smreki*. Logs, averaging 20 centimeters in diameter, were connected in the corners with a dovetail to create the walls. Openings were left for the doors and windows. Later, trees with a larger circumference were used, split with the aid of a wedge. Two *lupawice* (tree trunks split down the middle) were created from one log. They were further roughed down with axes, forming the basic element, the so-called *plaza* (beam for the walls of the house). Joining the plazas was complicated, often employing intricate "locks." The plazas were connected snugly in the corners and sealed with forest moss (later wooden wool). As in other matters, actual fashion played a role here. There existed a peculiar kind of rivalization in the matter of the width of the plazas. It sometimes happened that only four plazas fit on a wall more than two meters high. This attested to how successful the farmer was, since he was able to transport trees of about one meter's circumference. Such trees were split or cut with hand saws. Sawmills came later.

House construction was started with the placing of cornerstones, which delineated the size of the building. Between these stones were laid smaller ones set in boggy soil covered with sod. The interior area was filled with small stones mixed with river sand. The first logs were laid on the corner stones and anchored with dovetails. They were inclined slightly to the center. More logs or plazas were piled on top of them, joining at the corners to form the walls. The window and door openings were left to be completed later, and only the tops of the openings were fitted with traverse beams referred to as *lezuch*. On the highest logs rested the *sostrebiks* (longitudinal ceiling beams), to which ceiling planks were later attached. In the beginning there were only dirt floors in the dwellings; later logs were laid to cover the stones and floor boards were placed on top of them. Until sawmills made their appearance, the boards were split from logs or sawed by hand.

Roof construction consisted of inter-connected poles secured in notches in the walls. The roof framework, known as *krokwie* was covered with transverse slats overlapping for a tight seal, or later wooden shingles. The first row of boards were nailed from the top of the roof to the bottom, and the next row was attached from bottom to top.

Small windows were characteristic of highland architecture; old barns had no windows at all. There were two reasons for this: to keep as much warmth as possible inside the dwelling and to discourage crime. Animal membranes were first used to close in a window. Even after glass panes were introduced, the glazier was referred to as the "membrane installer." Early highland windows had frames with intersecting cross-bars.

When a house had two rooms and an indoor vestibule, the life of the whole family was concentrated in one of these rooms. The second room served as a kind of day room, where bedding, personal belongings and items only used "on holidays" were kept. Since the Dutch stove stood in the main room and there were no chimneys in the house, smoke escaped to the attic through an opening in the ceiling; with time the day room grew black from smoke. And this is how it was referred to, as "the black room," while the other room was called "the white room." The highlanders were charcteristically skillful in preventing fires in their houses. Despite the lack of chimneys, destructive fires were a rarity. An old-time cooking stove was called *bieganiec*. It had a twisted smoke pipe, so that the smoke escaping toward the ceiling did not contain any sparks. The soot blackened not only the top of the walls and the ceiling, but also the rafters and planks of the roof. This process served as a peculiar conservation agent for the roofing material. After twenty years, the roof shingles or boards were removed and turned with the black surface facing outward, to continue serving for more years to come.

In the white room, the ceiling logs were reinforced by a *sosreb* (carved ceiling beam) measuring about 30 centimeters wide and 15 centimeters thick, which extended into the corner logs. The central element of the carving was the star (rosette), with ornamental flowers going off to the side. The year the house was built was cut into one side of the sosreb and into the other a prayerful maxim and the first and last name of the owner of the house. The edges of the log were beveled, with decorative bands at the ends.

This was not the only ornamental element of the highland home, since the frames of the entrance door were often decorated with carvings and circles. The protruding logs holding up the slope of the roof were carved in fanciful ways, and the top of the roof was adorned with stylized crowns called "kings." The upper attic walls were decorated with "the sun": a semi-circle on the bottom with extending slats in the shape of sun beams.

A ledge was attached a half meter from the ceiling of the white room; it was a sort of shelf with a carved edging on which religious pictures were kept, usually painted on glass. Another carved shelf held decorative bowls and other utensils.

The "discovery" of Zakopane by Tytus Chalubinski and the resulting influx of tourists to the Tatras forced highland house construction to adjust to the needs of the guests. First, the white rooms were rented out, and chimneys were added to improve conditions. Then houses were erected specifically for tourists. Initially, additional rooms were built in large attics, followed by two-story buildings. These houses called for the right construction methods, the proper foundations. Unique drainage conditions in the Tatras made it necessary to raise the houses up on high foundations, which were actually basements used for household needs. In the 1930's there was a proliferation of boarding houses, multi-room structures designed for seasonal guests. Attempts to maintain a uniform highland style in housing failed; utilitarian considerations prevailed over tradition. The end of the war brought an era of block building for communal needs, analogous in form to building in Warsaw, Cracow and other cities. With the shortage of wood from the highland forests, family housing also changed to brick and pre-fabricated materials. What has remained from the highland style are the steep roofs and basements constucted from granite river rocks.

CHAPTER V

Highland Dress

Life in a closed society imposed on the highlanders the need for self-sufficiency in the broad sense of the word. The first tourists to visit the highlands in the XIX century were constantly amazed by the skills of the highlanders, who were able to make "everything"—from the smallest household item to the construction of a whole house. The wrong conclusions were drawn from this about the "exceptional" abilities of the highlanders—in reality it was a matter of tradition passed on from generation to generation and a folk wisdom which enabled people to survive in the extremely harsh conditions.

The highlander also had to take care of his clothes and adapt them to the climatic conditions. From the raw material for clothing to its preparation, everything was processed and made at home. At most, weaving and felting were sometimes done by village workshops. For many years, highlander dress remained the same. Sporadic contact with the Slovak region of Hungary in quests for food did not play a major role. Fairs in Nowy Targ, which attracted visitors from Poprad and the area beyond Gorce, and in Czarny Dunajec, which the Slovaks often attended, were more influential in the addition of novelties into highland garb.

The basic raw materials the highlanders produced and from which they then sewed their clothes were sheep's wool and linen. Home-processed cow hides were also used for shoes and belts and sheepskin coats were popular.

Initially, the number of sheep tended was determined by the amount of land the farmer could reclaim from the forest; flocks increased when he learned to utilize the mountain-sides for pasture. The raw wool was cleaned and combed to equalize the strands, then the women spun the wool on a spinning-wheel. Wound on a warping mill, the wool was washed, dried, and rewound for further use, either making fabric which after felting became a heavy cloth, or yarn for sweaters, knee-socks, gloves, short socks and hats. Cloth weaving was done by people who had looms, although these looms were primitive, since they were homemade.

Felting, called *folowanie* in highlander jargon, was done on a *folus*, a contraption in which wooden hammers activated by a water wheel pounded the cloth while it was soaked with water. This caused a natural adhesion of individual wool fibers into a dense felt fabric. The piece of cloth achieved in this manner was then treated further. Black and white fabric was produced from the natural color of the wool. Also, a grey fabric was created by mixing black and white fibers. Another woven product was a highland blanket called *derka*. In the weaving, the wefts and warp were of black and white wool, which resulted in a black and white check. Blanket fabric was woven closely, so that it did not need folowanie. Special patterns were used to weave thick one-fingered gloves out of black and white woolen yarn. These were used for work in the woods, where a precise grip with the fingers was not necessary.

Clothing fabric was handled by tailors. For long centuries this was a strictly male activity, since the heavy fabric, sewn by hand with linen thread, called for strong fingers. The tailors made trousers (called *portki*) from the white cloth, as well as *cuchas*, an embroidered highlander overcoat, a wide jacket extending below the hips. The cuchas, made out of black fabric, were long knee-length garments, similar to present-day overcoats. The cut of these garments was traditional and basically never changed. It was only in the XIX century that the shape of the lower part of the trousers began to change; it was lowered so that the bottom of the trousers covered the foot. Previously, they had been cut off straight at the ankles. But the real "revolution" occurred in the decoration of highland garb. For centuries highland clothing bore no decoration; at most the tailor sewed in an edging here and there or added a colorful trim. Then, at the end of the XVIII and in the XIX century, the fashion of decoration first became popular among young highlanders. This bore a connection with the acquired wool dyeing skills and with growing Hungarian influence. Highlanders returning home from the Austro-Hungarian army brought their old uniforms with them. Those who had been attached to units of the Hungarian *honveds* wore tight red (sometimes green) trousers and jackets embroidered with various designs. Hungarian decorations called *parzenica*, embroidered on the hips and in the front, were the first to find their way onto highlander trousers. The name probably comes from the Hungarian word *paros*, which means "even." At first these designs on highlander trousers were very modest, since older highlanders strongly objected to this new fashion, but over the years the decorations evolved to their present form. Besides the parzenica decorations, fancy edgings were also made for the *przypory*, vertical openings in the front of the pants and by the pockets. Ribbon was sewn along the seams of the trousers, at first one and then several, in the form of a sash. Originally completely plain, the white cuchas went through several phases of colorful decoration. Today these are beautiful embroidered flowers, leaves, along with wide collar and sleeve edgings. The black cuchas, worn by older highlanders, have remained nearly unchanged. Their only decorations are red insets at the collar and sleeve.

The decorated trousers and overcoats described above were the highlanders' "Sunday wear." For every day, the highlanders wore the same clothes, but without decorations; these plain clothes were enhanced by cloth patches added in places worn by hard work. It was characteristic for the highlander to patch his clothes himself, not trusting his wife to do it for him. The highland clothing, made of pure wool, or rather pure felt, was especially useful in the mountain weather conditions. In winter it protected his body from the loss of heat and in summer it kept the heat from his body.

The highlanders sewed vests and sheepskin coats from tanned sheepskins. The remain sleeveless. Their original cut has not changed much, but decorations have been added to them as well. Borders made of Persian lamb skin (not native to the highlands) were introduced, and festive sheepskins began to sprout colorful embroidery and applique work.

The highlander's wife sewed her husband's underwear out of linen produced on the farm. The old-time shirts were short, just to the waist, and were not tucked into the trousers. The shirt had no buttons, and was closed on top by a brass clasp.

The highlander dressed his feet in so-called *kierpce*, sewed from one piece of leather, held up by woolen or leather straps wound around the calf. His feet were wrapped in linen cloth instead of socks.

The crowning glory of this outfit was the hat: in winter a fur cap. Felt hats were produced by craftsmen, so they had to be bought at the open-air market. And this hat was also embellished, at first simple decorations, in the form of small animal bones strung on a thread, and later with sea shells sewn to a red leather band brought by merchants from the south. In later times the shells were replaced by porcelain imitations, but this hat adornment is still called "bones" by the highlanders. Bachelors wore an eagle feather in their hats, or a wood grouse feather with bird down at the base. Customarily, as the bride "lost her garland" during the wedding, the groom lost his right to wear a feather.

A belt, *ciupaga* (highland stick with hatchet) and clasps completed the highland outfit. There were two kinds of belts, some wide, covering the whole abdomen like an armor, and others more narrow, covering only the top of the trousers. Both the wide belts, *bacowskie*, and the more narrow ones called *juhaski* were adorned with buckles, buttons and decorative elements embossed in the leather. Highland clasps, usually brass, were of various forms and uses: those for shirts in the form of parzenica with decorative chains, clasps for the cucha and finally small buckles for the *kierpce* shoes. The ciupaga could come in handy during a journey or mountain climb, useful in cutting branches for the fire or as a side-arm during a fight.

While wool was the basic raw material for the highlanders' clothing, linen was used for their women. It was commonly cultivated at home in the highlands, since commercial cotton fabrics only began to appear in highland women's clothing some 150 years ago. After a laborious process of hand treatment, three kinds of cloth were produced: the thinnest, called *omesne*, the medium weight known as *paciesne*, and the heaviest, referred to as *zgrzebne*. Underwear for women and children, as well as kerchiefs, were made of the omesne fabric. The paciesne cloth was for men's underwear, sheets, clothing for small children, women's skirts, blouses and aprons, as well as outercoverings for women called *oktusy*, which were thrown over the shoulders. Before sewing, the linen set aside for clothing was dyed. The thickest zgrzebne linen was used for sacks and canvas tarpaulins for carrying heavy loads, as well as to cover mattresses.

The highlander woman's every-day outfit consisted of a shirt, skirt, blouse and sometimes an apron. At first the skirts were long; later fashion shortened them, at the same time introducing short linen drawers for women. In earlier times, the highland women did not know or need this garment, since their long skirts, sometimes two, kept them warm, protecting their legs from the cold. The women wore linen throws over their shoulders and linen (later cotton) kerchiefs over their heads. From spring to late summer, the women of the highlands walked barefoot; when they had to dress up, they wore the same kierpce as the men. In winter woolen footwear was usually used; it was either short, without shoe tops, called *ponczochy* (stockings) or longer, reaching the knee, called *kapce*.

Fashion which came to the highlands from Cracow brought with it corsets, which were a sort of sleeveless waistcoat, decorated with embroidery, sequins and beads. The corset was tied together with a red ribbon. Also from the women of Cracow (or perhaps the Slovak region of Hungary) the highland women adopted mid-calf shoes with tops. Women's shirts had to be adapted to the waistcoats with rich embroidery on the sleeves and collar in special patterns. Like the men, highland women wear sheepskin coats and sleeveless jackets. Those who can afford it own genuine red coral beads. It is interesting to note that the highland women have not adopted the fashion from Cracow of wearing colored glass beads. Genuine coral is a traditional way to invest loose cash.

Along with the rest of highland folklore, highland dress has undergone an evolution toward modern uniformity. Economic structures have influenced this matter. Highland dress is expensive, and not everyone can afford it. Roughly speaking, a man's highland outfit costs 2000 (US $725) *zlotys* today, while he can buy a suit of decent practical clothes for about one-fourth of the price.

The traditions of highland garb maintained by regional associations which pay part of the cost of costumes for their members. The traditional is also nurtured by people who have not severed their ties with old highland roots. These costumes have special meanings for highlanders abroad.

Although they wear them only on "special occasions," the costumes attest to the emigrant's attachment to the land of his fathers, to the highlands which are his heritage.

CHAPTER VI

Highland Cookery

For early settlers in the Highland glades, basic staples of the diet were the harvest of a primitive tillage of the soil, products of animal husbandry and whatever was yielded by the forest and rivers. Trade with the lowlands was at first sporadic, and thus was not very meaningful in the highland economy. (Similarities to the situation of Scottish highlanders or American pioneers comes to mind here.) Often, the highlanders traveled to the other side of the Tatras, to *Uhra*, as they called it (which was actually Slovakia, then part of Hungary), where it was easier to earn money and where products necessary for every household were available.

Climate and soil conditions in the Rocky Highlands made the cultivation of wheat impossible, while rye succeeded near Nowy Targ, some 30 kilometers from the Tatras. The highlanders could grow oats or barley, which they called *jarzec*, since they only used the springtime variety of this grain. Of the root crops, potatoes enjoyed the greatest popularity—in slang they were called *grule* or *rzepa*, along with a variety of white pasturable turnip known as *karpiele*.

If the harvest was good, potatoes were consumed three times a day, but during a year of poor crops, potatoes were a rarity in many families. The potatoes were served with an *omasta*, which was vegetable or animal fat (lard, bacon) or sour milk. Potatoes were also an important ingredient of other dishes, such as *polywka* (broth), borsch, *kwasnica* (cabbage soup), and *zur* (sour soup). The highlanders also ate potatoes with cooked or raw sour cabbage, which constituted their only vegetable save for the greens they gathered in the fields and forests for a so-called *warmuz* (pre-harvest dish of the poor).

Made from ground oats and barley, flour was used for *kluska* (dumpling) or *bryjka* (mash), as an accompaniment to borsch and zur, as well as for highland "bread" which were round loaves called *moskole*. The *kluska* was made by pouring flour into salted boiling water until the mixture thickened. The kluska was eaten like potatoes, with fat or milk. A thin, runny kluska called *bryjka* was fed to children with sweet milk. Another way to prepare bryjka, handed down by tradition, nourished hunters who went out into the mountains for several days. The highlander took with him a bit of flour in a bag along with a little salt. Where he was to take his meal, at the side of a brook, he put the amount of water he needed into his hat and added the flour and salt to it. Taking a hot stone out of his fire, he dropped it in the water in his hat. The heat of the stone was enough to make the bryjka drinkable. It should be mentioned here that highland hats were waterproof.

Since there was no rye, the moskole replaced bread. The origin of this undoubtedly very old word is not known, but it is sure that it has nothing to do with Moskale (the residents of Moscow). The moskole were made of flour, water and salt. The kneaded dough was formed into round loaves which were baked on coals, heated stones and later on the ranges of modern stoves. Since there was no leavening agent in moskole, especially the ones made from barley, they were hard, but on the other hand durable.

Karpiele—a kind of turnip—is actually a fodder plant

meant for the feeding of livestock, but it is tasty enough to be eaten raw or baked on a fire, which children often did. Sliced karpiele was also added to *wodzianka* (panada) soup or to warmuz. Thus the highlanders were often faced with a dilemma expressed by a father's cry: "Children, leave these karpiele alone, what am I going to give to the cows!?"

As has already been mentioned, the only vegetable in the highland kitchen was sauerkraut. A barrel of it was prepared in every household for the winter. During lean years, its lack was sorely felt, since besides greens, it was almost the only source of vitamin C available. Another source of this vitamin essential for life was *mojki*, young buds of a spruce (in highlander language *smrek*) gathered from the trees in spring.

Animal husbandry, especialy cows, sheep and domestic fowl provided the highland table with essential protein. However, when early forms of barter appeared, animal products became the easiest to sell and thus grew to be the highlanders' most popular commodity. Even the poorest man had to buy salt, matches, a bit of flour or omasta once in a while when his own supplies ran out. Places for exchanging goods were the outdoor markets, one in Nowy Targ and the other in Czarny Dunajec. There were also Sunday church fairs, as well as taverns, either leased or built, which were designed to bring an income for the landlords. These often served as the first village shops. The lessees of these taverns and, in larger settlements, the inns attached to them, were mostly Jews. Just like with the karpiele (rutabagas or turnips) mentioned above, the highlander was constantly faced with the dilemma of whether he should eat an egg at home or take it to the Jew in exchange for some item needed in the household. The situation was similar with cheese, cream and butter; after he secured them with a great deal of trouble, they did not always serve to improve the highlander's diet—he had to sell them instead.

In old times many families in the highlands considered

meat an extremely desirable product. In poorer families, it appeared on the table only a few times a year. There is an old Polish saying that the peasant only eats a chicken if either the chicken is sick or the peasant is sick. This was also true of the highlanders. The raising of pigs was quite limited because these animals needed potatoes and ground grain for their feed—exactly what the people themselves ate. The highlanders found it difficult to maintain their body weight by eating only greens. There was also meat "on the hoof" in the forest to be hunted down. But as the number of settlers grew, the population of wild animals decreased. The introduction of primitive firearms reduced the chances for survival of game in the woods. By the end of the XIX century, only a few bears remained in the High Tatras. Despite the regulations introduced with time by the authorities, poaching was a constant phenomenon because people had to eat. Trout, grayling, millet and smaller fish which served as food for these predatory fish populated the mountain streams. People who lived near the streams took advantage of this, albeit seasonal, source of protein at will, until the royal and later Tsarist administration introduced interdictions on this practice. The regulations were mainly concerned with the salmon which swam to the mountain streams to spawn. The highlanders found it hard to accept that what was to be found in the forest and the streams was not a source of food for all, but was considered property of the authorities. Thus they poached in the mountain streams at will.

Geography and climate in the highland region do not provide a dependable growing season. Snowfall as late as May is not unusual, and it also has happened that potatoes had to be dug from under an early snow in September. When a so-called "bad year" came along, with a sort season for potato, oat and barley ripening, the harvests did not satisfy the needs of the population. Hunger threatened; chronic malnutrition and infant mortality increased, while disease staggered human organisms that offered little resistance.

Most often, this was in the form of infectious diseases which took a terrible toll on highland villages. Instead of grain, oat straw and pyrnica (soft wool from young sheep) were ground into a "flour" and used to thicken the warmuz. This dish, available only in the spring, was made of various chopped and boiled plants of the field, such as: wild caraway, young thistle, nettle, sorrel and rabbit clover. Not everyone had enough money to put salt on this starvation concoction.

Difficulties in providing for the family in their own region often caused the highlanders to migrate to the southern side of the Tatras looking for work. The areas of Slovakia and Hungary located there enjoyed better climatic and soil conditions which produced richer harvests. From their migrations in search of work they brought home the longed-for *dudki* (money) and often desirable products such as flour, fat, salt or matches. They also brought home "household innovations"—new methods of tilling the soil or tending animals which they had seen in the south. For instance, a clover that yielded greater harvests of feed for the livestock, making it possible to enlarge the herd and have more natural fertilizer to improve the quality of the soil. On the other hand, the highland women had something desirable to offer to the south in return: linen fabric. This was a hand-made cloth produced in three thicknesses. Besides livestock, sheep and cow hides were also sold at the local markets. The profit on sales of bartered products made it possible for the highlanders to survive even during the "difficult years."

With the passing of time, the ratio of "home produced" to "purchased" food shifted. The decisive turning point came in the second half of the XIX century when Dr. Tytus Chalubinski "discovered" Zakopane as a health resort and growing numbers of guests began to come for the summer season. A limited amount of industry also started to develop, based on lumber resources and the exploitation of metal ores, mainly iron, although the latter was not very significant in either quality or quantity. Work connected with these new branches of the economy brought in profits that had bearing on the affluence of the highlanders' kitchen, which also had to be adapted to the needs of the seasonal guests before restaurants catering to the visitors made their appearance. After the tourist season passed, certain elements of the "lordly" diet remained in the highlanders' household. Fruits and vegetables, mostly imported from the lowlands, became increasingly popular.

Experience from the old times and the early way of life (or rather of survival) came in handy for the highlanders during the Nazi occupation, when legal forms of procuring food from outside one's own farm were reduced to a minimum by the occupying forces. What is more, the highlanders were forced to turn over part of their crops and livestock for minimal compensation, far below the real value of the goods.

Today the "highland kitchen" is a concept from the realm of folklore. During festivals and other regional functions, there are sometimes presentations and contests on preparing traditional highland dishes made in the old ways. The tasting of these dishes is always a great attraction. For instance, baked moskole, no longer from oat or barley flour but from wheat, served with boiled potatoes and slathered with butter, "disappear" from the platters very fast. The proportion of homemade and "bought" food in the highland kitchen has been reversed. Today a cow might not be found on every farm. Milk and other dairy products are simply bought at the store. The book *The Polish Kitchen* can be found in nearly every highland family, especially where the lady of the house is young and well educated. *Tempora mutantur* ...yes, times have changed and we have changed with the times.

CHAPTER VII

Folklore and Mythology

In the early days when the peasant communities in the highlands were formed, the only social life were *posiady* (friendly gatherings in homes). From late fall to early spring, during the short days when there was less work on the farm, people gathered in one house or another to visit, talk or just sit together. The name for these social gatherings comes from the Polish *sit*. The black rooms of more spacious cottages were chosen for these meetings, ones where the farm animals no longer shared the room with the farmers. Every woman attending these meetings brought along something to work on. Usually the women spun wool or linen and prepared feathers for pillows and comforters. Meanwhile, the men occupied themselves with their pipes.

Lighting to illuminate the handwork was a problem. Richer farmers had oil lamps, but most used *szczypaki*. These were thinly pinched and dried conifer roots or branches, measuring about 30 centimeters. A boy delegated for the task kept one lighted. He prepared a bundle of szczypaki, lit one and stuck it into a space between the logs. When it was nearly burned out, he lit another from it. Ambers and resin fell into a bowl of water placed on a bench below.

In the times of posiady, people who could tell interesting stories were in great demand. Such people could always be found and they spun their more-or-less-true tales about what they had seen themselves or had heard from others. The group, especially the women, eagerly listened to tales about fantastic creatures, monsters, ghosts and dark forces. The return home late at night on these occasions was especially exciting.

Among the story-tellers there were some with special narrative talents and wild imaginations. Listening to highland stories, popularly referred to as *godki* (from *godac*, jargon for "speak") was especially fascinating for city dwellers who visited the Tatras for health and rest. They found early Slavic and even early Greek elements in these highland tales, and they raved about the highlanders' archaic vocabulary and the educational character of the morals of the stories.

When Tytus Chalubinski and the growing numbers of summer visitors virtually made their home in Zakopane, Chalubinski drew attention to a highlander, about 60 years old at the time, who stood out because of his traditional highlander garb, his ability to play a "homespun" fiddle called *zlobcoki* (from *Zlobek* or "cradle"), and his free and relaxed manner. These two men became friends. Chalubinski took the highlander along on his numerous excursions into the Tatras, where he became something of a tourist attraction. His fiddle playing and the tales he used to spin by the fire were enjoyed by all. This highlander was Jan Krzeptowski—Sabala. He was not the only accomplished story teller in the Zakopane region, but because many visiting members of the Polish intelligentsia from the three partitions got to know him from his excursions into the mountains with Chalubinski, he grew into a leading folk figure. His fame was established by Henryk Sienkiewicz when he published a "Sabala Fairytale" in the *Illustrated Weekly* of Warsaw in 1891. It was accompanied by drawings by painter Piotr Stachiewicz. One of the visitors, enchanted by the highlands and the highlanders, dubbed Sabala, "the highland Homer." It was a rather excessive comparison. Although neither Homer nor Sabala could read or write, their works were published and are known far and wide, and in both the stories of Homer and Sabala, reality is intertwined with fantasy. People contact, visit, converse with extraterrestial beings, and the world is peopled with ghosts, demons and goddesses.

Characters such as God, Jesus, the Virgin Mary and a whole pleiad of saints appear in highland tales. These religious elements are relatively new, just as church activity in the Tatras is much more recent than in other regions of Poland. Most probably the missionary monks who first made their way to the distant highland mountain settlements, wishing to make revelation accessible to primitive people, reduced it to forms understandable by these simple folk. This was the source of the many lovely godki about how the Lord's saints wandered the world, naturally ending up in the highlands. Belief in the fact that the saints could do anything seemed to authenticate this kind of tale. It was characteristic of these stories that the saints who came down among men became completely like them, in clothing, vocabulary, way of reasoning and behaving. The "gentlemen" carefully noted down and published the tales of the mountaineer *bajars*. More than once, two or three listeners to the tales of these highland bajars noted down the words of the same story-teller, and later there were found to be profound differences in the published text. Controversies erupted over which text was genuine, or at least more authentic. This dilemma was solved by one of the authors of the gadki— Andrzej Galica.

Folk gadki are seldom individual creations, but rather collective ones. Someone heard something somewhere, twisted it, added something, someone else dressed it up some more, elaborated on it. And that is how the gadka, legend or tale whose author cannot really be established came to be. But when it comes to expressing these tales in literary, written form, this is where the writer's individuality is revealed along with his literary invention, character, form of expression, and the moral he wishes to draw from the given *gadka*.

About 100 years ago the highland bajars were illiterate. The gadki they told about a given subject varied in certain details from teller to teller. What has remained of these tales are the writings of people who listened to them and then wrote them down. Nevertheless, in anthologies of folk tales the author of the stories is always the prototype highlander.

An exception was the "Story of St. Joseph," whose authorship several writers link with the person of Brother Albert, a monk from Kalatowki. The story was a clarification of the fact that St. Joseph is the patron of a good death—the protector of the dying. Brother Albert told the story that when he noticed souls in heaven whom he had not let in through the pearly gates, St. Peter began an investigation to find out how these "illegal" souls had gotten into heaven. After a long search it turned out that St. Joseph, who lived in a cottage in paradise that he had built himself (he had been a carpenter), left a hole in his floor and on his own was pulling souls up into heaven by a string. This whole story, presented by a certain class of *gawedziarz*, is a wonderful example of the idea that things are the same in heaven as on earth—well, maybe a little better—and those who have not achieved a lot on earth and are afraid that St. Peter might not let them in through the pearly gates, direct all of their adoration toward St. Joseph.

An example of the same story told by two bajars differing in the details is the tale about Jesus, St. Peter and highland robbers attributed to Tomasz Stopka Gadeja and Andrzej Galica. Galica was was 43 years younger than Gadeja, and was an educated man, while Gadeja could not read or write. Undoubtedly, then, Gadeja's story was the prototype in this case. In both versions, the action is actually the same: Jesus and St. Peter were spending the night at the inn, when the robbers arrived there. They took some refreshment and then began to dance around the room. One of them noticed people sleeping in the corner and hit the one lying near him with his ciupaga. When there was a pause in the robbers' dancing, St. Peter offered to change places with Jesus, supposedly because he was worried that there was a draft from the wall. They changed places and the robbers resumed their dance. The same robber was about to hit the man lying closer with his ciupaga when he decided to torment the one lying closer to the wall. The moral of this tale is different for each author. Gadeja ends his story by saying: "If something is to happen to you, it won't pass you by, no matter how you try to avoid it." But Galica concludes as follows: "No matter how you try, you can't fool Jesus." A fundamental *novum* introduced on the subject by Galica is the beginning of the story, when the holy personages entered the inn. Here the author makes both saints just like highlanders in their behavior. Before eating, they downed two glasses of vodka and followed with a little beer.

A highland writer and poet of the younger generation, Aniela Gut-Stapinska (born in Poronin in 1898) left behind, among many stories, a lovely genre image entitled "The Crocuses." It is a story of the Virgin Mary, who descended with the Baby Jesus to the highland area on orders from God to see how people lived there and whether they had God in their hearts. It was winter and the Virgin Mary had already unsuccessfully asked for shelter in three cottages for herself and Her Little Son. But the rich farmers had no mercy in their hearts. Finally, at the edge of the village, the door of a miserable shack opened to the travelers and they were invited inside. The farmers were very poor and had ten children and two sheep. They heated water for the Little

Jesus' bath, in which the Virgin Mary later washed the youngest child who suffered from a skin disease. In the morning, when the farmers woke up, their strange visitors were gone. Looking out of their door, they saw footsteps leading away from their cottage. And everywhere the Virgin Mary's foot had stepped the snow had melted and purple flowers—crocuses—bloomed. Seeing that their child had been cured by the bath, the farmers understood who had visited them. This tale illustrates how riches numb the human conscience and how crocuses came to the highlands.

Gadki in which death, the devil, the peasant and the struggle between them play a role are kept at a somewhat different pitch. The "Sabala Fairytale" mentioned above begins with a meeting between a highlander-carpenter and death disguised as an old woman. The peasant was "psychic," so despite the disguise he knew who he was dealing with. Wanting to get rid of death, he took advantage of her innate woman's curiosity and lured her to a hollow in a willow tree. When death entered the hollow, the peasant nailed a peg into the hole and imprisoned death in the willow. And so it happened that people stopped dying. But finally the carpenter got tired of living and went to release death from the willow tree. Then death began making up for lost time and people died by the hundreds. Once death came to take a mother of seven, and a widow to boot from one of the peasant cottages. Death took pity on her and went to Jesus with a complaint. After hearing what death had to say, Jesus slapped her across the face once and then hit her again. "Go"—He ordered—"to the sea and bring me a rock lying on the bottom." When death returned with the rock, Jesus ordered her to bite into it. There was a small live worm inside the rock. Jesus demonstrated that He knew about every little living thing, so that He would not let these orphans perish when their mother was taken away by death. There are two elements in this fairytale worthy of our attention: one is the folksy explanation for the plague which visited the highlands in the 40's of the XIX century, when every fourth inhabitant of the highlands lost his life, and the second is a justification of the highland proverb: "Whom God created, He will not let perish."

In their gadki and fairytales, the highlanders had numerous run-ins with the devil, but always emerged victorious from these encounters. It seems from these tales that the highlander always managed to outsmart the devil.

Also from Sabala's repertoire there is the story of a highlander who, seeing that his *jarzec* (barley) was coming up poorly, cursed: "Let the devil take such a jarzec!" Despite poor forecasts, the barley grew admirably. The farmer got ready to harvest the barley, but the devil grabbed his scythe saying: "The barley is mine!" And indeed the farmer had to admit that he had given the barley to the devil. Nevertheless, he began to bargain with the devil. It ended with an agreement that whoever came back to the field on a more fancy horse would get the barley. The peasant went back home sadly, realizing that he had no horse at all. But his wife found a way out of the situation. The next day the devil was waiting for him, prancing on a beautiful horse. Suddenly the peasant appeared out of the woods riding his wife, naked as a jay bird. Seeing this spectacle, the devil gave up, since he had never seen such a horse—with a tail in the front, talons instead of hooves, and a mane in the back. And so the peasant harvested the barley as his own.

A different category of highland tales is connected with the mountains, mountain secrets and the strange creatures which exist there according to highlanders' fantasy. The most famous of these is the story of the knights asleep in the Tatras. According to the plot, a hussar unit returning from Vienna became lost in the Tatras and found its way to a huge cave, where both men and horses fell into a trance. Once a strangely dressed man came to a young blacksmith in a small Tatra village and asked him to follow him deep into the mountains, bringing along tools for shoeing horses. When they arrived at an entrance between two large rocks, they passed through a long corridor to a large cave where knights were sleeping mounted on their horses. The horses' shoes had to be exchanged, and the blacksmith was given gold bars to do this job. When he had finished, the man who had led the blacksmith to the cave poured a lot of shavings from the horse shoes into his bag as payment for his work and led him out of the cave through the corridor. The disappointed blacksmith spilled these shavings onto the ground with a curse. When he got home, he told the whole story to his wife, who checked his bag and found a few golden shavings in it. Seeing his mistake, the blacksmith went back to the mountains where he had spilled out the shavings, but he could not find the place nor the entrance to the cave. Maddened by this obsession, he wandered the mountains in vain until he died.

A whole series of stories and oral histories revolve around the most famous highland robber—Janosik. He was a real person, a Slovak born in Trchowa, who was condemned to death by the Hungarian nobles and was hung on a hook by his lowest rib. Many legends grew up around this man, first expressed in oral histories and later in folklore as well as Slovak literature. Special powers, granted him by witches, were attributed to Janosik. He received a leather belt from them which protected him from bullets and any blows he might suffer from a ciupaga, with which he himself could vanquish a regiment of soldiers. The witches also made him a gift of an eagle feather which assured him of eternal fame. Tales of the numerous adventures of Janosik and his comrades were often told at the posiady—tales of how he took from the rich and gave to the poor. Legends abounded about the treasures they hid in the mountains. Many were willing to look for these treasures, but the money is still waiting to be discovered. Many difficult tasks had to be fulfilled before gaining possession of the robbers' gold.

The highland mythology peopled the mountains, forests

and rivers with various monsters who, as in Greek or Roman mythology, one way or another coexisted with man, once harming and pestering him, and then helping him instead. The highlanders imagined the goddesses to be creatures similar to women, living in hollows near the rivers or swamps, lurking about, waiting for young men so they could enchant them and draw them into the water. In the rivers there lived water spirits of both sexes, with skin similar to fish, but without scales. The female water spirits gathered by the river crossings, waiting for the careless, while the male water spirits liked to choose tributaries of the river leading to water mills. The millers blamed all the damage occurring in mill-races on the presence of the water spirits. The "planetnicy" were believed to be something quite different. According to the highlanders' beliefs, they were the creation of the devil, who had made them out of clay and tried to breathe life into them as God had brought Adam to life. Nothing came of these efforts, and God took pity on these clay people. He brought them to life, but the question arose of what to do with them—since they did not deserve either heaven or hell. Finally, after a lot of thought, God sent them up to the clouds so that they could direct them, riding them according to God's orders. Sometimes, on clear days, the *planetnicy* went around the villages. Poorly dressed, always hungry, they willingly worked for the farmers for a spoon of food or a piece of oatcake.

The products of human fantasy mentioned above and others like them undoubtedly go back to pagan times. The Catholic religion spreading in the highlands did not have easy access to highlanders' minds. The highland imagination created its own world of notions about celestial matters out of the instructions given by early missionary monks and later parish priests. We have already noted the legend of St. Joseph; now we need to cite what journalist and publisher Ferdynand Hosick noted about how old Sabala imagined heaven:

The Old Father (God) is the richest farmer on earth. His fields and forests are brimming with game, so he gives things away to good people and cares about them, because he has so much. He created everything on earth, but he cares the most about people because he can communicate with them. The Old Father lives in a beautiful cottage carved all over, with ornate benches under the windows and the ceiling beams with carving lovely like a miracle. He goes around in highland garb, always in His Sunday best.

Most likely this description was not in keeping with the teachings of the Church, but it was understandable and dear to the highlanders. The highlanders were rather skeptical in their approach to God. "Believe in God, but don't trust Him!"—means that if man does not help himself, God will not be of much help to him either. Or take this advice: "Have trust in God, but carry cheese in your knapsack."

The beliefs cited above, or even semi-beliefs, were a rich subject for highland bajars during posiady on autumn and winter evenings. But the themes discussed above only formed part of the "bajar's" interests. Other subjects they covered were people, their shortcomings, adventures, successes and failures. They told the tale of a farmer who was very much afraid of death and his humorous vicissitudes in trying to wiggle away from it. Or another story about a man who fell on the road under a heavy burden, and was sure that he was already dead and the devils were dragging him to hell. It turned out that it was a pig which was pulling at the sack that had fallen on the peasant. Other stories dealt with marital mishaps—men with shrewish wives and women with drunken husbands. There was talk of old folk cures, preventing the casting of spells and ways of breaking these spells once cast. But the most popular stories were those told by old hunters, of their adventures with bears and mountain goats, as well as their sometimes bloody encounters with the inhabitants of the southern side of the Tatras—the Luptaks.

In the highland tales, it was hard to separate truth from fantasy, beliefs from imaginings, convictions from suppositions. There were lots of details in these tales, undoubtedly creations of the speakers' imaginations, which served to authenticate them and stretched out their length. No one minded this—there was plenty of time and everyone was glad to listen to the spinners of yarns. The younger generation of highlanders, many of whom completed studies in secondary as well as higher education at the turn of the XIX century, preserved the old tradition of the highland gadki in literary form. That is how many of these tales of the old days survived. New versions of the old patters survive still, even though new communication media such as television have spelled an end of the traditional posiady. But the name has remained and is still given to meetings in cultural centers and community halls where highland folklore is cultivated.

CHAPTER VIII

Highland Customs and Celebrations

Folk customs are as old as humanity itself. They stem from ancient beliefs and traditions cultivated for centuries, connected with specific activities, times of year, or natural phenomena, and are designed to stress their special significance. And so, for instance, the drenching of madder symbolized the recession of winter in face of the approaching spring, the celebration of *Kupala* on the night of June 24 (St. John's Midsummer Eve) stressed the turning-point in the relation between earth and the sun; wedding celebrations were designed to emphasize the importance of the state of matrimony; while the holiday customs and celebrations increased the importance of the holidays observed.

As typical traditionalists, the highlanders attached great importance to observing customs of the old days and to keeping the celebrations inherited from their forefathers. Ancient beliefs, undoubtedly going back to pagan times and opposed by the Church, remained in the highlanders' consciousness for a long time. As late as the XVIII and XIX centuries the population of highland villages was largely illiterate. Without access to books, these people drew all of their practical wisdom from traditional oral history. Thus their knowledge was somewhat removed from scientific accuracy.

The highlanders, like the rural inhabitants from other regions of Poland, believed in the existence of various unearthly powers having nothing or little to do with the teachings of the Church. For instance, it was believed that some people, both men and women, had the power to harm others by casting spells. There were various ways of protecting oneself from these spells, the simplest being spitting to the side three times and saying: "Touch wood." Placing a silver coin on the forehead of a newborn on his way to christening was supposed to keep him healthy. To identify women who cast spells, it was necessary to observe the Easter procession through a hole made by a knot in a plank of wood, but the plank had to be one that was to be used to make a coffin. Special powers and skills were attributed to the *bacas*—flock-masters of sheep herds in the mountain pastures. It was believed that certain "bacas" were capable of milking other people's sheep from a distance into their own *gieletas*—wooden eating utensils. Such milk thievery was the reason for any decrease in milk production. But it sufficed to place a ciupaga (shepherd's cane) across a passage and chase the sheep across it to nullify the spell of the outside baca. Any unexpected strong wind was generally viewed to signify someone's suicide by hanging. When it rained for a long time, more than a week, and there was no indication that it would stop, a knowing baca explained the phenomenon by telling that the suicide had been buried in the ground. As late as 1911 there was a documented case of a suicide's body being exhumed and burned on a pyre. Unfortunately, it is not known whether this made the rain stop.

The bacas in the mountain pastures cherished various

customs connected with tending their sheep. For instance, when wood was gathered for the first fire after arriving at the pasture, great care had to be taken not to break the smallest twig, because the sheep could break their legs as a result. A knowing baca never offered anything to anyone in the pasture after sunset in the fear that the sheep might lose their milk. It is hard to say how much conviction there was in these beliefs and how much desire of the bacas to augment their importance.

Sheep breeding was very important to the highlanders so that everything connected with this activity was carried on in accordance with age-old regulations. The person of the baca was of central importance. He was a contractor who on one hand made agreements with owners of the pastures for permission to graze the animals, and on the other hand, by accepting the animals for the time of pasturing, took on the burden of caring for the sheep and financial responsibility to the owners and his helpers—the *juhas* and *honielniks* (shepherds and sheep beaters). The sheep were driven out to the pastures between mid-May and mid-June, depending on when winter loosened its grip. On the appointed day the farmers brought their sheep to the baca, after branding them. The sheep were gathered in a *kosor* (pole enclosure for sheep) on the baca's farm. When all the sheep were in place, the baca's wife placed glowing embers in a pot, added dried, previously blessed herbs and burned the incense around the sheep. She circled the entire kosor. After this ceremony the baca went out into the road, the juhas opened the kosor and the *redyk* (sheep drive) began. "Redyk" was the word used when the whole farm went up the mountain, men and animals, as well as the drive itself from the village up to the pasture. After arrival at the pasture, the sheep were gathered in an enclosure and the baca with his juhas or helpers entered the shack, referred to as a chalet. Here a ceremony was held to spread incense and bless the chalet, during which the baca mouthed the following: "Let Jesus Christ be praised! All you evil spirits, get away from this chalet. May this summer go well for us, let the sheep have enough grass and we enough cheese and *zyntyca* (whey of sheep's milk mixed with another type of whey)." After that the baca again burned incense over the sheep inside the kosor and sprinkled them with holy water.

According to an old custom, the baca had to make an accounting with the farmers who had entrusted their sheep to him. Three days after the arrival of the redyk (drive) in the pasture the sheep's owners came up from the village for a so-called *myira* (settlement). Every owner milked his sheep into one pail. The "baca" measured this milk with a stick called the *zomyirek* (sheep milk measure) and he marked on the stick the place that the milk had reached. Then the zomyirek was divided in two; the sheep owner kept one part and the baca the other, after marking it. Before the end of the pasture period, the owners again appeared at the pasture, and the settlement of accounts occurred. A scale was hung on a hook, with a kettle on one side and a weight on the other (usually a flat stone). Water was placed in the bucket to the height which the owner had milked at the beginning of the pasture period, measured by the zomyirek. The amount of water placed in the kettle was multiplied by the number of weeks the sheep had spent in the pasture. The kettle went down on the scale, and the sides were evened by placing cheese and cheese products on the stone. This is what was due to the sheep owner. The baca went through this procedure with all the owners in turn. Whatever was left was divided into two parts: one was the remuneration for the juhas and honielniks, and the other was the baca's earnings for his work at the pasture—for his leadership and the risks he took. This traditional custom survived until World War II. The war and the occupation put a stop to the pasturage in the Tatras, and after the war a more convenient monetary accounting was deemed to be preferable.

Just as the redyk was a ceremony for the whole village,

even for those who owned no sheep, a wedding was a custom celebrated by the whole village in the old days. Some took an interest because they were directly involved as family members and friends who expected to take part in the ceremony, but others who were not members of the wedding still viewed it as an event bringing color to village life, a subject for conversation, suppositions and gossip, and finally as proof that the young people were keeping the traditional wedding customs.

Everything started with the *namowiny* (matchmaking). As late as two hundred years ago, it was a rarity for couples to come together because of their feelings for each other. In the harsh highland conditions, it seemed more important what the young couple would live on and what they would feed their children with than whether they loved each other. In the highland dialect there is no expression for "I love you." It is supplanted by "I'm pleased to see you." Parents usually arranged marriages, unless the young people were so well suited with regard to property that their choice coincided with that of the parents. When matters were already on their way and a definite refusal was not expected, the prospective bridegroom went to the home of his chosen mate for the namowiny with his father or matchmaker. This was a long-established ceremony, during which the course of the conversation had to be suitable, the "circling" around the prime subject sufficiently lengthy and the metaphors used both pointed and witty. Finally the pertinent question was asked: "Well, will you give Marysia to me?" And although everything had seemingly been arranged earlier, sometimes the answer was negative and the results not always courteous. If the answer was positive, a bottle of vodka which the young man had kept in his pocket, appeared on the table, the mother of the bride put out snacks and a discussion of property settlements and details concerning the wedding ensued.

Another traditional custom involved invitations to the

wedding. Inviting is *pytac* (asking) in the highland dialect, so the engaged couple invited people to their wedding in the company of *pytacy*. The young people rode in a two-horse carriage, or sleigh in the winter, preceded by pytacy on horseback, dressed in black cuchas, wide belts with colorful ribbons at the shoulders. As they rode through the village the pytacy sang appropriate songs to a tune known as *pytacka*. For instance, they might sing before a house where they were to invite the residents to the wedding: "Let us in, let us in, hey, we will not spend the night here. We are only coming, hey, to invite you to the wedding."

After they entered the house, there followed the ceremony of asking the residents to the wedding, informing them of the time and place of the ceremony. As the people bid them farewell, the pytacy got back on their horses, the engaged couple went back to their carriage and were on their way. When the family was large, and some of its members lived in other villages, this ride could last up to three days. Today only the closest relatives are invited personally; the others receive invitations.

A few days before the wedding women friends gathered at the bride's house for the ceremony of *wicie rozdzek*. *Rozdzki* were long juniper tree branches which the girls decorated with artificial flowers and ribbons. Thes rozdzki were attached to the horses' collars on the day of the wedding. Little myrtle bouquets with white ribbons were also prepared for the wedding guests.

Traditionally, weddings were held at the bride's house. In old times the burden of the wedding expenses fell to her parents. The family had to provide enough food and drink to serve the guests for two, and sometimes three days. In keeping with tradition, the pytacy and groomsmen with the bridesmaids first went to the groom's house. As they rode their horses before the house, the pytacy sang:

> *Well, we are here, hey, to get the groom*
> *Since the bride, hey, sent us for him*

The groom's parents and the relatives gathered for a light meal went to the bride's house with him. There followed the ceremony of dressing the groom in a shirt made for him by the bride and tying a white ribbon to his cucha. The next ceremony was the blessing. The wedding-host addressed the gathering. Traditionally he reminded the young couple of their marital duties, gave them advice on their new life and finally turned to the parents to give a parental blessing to the couple. The young people kneeled before their parents, who blessed them with a sign of the cross and laid their hands on the young people's heads. After the blessing, the wedding procession set out for the church—the bride in the first carriage with her bridesmaids, the groom in the second with his attendants, then the parents, musicians and wedding guests. The ride through the village provided a diversion for its residents.

On the way home to the bride's house after the wedding, the procession was met with traditional obstacles in the form of gates. This was a barrier decorated with flowers closing off the road, with a "gypsy" family at its side (these were young men dressed up as Gypsies). They played on old frying pans, sang, danced and collected money from the wedding party, "ransom" for passing. A "baby" consoled by a "Gypsy woman" yelled at the top of its lungs. And here "modernity" has invaded the old customs: sometimes a "group of health officers" appeared at the barrier and a nurse took the young couple's pulse.

The young couple, who customarily return from the church together, approach the door to the house, where they were met with bread and salt, and the groom carried the bride over the threshold. The groomsmen waited for this opportrnity to take the groom's hat away from him. Since his hands were busy, he could not defend himself, and had to pay ransom for its return in another ceremony to follow.

The wedding festivities began with a traditional dinner

and when its was over the guests amused themselves according to their preference—they danced, sang, enjoyed of the delicacies. Traditionally, the groom's father made the rounds of the house with liquor bottles, seeing to it that no one went thirsty. When the house was small, the dancing usually took place in the barn, decorated for the occasion.

About 8pm was time for the next wedding custom— *oczepiny*. Just as the symbol of maidenhood and virginity is the garland, so the attribute of the married woman is a head covering called *czepek*. This czepek can be a hat or cap, or can also be a properly arranged kerchief. The ceremony of oczepiny during a highland wedding symbolized the passage of the bride from the group of girls to a group of married women. The sequence of events of the oczepiny ceremony has been long established. The wedding-hostesses, or "czepia," place the head covering on the bride. But then the groomsmen take her in their midst and a "bargaining" begins between them and the wedding-hostesses. All this takes place to the accompaniament of song and dance: "Hey, I will not give up the bride, hey, I will not give her up, Until the wedding-hostesses come here with a little booze."

The wedding-hostesses bring the drink, but that is not enough; there follow additional demands from the groomsmen—sausage, cheese, wine, etc. Finally the bride is handed over to the wedding-hostesses, who perform the proper oczepiny and settle down in chairs in anticipaion of the presents for the young couple. Then the bridesmaids approach the bride and dance with her, first singing as follows:

"Now you, Hanus, took the plunge, now you will have a guy. I have to knock myself in the head, I still have to search for one."

After the bridesmaids, the groomsmen dance with the bride, then relatives, and finally the remaining wedding guests. Every dance is preceded by a couplet and followed by the presentation of good wishes and gifts, which the wedding-hostesses place on a pile. Everyone who offers a gift is presented with a glass of vodka and a piece of sheep cheese, the *oszczypek*. Finally the groom comes up to the bride, but the best man bars his way demanding that he ransom his hat. After he does that, he can finally dance with his wife and the oczepiny ceremony is over. Besides the symbolism of the ceremony, oczepiny also serves to equip the young couple with the things they need to set up housekeeping. In very old times gifts were usually a piece of linen, woolen or linen thread, pillows, comforters, household items or even a small pig or calf. Now the gifts usually consist of money, and the amount depends on the prosperity of the village.

Funeral ceremonies were also considered family customs. As a rule the deceased awaited burial at his own home, or sometimes in the home of a family member (if that home was closer to the church or the cemetery). Relatives, friends and acquaintances visited the dead person as he lay in his coffin surrounded by candles. Prayers were said on these occasions and religious tunes were sung. On the day of the funeral the residents of the village, in their Sunday best, bid farewell to the deceased along with his family. The four men carrying the coffin were dressed in black cuchas. As they carried the coffin out of the house, they struck the threshold with it three times. This was a symbol of the host's bidding farewell to his house. After the funeral the family usually invited the dead man's friends and relations for a wake, which was a modest reception without liquor or singing.

Highland customs were also connected with the change in seasons and church holidays. The approach of spring and Holy Week before Easter were an occasion to bless palms and other plants which, in the approaching months, were to do good to man and beast, often as medicine. Young people made wooden rattles which replaced the sound of the bells which fell silent on Good Friday. They also fashioned puppets of Judas and Marzanna, referred to as *smierztecka*. These puppets were drowned in the stream, but the girls went around the village with the smierztecka collecting contributions usually in the form of eggs.

As in other regions of Poland, decorated Easter eggs were popular in the highlands, but they were rather modest in color. One method of coloring them used dye from onion skins. First designs were drawn on the shells with wax. Then the eggs were simmered in a pot of water and onionskins. The wax melted, but where it had been the onion did not color the egg shell and the design remained. The Easter eggs were blessed and their shells were carefully preserved after the eggs were consumed because special properties were attributed to them. The addition of powdered egg shells to animal feed was to have a salutary effect on the fertility of the livestock. The egg shells were reputed to protect a home from calamities and sickness, as well as evil spells. Powdered shells were added to grain to assure a good harvest. On Easter Sunday, the whole family traditionally sat together to eat the holiday breakfast. This was a long-awaited meal, since the old-time highlanders strictly observed the fast imposed by the Church during the period of Lent. Care to avoid eating even a gram of animal fat was carried so far that before Ash Wednesday pots were boiled in cauldrons to remove every trace of grease. On the second day of Easter, the traditional *smigus-dyngus* (custom of dousing womenfolk on Easter Monday), called "polywacka" by the highlanders, took place. According to tradition, water was indispensable to life and brought health. Old highlanders explained the genesis of this custom as follows: in Jerusalem, on the Monday after Jesus' burial, crowds began to gather whisper that Jesus had been resurrected. The Pharisees sent their servants into the streets to douse the crowd, forcing it to disperse.

One of the oldest Slavic customs is the holiday of *Kupala*, when people greeted the approaching summer. The Tatra highlanders combined this holiday with Whit Sunday. Fires were lit in the hills and music and singing continued through the night. Boys prepared torches for this observance, and ran through the hills with them. Young couples regularly disappeared in the dark of the woods. In the morning the ashes from the fires were spread over the fields, which was believed to bring a better harvest.

The period of Christmas, called *Gody* by the highlanders was the richest in customs and celebrations. This period began on the feastday of St. Lucia on December 13. From conditions on this day, predictions were made about the months of the coming year. And so, the weather on December 13 was to indicate the weather conditions for the month of January, the 14th for February, and so on. These predictions were tested from December 25 to January 6. The actual holiday began on Christmas Eve—December 24. Many beliefs and customs were connected with this day. First of all, it was a day of especially severe fast. The most popular meal was raw cabbage with baked potatoes and coffee made from roasted barley. Care was taken that the first visitor to the home should not be a woman. She brought bad luck. But men, as augurs of success, were most welcome. Women had plenty of work to do on Christmas Eve, but the men traditionally went off into the forest. Why? Truth be told, it was to try their luck; to bring something back home even if it was not completely legal. It was believed that Christmas Eve influenced events for the whole coming year: children tried to be especially good, a wife avoided fighting with her husband and vice versa, hunters' good luck on Christmas Eve boded good hunting all year, the peasant who brought home a sleigh full of wood could count on the same success in the coming year.

As darkness on Christmas Eve approached, children watched for the first star to appear in the sky—this marked the beginning of the festive meal. The host, carrying a sheaf of oats and a handful of hay entered the room where the family was already gathered. He placed the sheath in the corner and put the hay under the tablecloth. Then he picked up previously prepared fir branches, called *podlazniczki*, which he shaped into a cross and used to bless the house and the people gathered in it. They accompanied him to the barn, where he blessed the cattle, the horse, the sheep and pigs. After this he placed the podlazniczki above the barn gates. After returning to the house the family exchanged good wishes and holy wafers, which were dipped in honey before eating. The Christmas Eve dishes were meatless: sour soup, red borsch with beans, sauerkraut with mushrooms, sweet noodles with poppy seeds. In more affluent homes there was also fish fried in oil. At the end—a rare tidbit for the children—a compote of dried fruits. As late as 100 years ago, it was usual to eat meals with wooden spoons out of a common bowl. After supper, the leftovers were carried to the barn and given to the cattle, the hay from under the tablecloth was also for the livestock, and the oats from the sheath were added to the grain prepared for sowing, which was to assure a successful harvest the next year. The children lit candles on the tree, and the whole family sang Christmas carols before leaving for midnight mass. The mother took the leftover pieces of holy wafer and attached to the frozen window pane as many pieces as there were members of the family in the house, naming each of them. If a piece fell off the window pane, this meant that this member of the household would not live to see the next Christmas. Girls went outside listening to see which direction a dog's bark was coming from. This was the direction that a young man was to appear from for *podlazy* (traditional visits to a girl's house after midnight mass). Podlazy was an old highland tradition following midnight mass. A young man would appear at the house of a girl he had his eye on, express the traditional Christmas greetings, and scatter oat seeds which he had brought in his glove. If the girl and her parents were well disposed toward the visitor, they brought out some food, and he reciprocated by offering a bottle of liquor. This led to preliminary negotiations over a future marriage and its conditions.

The first day of Christmas was a day to be spent with family. The second day brought visits from friends and carols in the village by singers known in the highlands as *jaslikarz*, from the term *jasla*, meaning creche. The carollers carried a creche with them, and were dressed up as various figures, such as the devil, death, Herod, shepherds and more familiar persons connected with Christmas. Going from house to house,they reinacted the story of Christ's birth. For this they received treats, and sometimes money.

Carols and pastorales were sung in churches and homes all through the Christmas season. While the carols were songs of a religious character, the pastorales were folk songs on the subject of Christmas. The oldest printed Polish pastorales are dated 1843. New Year's Eve celebrations were unknown in the highlands, but after the new year, groups of young people, accompanied by music, paid visits to rich farmers, wishing them a happy new year. Impromptu parties erupted, with dancing, playing and singing, and then the revelers moved on to the next place.

The highland customs and celebrations are relics of old times, forming an important element for social bonds. They emphasize the age-old roots of the Tatra folk, and attest to their affiliation with Slavic culture. In the midst of today's commercial world, regional folk groups reach back to these old customs and celebrations.

CHAPTER IX

Song, Music and Dance

Highland song is different from similar melodic forms of other regions of Poland. First of all, the highlanders sing in a loud high-pitched tone, sometimes breaking into a falsetto. This makes a strange impression on outsiders, who may interpret Highland singing as shouting. There exists a theory that people living in the mountains have gradually developed specific calls, exchanges of brief information in the form of voice signals which gave a start to melodies when performed in changing tonations. This is why instruments such as alpenhorns and wind music makers, and characteristic ways of singing, such as yodeling (by Alpine highlanders and the residents of the Harz Mountains), or the way certain primitive tribes sing, are similar in the mountains of various countries.

A peculiar yodeling by the Tatra highlanders is called *wyskanie*; increasingly high pitched calls are sung by a woman and then by a man. This was undoubtedly once the way shepherds and shepherdesses communicated with each other over great distances. Although every highland melody can also be sung an octave lower, and that is what those who cannot sing so high do, this is not really "the highland way."

Another characteristic of highland singing is a diversity of melodies which only seldom are connected with a specific text. In most cases, various lyrics can be sung to one melody, with differences resulting from varied rhythms and building cadences. As late as 150 years ago, highland folk songs were unknown outside the Tatra region. It was only in the middle of the XIX century, thanks to Ludwik Zajszner, a geologist also interested in ethnography, that the texts of some highland songs were published. Zajszner was not a musicologist, so he did not record music scores. In 1883-84 Jan Kleszczynski undertook the task of noting down Highland melodies with the help of Jan Ignacy Paderewski. They made "excursions" to highland villages, seeking out the most celebrated musicians, and managed to preserve both words and melodies of folk songs, which were subsequently published. Later well-known composers intrigued by the originality of the highland melodies included Mieczyslaw Karlowicz and Karol Szymanowski. Szymanowski used them for his "Harnasie." An anthology of *Highland Songs* prepared by a team from the Art Institute of the Polish Academy of Science was published in 1971. It was the result of several years of study by a large group who in the years 1950-1955 visited nearly all significant highland localities, and recorded original highlander performances on tape. A total of 143 melodies were isolated for the anthology, in both basic forms and variations, since "in every village there is a different song." If this number of melodies (in highland dialect "notes") seems large, the collection of texts to highland songs is truly impressive. About 20,000 have been written down—and that is not all of them. Songs, like people, are born, live for a short time, a longer time, or even a very long time, and then many are forgotten and simply die.

Song, Music and Dance

The anthology lists only 1,250 selected lyrics. Most highland folk songs are short couplets consisting of two lines, sometimes four. There are also some ballads which take twelve or more lines to tell the story of people or events. But these ballads are usually not of highland origin. The authors of the anthology divided highland songs into eleven categories: reflective, social, military, highland robbers' ditties, hunting, shepherding, blustering, flirtatious, love songs, family, and comical. Although there are many, wedding songs are not listed separately, but were included under family songs. Following is an example of each type of song:

Reflective
What did you come here for, grey fog, grey fog
You barred the way to my girl.

Social
Gentlemen, gentlemen, you will be gentlemen
But you will not lord it over us.

Military
Do not be sad, do not be sad, you miserable
  recruit,
You will be issued a carbine and shapely boots.

Highland Robbers' Ditties
While robbers danced at the inn by the wooded
  mountainside
The Hungarian sentries fell on them from above.

Hunting
When the eagle soars over the steep mountain
  peak,
A goat whistles, sensing something.

Shepherding
When I go off to the pastures with my sheep,
I have them eat their fill in the mountains.

Blustering

When you were dancing, I did not get in your way,
Now I'll be putting you out the window.

Flirtatious
Do not lure me, do not lure me, 'cause you will not seduce me,
Until you come on horseback for me.

Love
I fancy you, I fancy you, my little darling,
You who only have eyes for others.

Family
My mommy gave me some sweet milk
So that my face should smile at the boys.

Comical
I'll not marry an old man, since I will have no use out of him,
The minute he lies down, he begins to snore, he does not grab me even once.

Another characteristic of highland singing is its natural dipthongal quality. One person sings the melody and others take a second part, which always provides a good complement. Sometimes it is only an octave lower, and at other times it is a variation on the main melody. Since there are usually more people singing the second part, they often muffle the sound of the main melody, as everyone sings very loudly.

Most highland lyrics can be set to various melodies, but there are texts associated with only one tune, either by custom or because of the rhythm of the melody and syllabic verse of the text. When highlanders sing *a capella*, their music is free, its phrases broadly drawn, with elongated endings. This provides singers with an opportunity to melodically blow off steam, to show off their voices.

Highland music is closely connected with singing. In the

highland dialect, the word "music" has three meanings: 1. the art of organizing sounds, 2. a team of musicians, and 3. a social gathering, during which people sing and dance "to the music." It has already been mentioned that in the highland dialect the word "note" has a special meaning. The highlanders use the word "note" to mean music.

The first string instruments to reach the Highlands and be adopted by the population were extremely primitive. Later they were produced by people familiar with woodworking techniques, usually carpenters; the profession of violin maker appeared very late in the Tatra region. Early instruments were made of a solid piece of wood, from which the center was hollowed out, leaving only the rim, something like a bowl or trencher. A slat with openings was attached over the top, a neck with pegs for the strings of sheep gut was added—and the instrument was ready. The bow took even less work. These primitive violins, called "zlobcoki," served the highlanders for many years until instruments fashioned on the Italian model made their appearance.

Highland melodies can be divided into several groups:

Sabala melodies—played most readily by the legendary Jan Krzeptowski-Sabala in his own style

Marches—melodies of greeting and farewell, as well as introduction to highland robbers' melodies

Wierchowe (mountain melodies)—from the word "wierch," and denotes a melody sung at high pitch, providing the opportunity for full outlet of one's energies in song

Ozwodne (one strain of highlander melody)—from the word "ozwodzic," which means to spread the melody out broadly by precisely including all nuances and a decelerated finale

Krzesane ("stricken melodies")—tunes for dancing characterized by rapidity and execution of difficult, quick dance steps on a small surface, almost in place (derived from shepherds' dances originally on very limited surfaces in the mountains); today dancers show off their skills by dancing these krzesane steps atop a tree trunk 30 centimeters in diameter and 60 centimeters high

Green melodies—tunes ending the performance of a dancing couple; name comes from the following melody:

> *The linden tree glowed green, the girl sat under it,*
> *The sparks fell on her, "zygaly" pinched her under*
> *her shirt.*

Wedding melodies—connected with wedding ceremony, further divided into *pytackie* (invitational), *wywodne* (sung while bride is led out of her house), and *ocepinowe* (performed during the ceremony of *oczepiny* or capping the bride)

Highland musicians revel in creating new variations of melodies by adding grace-notes to the basic score. This "decoration" (called *cyfrowanie* or musical variation) attests to the performance skills of the musician.

Besides violins, *kozy* (bagpipes, also known among highlanders of other counries) were also in use in times gone by. The *koza* was made from an airtight goatskin with a wooden funnel attached, through which the player blew air; two fifes were tightly connected to the bag, one base fife with a constant tone and another with openings through which melodies could be fingered. The melodic fife was joined to the sack through a sculpted goat head, which the highlanders also referred to as "koza." Before world War II there were only two or three bagpipe players in the Highlands. The most famous was the Budz-Mroz family from Poronin, which traditionally played the bagpipes. Now the practice of playing bagpipes is being revived by regional groups.

The highland dance, as one of the important elements of the highlanders' folk culture, is closely connected to the music. People dance "to the music," but the dancer himself chooses the tune he wishes to dance to, singing before the musicians the text he wants played while he is dancing. According to highland tradition, only one couple dances at a time. The rest of the dancers patiently await their turns. The custom was for a couple to dance three dances, the third ending with a "green" melody and *wyzwyrtanie* (rotating dance) with the female partner. At weddings, christenings and neighborly "musics," a dance was occasionally played, such as the polka, which everyone danced together. When it was over, the traditional dance by one pair was resumed.

According to Ch. Winnick, "The dance is the movement of the whole body or only the feet, in keeping with rhythm. It is a universal expression of human emotion, regardless of age or nationality and constitutes a basic sort of relaxation for primitive tribes. It may be performed for visual effect or for the personal satisfaction of the dancers" (*Dictionary of Anthropology*, under the entry "dance").

In the traditional highland dance, both stated purposes of the dance undoubtedly played a role. Rural society had great respect for refined skills of dancers, so that a dance exhibition was an important element in gaining respect. The primary purpose of a dance, however, was to demonstrate how partners felt about each other. There existed a whole system of signs and behavior for those who danced to convey their feelings to others watching them. This is based on a man's choice of his partner. While waiting in line for the dance, a fellow agrees with a friend what partner he is to lead out to the floor for him. Not just any girl, but that special chosen one, which right away defines his feelings for her. Custom does not allow the girl to refuse to dance, even if she does not reciprocate his interest. Then she can let him know during the dance in the generally accepted way (by the reserve in her smile, distance kept from her partner, a proud posture) that she does not return his feelings.

A dance began with the dancer's entry to face the music. It was customary for the dancer to greet the musicians and toss the usual fee for the playing. Then the dancer sang the chosen melody and the band slowly followed him. After the singing was over, the band took up the rhythm proper for the melody and the dancer's friend, bowing to the chosen partner, led her to the floor. He began the so-called *zwyrtany* (turning) dance with her, which is to say he turned first one way and then the other with her, and then bowed and moved away. Then the actual dance of the couple followed, and everything depended on them. If there was "something between them," they would show this during the dance by smiles, looks, hugs, the man's feigned aggressiveness, and the woman's coquettish tractability. All this was during the dance, i.e., during foot movements carried out in accordance with generally accepted rules, but still demonstrating individual imagination. The male dancer stopped the dance by going up to the musicians to perform the next couplet. The custom ws that the first dance was calm, a walking dance, usually set to an *ozwodna* melody, during which the boy followed the girl who retreated with dance steps. When he changed the form of the dance into "ozwodna from behind," his partner advanced toward him. Once in a while he made her turn around on her own axis by clapping his hands. The next couplet and dance was to the rapid rhythm of the *drobny* or *krzesany* tunes. Here the dancer exhibited his whole skill with perfect execution of dance steps. While she danced at his side (*boczkowanie*), the girl showed that she admired his skill. The third dance was of a slower tempo, traditionally a melody known as *brzozowicka* or *wiecna* (eternal). Here the precision of the boy's foot movements, the dance's consistence with the melody's rhythm and occasional changes to the *chodzony* (walking) tempo played an important role. As he concluded his dance, the boy shouted in the direction of the musicians: "Zielono! (Green!)" and the band changed to the melody indicated to them, while the partners danced the *zwyrtany* (turning) dance as they put their arms around each other. Then there followed thanks to the girl partner and to the musicians. Sometimes, and this was also acceptable, other women joined the "zwyrtanie" before the second and third dance, forming a dancing circle.

The *zbojnicki* (highland robbers) dance is a man's dance performed by at least four dancers with a ciupaga in hand. The dance is preceded by a couplet to the tune of a march and after the band takes up the melody, the dancers march around with an elongated dance step. During their march, they turn to each other in pairs and clang their ciupagas. Standing before the musicians, they sing the melody of the zbojnicki tune and again go around in circles. After one of them gives the sign, they begin a dance with knee bends: knee bend and one foot forward, knee bend and the other foot forward. Then again a couplet and the second part of the dance. Here sometimes you can see a lively step called *hajduk* (XVI century dance), when the dancers thrust their legs forward in turn without coming out of the knee bend. This difficult step is seldom performed.

Sadly, the highland dances performed these days are far removed from the old standards. The visual side of the dance is now brought to the forefront, without regard for the whole traditional side of this cultural phenomenon. Tawdry showiness reduces the dance to the level of circus stunts, without dignity or responsibility of the male partner toward the woman, who becomes nothing but a background for him. The universality of the dance is also disappearing; more and more highlanders, especially young ones, do not know how to perform the highland dances. The folklore troupes are also following the fashion of "giving the public what they want," making clumsy attempts to ape such professional song and dance troupes as Slask and Mazowsze, which present stylized folk dances without sparing the highland dances among others. The posiady and neighborly musics have been supplanted by discotheques. In the field of song and dance, we can see in the Highlands the leveling influence of relentlessly advancing unification.

Old houses in Chocholow.

Interior of old highland dwelling.

Photos of old Podhale by Ryszard Bukowski, courtesy of Tatra Museum in Zakopane. Other photographs by author.

Shepherds' huts in Chocholow valley.

Zakopane around 1850.

Chapel in Jaszczurowka built in 1910.

Pre-1810 Gasienica chapel at entrance to old cemetery in Zakopane.

"Koleba" Zakopane-style house designed by Stanislaw Witkiewicz

Desk, table and chest built around 1910 in Zakopane style.

"Robbers' dance," a highlander dance for men.

Highland robbers in a Christmas creche painted on glass.

"Janosik with Girlfriend,"woodcut by W. Skoczylas (1883-1934).

"Janosik Fighting the Bear," woodcut by W. Skoczylas.

"Janosik and the Robbers," woodcut by W. Skoczylas.

"Kostka Napierski at the Head of His Highlanders," woodcut by W. Skoczylas.

"A Tatra highlander," woodcut by Wladyslaw Skoczylas.

Pieniny.

Chalubinski villa.

Highland station in Zakopane.

*Chapel in Koscieliska valley,
painting by Janina Kaminska.*

The old church in Zakopane, painting by Janina Kaminska.

Wooden church in Chocholow, painting by W.E. Radzikowski.

Another view of the old church in Chocholow.

Steczynski, view of Zakopane.

Steczynski, Pieniny.

Steczynski, view of a castle.

Steczynski, Eye-of-the-Sea Lake.

The church in Debno, painted by J. Pieniazek.

Lopuszna, the Tetmajer manor.

The church in Brzegi.

In the Jan Zietawa workshop in Chocholow.

One that didn't get away.

CHAPTER X

Highland Folk Art

Enhancing utilitarian objects with artistic decoration is a spontaneous and common phenomenon in the Highlands. It is really decorative art and the work of individual artists is clearly identifiable. The shapes of objects and the methods of producing them have evolved over the centuries from primitive, simple forms to increasingly complex ones, showing the influence of neighboring lands—the Cracow region, Slovakia and Hungary.

In the Highlands, decorative art is seen on residential buildings, household furnishings, tools, utensils and other articles used daily, as well as clothing.

Kings ornament Highland roofs.

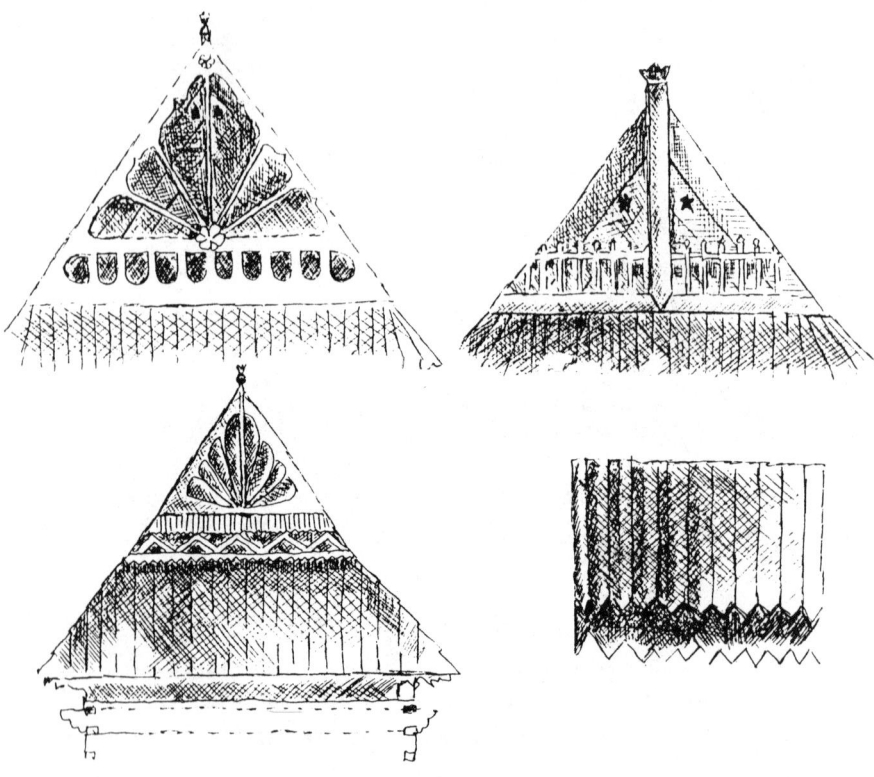

Peaks are topped off with a variety of symbols.

Highland roofs are ornamented with so-called "kings," and the very peaks of houses are topped off with representations of the sun and other symbols. Roof beams end in carved *pazdury* or claws, and the lowest rows of shingles have a *pilka* or sawtooth edge.

Entry doors and windows are an integral part of the design of a Highland building, but their very construction is decorative, and wooden pegs with beveled and fluted heads placed symetrically in the jambs add further ornmentation.

In homes, the carved ceiling beam (*sosrab*) of the "white" room may be decorated with simple geometric or plant

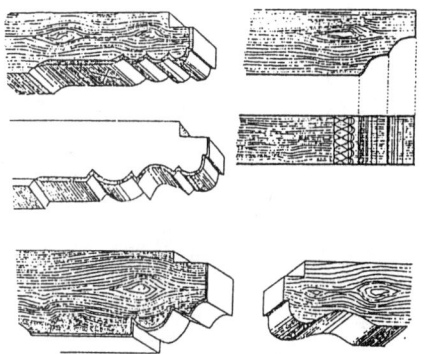

Roof beam claws or "pazdury."

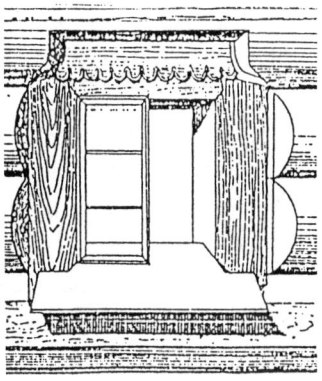

Windows and doors are an integral part of the design. Ornamental pegs are used as a decorative element.

forms or very intricate artistic forms. Usually the date the house was built is carved into the "sosreb."

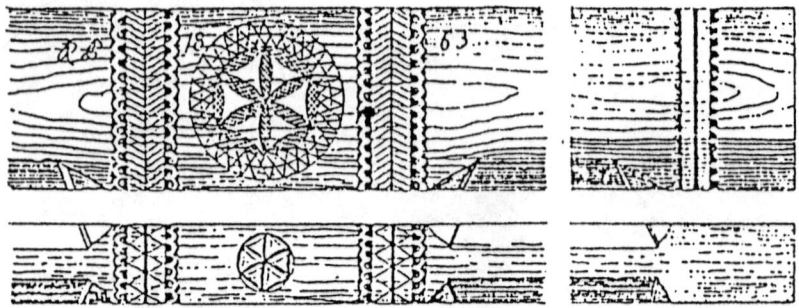

The date the house was built was often carved into a ceiling beam.

Household furniture, especially shelves, are frequently decorated. The *listwy*, a shelf placed about half a meter below the ceiling, was used to display the popular paintings on glass. A small shelf with openings in the horizontal board to hold spoon handles, *lyznik*, was an important decorative element in the main room.

Highland tables and stools, initially simple in form, in time came to have a variety of shapes and carvings. When visitors to the Tatras purchased these pieces as folk art, demand for them grew. The Zakopane style of decoration was distinctive. Two artists of merit are Stanislaw Witkiewicz and Wojciech Brzega, the first highlander artist with professional training.

Carvings enhanced many items in a household, including the edges of shelves.

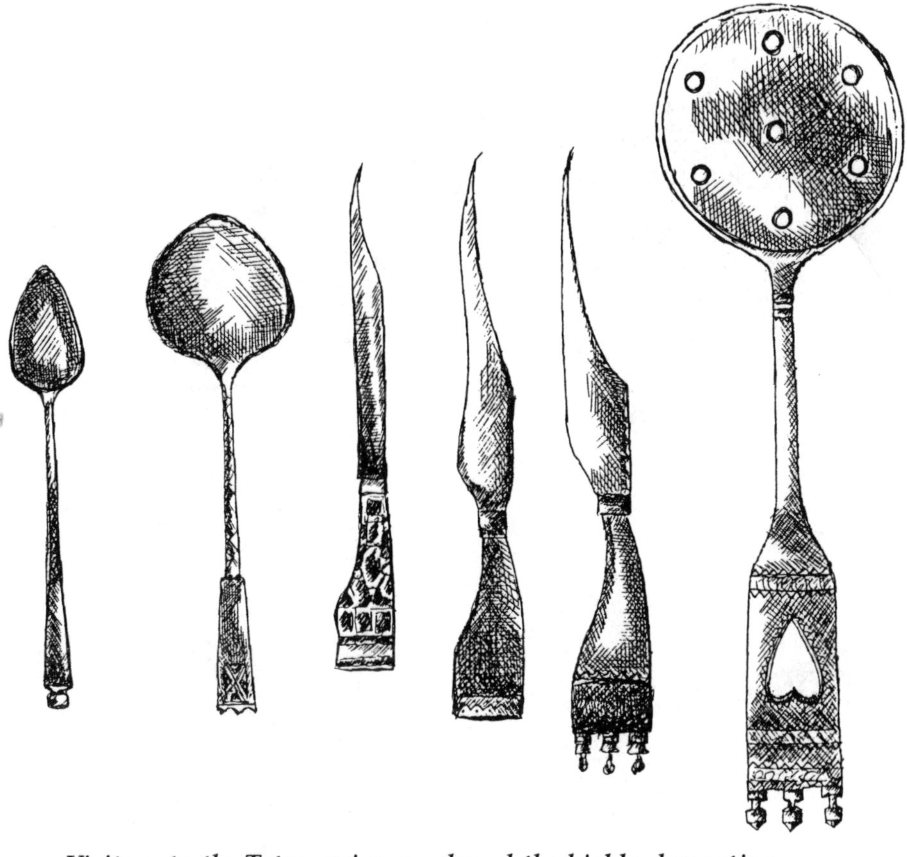

Visitors to the Tatra region purchased the highly decorative household items, such as these utensils, and the demand for them grew.

Artistic iron work flourished. Door and gate hinges used outside had a ramified shape, modeled on the *gadzik* (snake) form often used in shelf decoration. Gratings used inside, as well as smaller objects such as knives, *ciupagas* (highlander sticks with hatchets), large spoons for stirring milk in kettles, the *grudzielnice* and even small spoons for every-day use were made more attractive with ornamentation.

The desire to beautify objects was often expressed in shepherding motifs. Popular wooden utensils called "czerpaki" (dipping cups) had shaped carved handles. Molds

Popular wooden utensils included dipping cups with carved handles and molds for smoked cheeses.

used for smoked cheeses were made of two cone-shaped parts, carved on the inside. Pressed between the two parts of the mold, the cheese took on the form of the carving inside the mold. Such cheeses, still popular today, are called *ozcypki*. Little birds (ducks) and deer were common shapes.

Decorations cut into wood may be geometric shapes, plant motifs, or representations of animals, even people. The simplest geometric form is the *skiba*, a plain cut (groove), one next to another, which may be patterned on the surface of an object either vertically, horizontally or on a slant. Grooves intersecing at a right angle form a *recica* (sand strainer). They may be straight or slanted, or *koziato* (uneven). *Mirwa* (criss-crossing) is formed of lines of the letter X. *Pilka* (saw), either one or two-sided, refers to a sawtooth edge cut into wood.

Simple geometric patterns covered surfaces of objects.

Designs based on plants were used on larger surfaces. They bore the names *ostrewka* (pole with crosswise sticks for drying hay), *klosko, goje, podstol* among others. Rosettes were also an important element in Highland decorative art.

Plant and animal motifs were popoular.

Among animal motifs, the most widely used were the *gadzik*, a stylized snake with a head, and an eagle rising in flight. When early beekeepers shaped hives from a single tree trunk, they often took on human images of saints, old bearded men or even bears.

Ornamentation of highland clothing developed with the decoration of homes and their furnishings. The oldest surviving illustrations from the XVIII and XIX centuries show plain highlander clothing, with no decoration, made from sheep wool, sheep skin and the readily available linen. The first items of ornamentation were the *listwy* (ribbons of colored linen sewn on to women's attire), and *snurki* (thick woolen, usually black or navy, pieces of twine) sewn along the side of men's trousers. In time additional pieces of *snurki* were added to show the wealth of the owner.

Highlander women were happy to buy novelty items from merchants at fairs in neighboring districts. The decorative traditions of Cracow (as seen in women's vests) and Hungary (the *parzenice* embroidery on the front of trousers) dominated highland regional costume for many years. Over time, a stylized Parnassus grass motif (*carlin aculis*) replaced the Cracow plant motif on vests. However, recently a return to the old forms in male and female garb has been initiated by young people.

The collars and sleeves of highland women's blouses are decorated with "white embroidery," in a pattern of small openings edged with white thread. The same type of embroidered plant motifs has been a fashionable ornamentation on men's shirts for the past decade.

Leather goods are another material that folk artists in the Highlands like to decorate—wide flock-master's belts (*bacowskie*) and narrower shepherd's belts (*juhaskie*), as well as Tatra mountaineer's moccasins (*kierpce*). They are stamped in various designs and enhanced with pins, knobs and buckles of metal.

Highland pins are a special element in the field of metalwork. In the beginning, when the highland shirt had no buttons and was tied at the neck with a linen ribbon, it was pinned at the chest with a piece of metal with a hole in it, through which the edges of the shirt were drawn and pierced with a pin. These pieces of metal were decorated with

The decorative traditions of Cracow and Hungary dominated Highland women's costumes.

semi-circles around the edges. Further development in the ornamentation of pins included the addition of a cross at the top, dangling *kistki* and a pipe-cleaning gadget.

Over time, the highland pipe also became very ornate. The most beautiful and thus the most desirable pipes were made by highlanders in the village of Ratulow.

Native ceramics of the Rocky Highlands were poor because of the shortage of the kind of clay necessary for its production. The highlanders stocked up on ceramic products at fairs in Nowy Targ and Kezmark in Slovakia. The situation was similar with paintings on glass. Such paintings, usually with religious themes, were sold by itinerant merchants from Slovakia. After World War I, this form of painting nearly died out, except in the Highlands, from where it radiated back to Slovakia.

The highlander loves horses, so on the occasion of great celebrations, he takes care that the equipment worn by the horse is not only utilitarian, but also beautiful. Patterns for parade horse gear came originally from Cracow, but were developed in the Highlands into a rich form of folk art.

Highland folk art underwent several different periods in its not always natural development. When, in the second half of the XIX century, Zakopane became famous and a growing number of visitors came to the Tatras and interest in original highland artistic output was great, efforts were made to improve it. A wood-carving school for developing the talents of local youths was opened in Zakopane in 1880, which offered education in the trades as well as the decorative arts. Its first directors (it was the Austro-Hungarian empire) were foreigners, Czech and Hungarian. They promoted the "Tyrolean" style then fashionable in Europe. In time, however, through the influence of Stanislaw Witkiewicz and Wojciech Brzega, this was reversed. But folk art in the Highlands is still "living a double life": one of mass production for commercial sale and the other of handwork by recognized folk artists who belong to a country-wide art cooperative.

Highland pipes were very ornate. Shirts were fastened with met-al pins, some of which had a dangling pipe-cleaning gadget.

PART THREE

TRAVELER'S GUIDE
TO PODHALE

EXCURSION I

Nowy Targ

Situated at the southern foot of the Gorce elevation is NOWY TARG, the historic capital of the Tatra highlands (Podhale). Where the streams called White Dunajec and Black Dunajec converge to create the Dunajec River rushing east toward the Pieniny Mountains, during the Middle Ages there ran a communication route linking Hungary with Cracow. The oldest preserved historical sources from the XIII century also mention settlements such as Stare Clo (Antiquuum Theloneum), Dunayetsh, Dlugie Pole (Longi Campi), but whatever stood at the confluence of the two Dunajec streams was destroyed by the Tartars in 1260. In documents from the time after the Tartar invasions, there appear names such as: Nowe Miasto (Nova Civitas) and Nowy Targ (Novum Forum), which means New Market. In 1346 King Kazimierz the Great granted this town a foundation charter and commercial privileges, which played a decisive part in its further development. A document from 1409 already mentions a castle and the town of Novitarg. A starost appointed by the king resided in the castle and governed over the whole area described as the Nowy Targ administrative district. It was a very sparsely populated region, with only a few settlements within close proximity of the town. Six kilometers south, near the settlement of Szaflary there was another castle, or rather a fortress in the defense system of the border regions of the land of the Polans.

Carriage-worthy roads branched out from Nowy Targ in six directions, mostly running along the rivers, but sometimes also through the mountain ridges. Villages sprang up along these roads, as the population increased in the new territories from Nowy Targ toward the Tatras. For centuries, Nowy Targ was the economic center of Podhale because weekly fairs were held there by way of royal privilege. Thursday was the traditional day for these events. Highlanders from all over the region gathered on these occasions, from as far away as Spisz and Orawa. Nowy Targ was also the administrative center and district headquarters, with the court, and institutions for education and care of the ill. Many craftsmen and tradesmen made their living by supplying household goods. Today the production and economic importance of the town has decreased, but still on Thursdays hundreds of people—including visitors to the region—gather in the Market Square or adjoining squares.

Fires have destroyed the wooden structures of Nowy Targ constructed during the Middle Ages. The oldest remaining building is the St. Catherine Church, whose Gothic presbytery dates to 1346. Its Baroque nave was added 300 years later. Many sacral elements of the church date from the XVI to the XVIII century. The free-standing belfry was built in 1702. This church, located near the Market Square, at 1 Koscielna Street, served as the parish church for many centuries. When it became too small for the growing community's needs, a new parish church was built. The new church on Queen Jadwiga's Street was finished in 1951. A small larch wood church named for St. Anna, probably built in the XVI century in the traditional highland style is more renowned. Legend has it that highland robbers founded this church to beg God's forgiveness for their sins. The little church stands on the other side of the Dunajec River, on St. Anna Street near the cemetery. The way to the Market Square leads over a foot-bridge next to the ice house.

Surrounded by old tenement houses forming a square, the Nowy Targ Market Square has a Town Hall in the center, housing a highland museum upstairs. The rather modest exhibition includes tools and products of Nowy Targ from the XIX century, sacral painting and sculpture, old photographs depicting the town and persons of merit connected with its history. It is worth mentioning that in 1919 General Galica (then a colonel) was granted the title of Honorary Citizen of the Town of Nowy Targ. In 1918 General Galica organized the regiments of the Highland Riflemen of the Polish Army in Nowy Targ.

A dozen or so exhibits and photographs call to mind the memory of Nowy Targ Jews, who until 1939 formed a sizable percentage of the town's population. They were all wiped out by the Nazis, and their belongings disappeared. There remain only small fragments of this significant part of Nowy Targ's history.

A statue of Wladyslaw Orkan erected in 1934 through the efforts of the foundation of the Highlanders' Association in North America stands in front of the Town Hall-Museum. This fact is commemorated by a plaque at the base of the statue. Wladyslaw Orkan (actually Franciszek Smreczynski /1875-1930/) was a writer and poet who focused his literary output on the highlands and Gorce. He was a son of the region himself, born to a poor farmer's family in Poreba Wielka. He introduced into Polish literature the highland village and its people at the turn of the XX century. His writing linked the regional viewpoint to the highlanders' emigration to North America.

The post-war (WWII) building boom in Nowy Targ was due to the construction of a shoe manufacturing plant near the town. New residential areas were developed on the southern outskirts of the town, while single housing was located on the other side of the river, on the Kowaniec hill. Following the administrative reforms introduced in the seventies, which involved the liquidation of districts, Nowy Targ lost its earlier role of administrative center and became one of the communes in the Nowy Sacz province. At the same time Zakopane, located at the foot of the Tatras and referred to as "Poland's Winter Capital," continued to expand. Thus now the highlands have two capitals (not counting Warsaw). However, Nowy Sacz province remains the best starting point for visiting Podhale. It is a communication center from which you can make walking excursions into Gorce and car journeys through the settlement trails of the Podhale highlanders. The main road linking Cracow with Zakopane runs right by the town. It connects with the route from the south and southwest of Europe which enters Polish territory in Chyzno (32 kilometers from Nowy Targ). From a junction on the eastern outskirts of town travelers had head for various destinations: Cracow, Zakopane, Szczawnica, Bukowina and the border crossing in Nowa Polana, to Orawa and through Ludzmierz, Chocholow to the border crossing in Sucha Hora. The National Automobile Communication—with an access network for fifty or more localities—is located at 20 Ludzmierska Street. There is a hotel near the station, with many restaurants in the vicinity as well. A fifteen minute ride down Kolejowa Street brings you to the rail station for the Chabowka-Zakopane line. On the edge of town, from the direction of Szaflary, there is a twenty-four hour gas station with a large repair and parts garage nearby. There are also many stores in Nowy Targ, where it is easy to stock up on supplies for a journey by car.

Podhale has three main tourism centers: Nowy Targ near Gorce, Kroscienko-Szczawnica in the east near Pieniny, and Zakopane by the Tatras. Nowy Targ is also a good sally-port for excursions into Gorce. It is a good idea to make this trip with someone who knows these mountains, so that nothing worth noting on the trails will be missed. Two of the most popular excursions can be made on your own, but always (after all, these are the mountains!) in someone's company. The first is to Turbacz, an elevation overlooking the town. The way leads over a bridge on the Dunajec and by the settlement of Kowaniec along the side of the road. Then over a marked trail, through meadows and woods to the Wszolowa Polana and Dlugie Mlaki to the Orkan Hostel near Turbacz. This is a central point for further excursions into various parts of Gorce. The hostel has sleeping accommodations with sanitary facilities, a restaurant and a club room. The excursion takes about five hours round trip. Another excursion easily made from Nowy Targ is Rabka; aside from the beautiful views in Gorce and the panorama of the Tatras to the south, it is interesting to see this famous resort, considered especialy beneficial for children. The walk there should take some five hours, with a return trip by bus. There is an active branch of the Polish Association of Tourism-Sightseeing in Nowy Targ, where visitors can obtain information and help.

EXCURSION II

Nowy
Targ-Szczawnica

The main road leading through the southern slopes of the Gorce toward the east initially goes through populated areas. Thus it would be better to select a way that avoids the center of the town, traveling down a street that leads over a bridge on the Bialy Dunajec near the settlement of Bereki, directly to the village of WAKSMUND. Historians date this village at the XIII century and connect it with the migration of German colonists from Spisz (Szepes) toward the Dunajec. They blended with the local population, leaving behind only a German-sounding name. Until 1519 Waksmund was an independent parish, later abolished in favor of nearby Nowy Targ. Old documents provide information about a parish school in 1598, (that is after the parish had been liquidated), as well as a survey of 1638 when the village had "10 inhabitants and 5 farmers." The village administrator's office was held by the Waksmundzki clan for many years. During the time of Nazi occupation, Waksmund was an important center for the partisan units active in the Gorce region. In revenge for their help to the partisans and the villagers' participation in anti-German activities, the Nazis executed some 20 villagers in the years 1943 and 1944, and fifty or more of those arrested later died in prisons and concentration camps. It is worthwhile to stop in this village to visit a brick church located near a bridge over the Dunajec. It was built in 1887, but its paintings and baptistry are from a somewhat earlier period. There is a cemetery near the church where some of the partisans who fell during the war are buried.

The houses are built close together on both sides of the road and there is only a sign to let you know that you have already reached the next village—OSTROWSKO. Part of the village lies on the left side of the Dunajec with the towering Czuba Ostrowska, measuring 916 meters above sea level (abbreviated *m. asl*) in the background. The village came into being in a way similar to Waksmund in the XIII century, as a knight's estate, and in 1519 it formed its own independent parish. After 250 years, the royal tenant built a new wooden church, which survived until a fire in 1915. Construction on the present church, located to the right of the road to Gronkow, was completed in 1927. Tourist trails depart from Ostrowsko to Czuba Ostrowska (1½ hrs.) and to Turbacz (3 hrs.). A sizable group of emigrants from Ostrowsko are living in the U.S.A. and belong to Circle No. 51 of the Polish Highlanders Alliance in North America located in Chicago. This is evident in the looks of the village, where new houses predominate and the church is well taken care of.

Near the last houses of the village, there is a bridge over the Lesnica Stream which flows into the Dunajec. About one kilometer from this bridge can be seen the first houses of the village of LOPUSZNA. It is located along the highway and a road leading left to the banks of the Dunajec and, after a bridge, more than four kilometers uphill on both sides of the Lopuszanski Potok. Documented beginnings of the village go back to the XIV century, but its sparse population caused its parish to be incorporated into neighboring Ostrowsko in 1596. Its independent status was returned two hundred years later. The wooden church in the village has been altered and repaired numerous times, resulting in a mixture of Gothic and baroque. The Gothic triptych of the main altar dates back to the XV century and many old scultpures and decorative elements, along with two bells, the older of which goes back more than 400 years, make this venerable church worthy of a visit. Another place worth seeing is an old estate in Lopuszna, since 1800 the home of the Lisicki family. In 1824 the Tetmajers received this estate through marriage. A member of this family, Kazimierz Przerwa-Tetmajer (1865-1940) was a renowned poet, writer and playwright. His poems and works written in prose, based on highland folklore, such as the novels *The Legend of the Tatras* and *On the Rocky Highlands*, were instrumental in popularizing highland subjects in Poland. The renovated mansion now houses the Museum of the Culture of the Nobility. The Stocking Center for salmon-like fish of the Polish Fishing Association, the only one in Poland, is located by the Lopuszanski Potok. It has six buildings, 18 ponds (0.7 hectares of water-level) and 120 breeding devices with a capacity of two million units of roe. The center supplies fishing associations throughout the submontane district with stock fish, and breeds up to 200,000 palcaks (fries—fish to 5-8 centimeters in length), which are let into the mountain rivers. There are trout and Dunajec bulltrout. A Scientific-Experimental Station and a Home of Fishing Culture are attached to the center, which also offers accommodations. There are many other room and board facilities in Lopuszna. Some residents have full accommodations for visitors with all meals. There is a post office and restaurant. A regional group organized in the village, called "Lopusnianie," has taken part in many recitals and won prizes at festivals and regional contests.

A scant three kilometers beyond Lopuszna lies the next village, called HARKLOWA. It was founded before 1335 as a knightly settlement of the Sreniawit Order. The parish dates back to 1354. Together with the villages of Knurowo and Szlemberk which lie on the other side of the Dunajec, it formed one property in an area owned by the king. There was a mansion and a defensive blockhouse, fragments of which remain to this day along the roadside. A little church in Harklowa, which now serves as a museum of medieval art, is worth a visit. The triptych of the main altar and the fragments of its wall-paintings are more than 450 years old. Harklowa is a center known thoughout Poland by fishermen anxious to try their skills on the Dunajec. From this rather small place, many residents have emigrated to the U.S.A., forming Circle No. 25 of the Polish Highlanders Alliance in North America with headquarters in Chicago, Illinois.

About a kilometer from the last houses of Harklowa, a road veers off to the right, over a bridge to Knurowo. Another kilometer later, the houses of the village of DEBNO appear on the right side of the road. It is necessary to leave the highway, turning right among the houses, then at the crossroads left, to arrive at the historic small wooden church, among the most interesting in this region of Poland. The village dates back to the end of the XIII century, while Urban from Grywald received the document authorizing him to found it in 1335. The little church, surrounded by trees more than 400 years old and representing a relic of nature, was built late in the XV century. The upper walls, the ceiling and many other interior elements are covered with unusually beautiful wall-paintings from about 1500. The church contains relics of earlier sacral buildings, such a crucifix on a cross beam, the so-called "rainbow," from the end of the XIV century. The appointments of the baroque side altar, decorated with figures of the Madonna and the "holy ladies" from c. 1440 are noteworthy. A curator gives tours when the church is not in use. He also has tapes in several languages for visitors on the history of the village and the paintings in the church.

Right outside of Debno the highway crosses a new bridge over the Dunajec which puts you on the left bank of the river. This is the beginning of the road built to bypass a huge water storage reservoir with a dam and hydro-electric plant near Czorsztyn. To see the upper section of the future lake, it is necessary to turn right after Debno to the road to Niedzica. To the left can be seen the houses and church steeple of Debno, shielded with a tall soil and cement embankment. This village survived because of its special historical significance. To the right, high on the slope, is the village of Nowe Maniowy, which is unique in this region because of its building style characteristic of urban one-family homes. Other villages, such as Kloszkowce, Mizerna, Czorsztyn, Niedzica and Sromowce Nizne shared the fate of Stare Maniowy to some extent, being moved to higher ground.

The idea for a system of dams developed after a catastrophic flood caused immense damage along the Dunajec all the way to the Vistula in 1934. From the very beginning experts, followed by public opinion, were divided into two camps: one in favor of a final "subjugation" of the Dunajec and of making it a river serving man, and the other representing concern that the unique natural and scenic attributes of this lovely corner of the country be preserved. Heated discussions on this subject, involving people in high authority, raged until the outbreak of the war. After the war and subsequent floods (though not as devastating as the one in 1934), the concept of building a dam and a retentive water reservoir won out. It is a massive undertaking, requiring tremendous outlays in money and materials, which are always in short supply. This is why it is taking so long. Actually, in 1994 there was talk of a speedy start to fill the reservoir, which is expected to take several years. It all depends on the springtime rain runoff from the whole Dunajec river basin. The river cannot be completely closed off.

After returning to the highway near Debno and traveling

about five kilometers beyond the bridge, there appears on a hillside to the right the settlement NOWE MANIOWY. It is a completely new settlement, not more than twenty years old. The modern outline of the church dominates the view, with a nearby new school building and a fire house behind it. Nowe Maniowy was conceived as a resort center near the reservoir. There already exist rooms to rent with all facilities, a restaurant with a cafe and numerous shops. The people of Nowe Maniowy are anticipating new opportunities. Not all, however, since many residents of Stare Maniowy emigrated to the U.S.A. a long time ago. They are organized in circle No. 22 of the Polish Highlanders Alliance in North America.

The highway continues along the shore of the future lake and, after three kilometers, approaches the village of KLUSZKOWCE which lies at the foot of the Luban elevation (1,211 m. asl). According to documents, this village has existed since 1660 (earlier called Klioskowice or Kluskow) as an independent parish. In 1811 a fire destroyed an old wooden church, then the whole village went up in smoke five years later. The rebuilt town survived on agriculture, animal husbandry and the exploitation of the local quarry, which employed 300 people. Shortly before the war a community center was built in the village, which temporarily housed the village chapel. In connection with the construction of the reservoir on the Dunajec, the lower part of the village was liquidated. Many residents of Kluszkowce emigrated to America. In Chicago they formed their own circle of the Polish Highlanders Alliance under No. 49.

About one kilometer past the village, the highway crosses the Snozka mountain pass (also called the Krosnicka Mountain Pass—653 m. asl) separating Gorce from Pieniny. A nearby sign indicates the direction to CZORSZTYN. About two kilometers over a paved road brings you to this settlement. In part, it is composed of new housing, since Lower Czorsztyn found itself at the bottom of the future lake. The main attractions of this locality are the remains of a fortified castle which dates back to the XIV century, when it was built by King Kazimierz the Great (who ruled from 1333 to 1370). On a limestone hill rising ninety meters above the valley, it was a defensive structure on the route between Cracow, Slovakia and Hungary. Both Polish and Hungarian kings stayed at the castle, since it was the place of their diplomatic meetings. All that remains of the castle today is a massive, quadrangular tower, preserved to the third floor, and a 30-meter protective buttress. Both of these relics are from the earliest history of the castle. Many years of restoration and conservation work have already made possible visits to one castle chamber and two scenic terraces. These terraces afford a view of a wonderful panorama of the Tatras to the south, the eastern part of the highlands and below—the massive dam built under the castle and the tail end of the area to be occupied by the future lake. There is parking for cars at the end of the road, and the rest of the way to the castle gate, c. 300 meters, has to be made on foot.

After visiting what is left of the Czorsztyn castle, you should return to the highway leading to Szczawnica. After the Snozka mountain pass, you reach the settlement of Krosnica and to the right of it the road leads to Katy. KATY is now the starting point for rafting down the Dunajec River. The 1960 resolution of the World Congress of the International Union of Nature Preservation attests to the natural and touristic qualities of this small corner of Poland:

> Because of the deep impression made by the magnificence of the gorge of the Dunajec and the Pieniny National Park, the Seventh General Meeting expresses the opinion that from the botanical standpoint, as well as because of the beauty of landscape, it is one of the most lovely and precious spots in Europe. It deserves to the popularized all over the world.

One way to become acquainted with this enchanting area is to take a rafting trip down the Dunajec to Szczawnica. At the start of the rafting expedition in Katy, there is a large parking facility, a waiting room, box office and many stands selling souvenirs from the Pieniny district. From May to August, the box-office is open from 8am to 4pm, and in September and October to 1pm.

From the starting point to the end station in Szczawnica Nizna, the rafting trip takes about three hours. The rafts are made of five wooden skiffs, 5.75 meters long and 45 centimeters wide, tied together. Such a raft, equipped with benches, accommodates ten adults or eight adults and four children. Two raftsmen—a master and an assistant—steer the raft by means of long wooden poles. They are properly trained and experienced in rafting down the Dunajec. They have to undergo examinations, which ensure that the passengers will reach their destination safely.

The first part of the expedition leads down the flat valley of the Dunajec, where the river forms the border between Poland and Slovakia. Elevations appear on both sides: the Polish hamlet of Sromowce Srednie and the Slovak Majery. Then the river turns sharply left and flows directly east for about a kilometer and a half. On the left it passes the village of Sromowce Nizne and on the right, partly concealed by trees, can be seen the roofs of the Red Monastery. The magnificent view of the Three Crowns massif is slowly revealed to the north. A kilometer past Sromowce Nizne begins the actual gorge of the river through the mountains. In the next three kilometers, the Dunajec takes seven bends for a total eight kilometer length of water. As the drop in the river increases, the rapid current is interspersed with calmer sections. In its most narrow spot, near the so-called "Janosik's Leap," the river is reduced to some ten meters in width, and its depth measures eight meters. The remainder of trip involves changing currents, meanderings, rapids and ever changing magnificent views. The raftsmen supply supply information along the way, and amuse the tourists with guessing games as to where the Dunajec will turn after the approaching mountain, which is not always obvious. After the Lesnicki Potok enters the Dunajec, the Polish-Slovak border moves away from the river over hillsides to the east. From there on, the trip to the final destination in Szczawnica Nizna, is made over a Dunajec which has been "soothed" after the difficulties of a fast run.

It is possible to return to the parking lot in Katy from Szczawnica by bus, unless someone who has already made the trip earlier is willing to bring the car around to a parking lot near the final landing-place in Szczawnica.

Those who return to Katy after the rafting trip, or give it up at the pass, will reach KROSCIENKO after six kilometers. The existence of this town has been documented since the XIV century; it bears the characteristics of a small country town. During the Middle Ages it was generously endowed with privileges by the Polish kings, and bravely resisted pressure from the magnates who sought to subjugate the Kroscienko townspeople. At the start of the XIX century, there was great interest in the mineral sources which the inhabitants had utilized for household and medicinal purposes. Scientific research confirmed this, and the estuaries of springs called "Maria," "Stefan" and "Michalina" were enclosed and adapted to large-scale exploitation. The oxalate compounds contain bicarbonate-chloride-calcium-soda, from 3 to 8 grams of solid components per liter of water. They also contain free carbon dioxide. Because these waters were advertized and distributed in bottles in the larger cities, people seeking treatment began to arrive in Kroscienko in increasing numbers. Baths and boarding-houses were constructed in the town, but it failed to develop as a large resort because of the proximity of the flourishing "queen of Polish waters"—Szczawnica.

The most interesting historical monument in Kroscienko is an old parish church standing at the crossroads near the Market Square. It is one of the few historical brick churches in the region, built in the XIV century with Gothic elements. Besides the many interior fragments worth seeing, which are explained in detail at the entrance, the crowning glory of this church are the wall paintings resurrected from under many layers of plaster—paintings dating from the XIV, XV and XVI centuries. The discovery of these paintings and their restoration caused a sensation in its time and was a major achievement. Jagiellonska Street leads to a bridge over the Dunajec, beyond which, in a part of town known as Zawodzie, can be found the local mineral springs.

A four-kilometer ride over the highway brings you to one of the important Polish resorts—SZCZAWNICA. The beginnings of this locality are somewhat unclear, but there was definite historical mention of it in the first half of the XV century. Its houses are picturesquely scattered over the hillsides, by the Grajcarek Brook and the Szczawny Stream, reaching the banks of the Dunajec. The development of Szczawnica began in the XIX century, when the local mineral springs, called "sour waters" or "oxalates," were first exploited for medicinal purposes, on a large scale after 1828. The real boom of the resort dates to 1839, when a new owner Jozef Szalay invested in health resort facilities, villas for the guests, baths and a park. The mineral composition of the waters was tested and deemed to be superior because of the variety of its components, especially bromine and iodine. In the 60's and 70's of the past century, several thousand people visited Szczawnica each year. After 1900, another resort some 50 kilometers to the east, also rich in medicinal mineral waters, became fashionable. This was Krynica. Before World War II, an electrical plant and sewer system were constructed in Szczawnica. A modern "inhalatorium"—a sanatorium to treat certain lung diseases was built as well. After the war, a center for the treatment of anthracosis and silicosis—the occupational illneses of miners and metallurgists—was installed there. At present Szczawnica is still one of the top centers for treatment of pulmonary diseases, along with less serious diseases of the alimentary canal and circulatory problems.

During your stay in the Tatra highlands, it would be worthwhile to restore your health in Szczawnica. Visitors have a wide choice between luxurious and modest accommodations. They can also avail themselves of various forms of medical care and good alimentary fare depending on their tastes and the depth of their pockets. Prices are subject to change seasonally, but they are undoubtedly lower than spas in Czechoslovakia or Switzerland.

When taking the cure in Szczawnica for a week or two, you should take advantage of the chance to visit interesting places in this town—picturesquely located by the Dunajec River on the slopes of the Pieniny Mountains—and to make a few enchanting trips into the mountains. First of all, natural mineral waters from springs bearing names such as Waleria, Szymon, Magdalena, Wanda, Stefan and Jozefina, should be tried. They should all be tasted, of course, with emphasis on the one prescribed by the doctor. Outstanding among them is the water from the Magdalena spring, the most strongly mineralized alkaline-saline oxalate, containing 26 grams of mineral components per liter, primarily iodine and bromide potassium.

In order to grasp at least a rudimentary idea of the history of the region, you have to visit the Pieniny Museum located on the top floor of a building on the Jozef Dietl Square. The museum is open daily, except Monday, from 10am to 1pm and 2pm of 4pm. The main room houses an exhibition entitled "Folk Culture of the Pieniny Region." The exhibits displayed there present the past and the present in the life of the Pieniny highlanders. There follows a history of the Szczawnica health resort, the martyrdom and struggle of the population during the German occupation and a re-creation of Szalay's house from the XIX century. A valuable collection of folk sculpture, paintings on glass and canvas by well-known artists decorate other rooms of the museum. There is also a series of portraits of persons instrumental in organizing and furnishing the museum. The Zdrojowa cafe is located on Dietl Square, housing the "Zbojnicka Piwnica" (Highlander Robbers' Cellar), maintained in the regional style.

Highlanders from Kroscienko, Szczawnica and surrounding villages who emigrated to North America are gathered in Circle No. 50 of the Polish Highlanders Alliance headquartered in Chicago.

From Szczawnica to the Pieniny

When making an excursion into the mountains to an unknown and sparsely populated terrain, it is necessary to take some precautions:

- If you have any kind of health problems, particularly in breathing or the circulatory system, it is necessary to ask a doctor's opinion before setting out on the excursion.
- Even if the weather is beautiful in the morning, you must take along some covering in your knapsack in case of an unexpected change in the weather, a common occurrence in the mountains.
- You must never set out into the mountains alone. At least one member of your party should be familiar with the route of the proposed excursion.
- Wear comfortable shoes, heavy socks, and slip-resistant shoes for steep areas.
- Carry basic first-aid materials.
- Particularly in scenic parks, you must comply with the requirements of nature preservation, and stay on marked trails.

With Szczawnica as your base, you can make your first excursion to Sokolica (747 m. asl, about 120 meters above the town). After reaching the shores of the Dunajec, near the final raft landing-place, the trail leads over the Pieniny Way to the boat basin near Biala Skala. There you travel about ten minutes to cross the Dunajec. From there you zigzag to the top of the mountain, from which there is a beautiful view of the gorge of the Dunajec and the neighboring elevations. You return by the same route. The whole excursion lasts about four hours.

The destination of the second excursion is Trzy Korony (Three Crowns), with an elevation of 982 m. asl. This is the highest peak in the Pieniny proper. The top of the mountain is composed of five steep limestone crags formed in the shape of a natural crown. Three of these fells, called Okraglica, Plaska Skala and Panska Skala make up this crown. Only Okraglica is accessible to tourists. At its peak there is a viewing platform with a metal barrier. The trip to Trzy Korony may be made over two trails. The first leads from Szczawnica over the the slopes of Sokolica to the Maly Sosnow pass and then over Sokola Percia through Zamkowa Gora and Polana Kosarzyska to the top of Okraglica. The other possibility involves walking to Kroscienko over the highway (which takes about 50 minutes) and from there, after crossing the Pieninyki Potok, going on to the Szopka and Siodlo passes on the way to the top of Okraglica. The return should be by the trail over Sokolica to Szczawnica.

If conditions allow and you find a group to travel with, you might be tempted to make a whole-day excursion to Male Pieniny and the Homole ravine. The trip begins by the final rafting station in Szczawnica and, passing the "Orlica" hospice you arrive at Salamonow, which marks the border of Poland. The trail continues along the border. Passing many steep ups and downs, you reach Dubantowska Dolina and before long the gorge of the Homole ravine. The canyon of the gorge is 120 meters deep and constitutes a marvelous geological-natural attraction. After crossing this gorge, the trail reaches the paved road between Szczawnica and Jaworki, from which buses run to Szczawnica (c. 6 kilometers). The length of the trail is about 20 kilometers, and takes 8 or 9 hours. It is necessary to carry food and drink with you, along with extra clothing in case of a change in the weather.

Szczawnica is also agreeable in the winter, not only because of the year-round medicinal treatment possibilities, but also owing to the skiing trails on the Palenica mountain. There is a ski lift available, taking tourists to the summit in ten minutes. Two restaurants serve visitors at the top of the mountain, while a snack bar and a hotel await them at the bottom of the lift.

Among other attractions of Szczawnica, to be enjoyed only in the summer, are mountain kayak races. Gates for a mountain slalom are erected over a rapid-flowing section of the Dunajec. A high embankment forms a natural viewing place for spectators.

The host of the town's tourist-sanatorium facilities is the State Enterprise called Szczawnica Health Resort. It also coordinates the activities of sanatoria belonging to Trade Unions and the Vacation Fund. Information about conditions for accommodations and treatment in Szczawnica can be obtained from the office of the Enterprise, and reservations can be made with them as well. Tel. No. 22 11—from Poland 1872—22 11—from the U.S.A. No. 0 1148 1872 2211.

The nearest gas station is located on Jagiellonska Street in Kroscienko. It is open from 7am to 6pm, Sunday from 8am to 3pm. A gas station on Szaflarska Street in the outskirts of Nowy Targ is open twenty-four hours.

EXCURSION III

"Dunajec" Castle in Niedzica

During a visit to the Tatra highlands, one must find time to visit the fortress castle in Niedzica on the Dunajec River. Niedzica is a small village on the shore of the Dunajec, built on the banks of the Niedziczanka stream, so that territorially it belongs to Spisz (Hungarian Szepes). It is easy to approach Niedzica from several directions: from Nowy Targ by the road near the Gorce, or by the southern route through Trybsz and Lapsze Wyzne (about 25 km). While in Szczawnica, it is also possible to travel to the departure point for a rafting trip down the Dunajec at Katy, and from there over the dam to Niedzica. In the village is a XV century church with Gothic, baroque and rococo portions preserved. But the main attraction is the castle, which is in fairly good condition. Situated on a cliff some 75 meters above the level of the river (566 meters above sea level), it was built in the XIV century by Hungarian Baron Rokolf Berzeviczy, according to documents dating 1325. There have been a variety of owners of the castle over the years, among them the Pole Olbracht

Laski, and from 1857 to 1945 it remained in the hands of the family Salamon.

There are three distinctive parts in the castle:

- Upper Castle, the oldest part dating from the XIV—XV century
- Middle Castle, from the XV—XVI century
- Lower Castle, from the end of the XVI to the XVII century

In those times, it was an important stronghold, one of four protecting the northern frontiers of the Hungarian state. Near the castle ran the ancient track from the south of Europe to Cracow and then on to the Baltic. To counterbalance the Niedzica castle, another was built by the Polish king in Czorsztyn on the opposite bank of the river, within sight of Niedzica. The entire Spisz area belonged to the Polish kings after 1412, when it was pawned to guarantee a loan given to Hungarian King Zygmunt of Luxembourg by King Wladyslaw Jagiello. This loan was never repaid.

Conservation work on the castle itself has been going on since 1949, along with the fortification of the castle hill in order to raise a retaining wall. Guest rooms for visitors have been available since 1950 and a castle museum was opened in 1963. This museum contains many archeological exhibits, documents, drawings and paintings, along with ethnographic collections and examples of the material culture of Spisz. Trained guides evoke visions of olden times, recounting legends connected with the castle, such as one about a well 60 meters deep dug out of solid rock, or showing visitors the torture chamber where prisoners were persuaded to see things their captors' way.

After the war in 1946, a story linking Niedzica with the Peruvian land of the Incas was added to the medieval tales. In the XVIII century, Niedzica castle owner Sebastian Berzeviczy married a Peruvian Indian during a visit to South America. Their daughter Umina married Tupak Amdru, the last descendant of the royal line of the Incas. Their only son, named Antonio, was cared for and adopted in 1797 by Waclaw Benesz-Berzeviczy after the death of his parents. Together with Antonio, Berzeviczy took over the testament of the Incas, which supposedly indicated the hiding place of the royal treasure in Lake Titicaca. In 1949 a descendant of Antonio, named Andrzej Benesz, appeared in Niedzica where, in the presence of witnesses, he removed a lead tube from a hiding place described in the 150-year-old document. The tube contained nothing but a moldy bundle of straps knotted in various ways. This was the *kipu* that the Incas used for writing. Unfortunately, there is no further news of this find, and no one knows if the Inca treasure was ever recovered from Lake Titicaca.

Various reflections come to mind during a visit to Niedzica Castle:

- There is a magnificent view of the Pieniny Mountains and the Tatras to the south from the terrace of the upper castle, making us aware of the beauty of the highlands.
- The huge excavations under the water reservoirs, dams and waterside fortifications illustrate man's constant conflict with nature.
- The thick stone buttresses of the castle make us think of the people through whose toil and sweat these walls were built.
- The palatial rooms and their beautiful furnishings create an unforgettable opulence far removed from the present time.

If only for a few days, one can pretent to be a resident of Niedzica by renting an apartment in the lower castle. There are two and three-person accommodations with bath, along with simpler lodgings. All meals are served in the castle dining room. There is also a cafe furnished with period pieces. In winter there are enjoyable sleigh rides organized by the locals and skiing is available at nearby Czorsztyn-Nadzamsze.

The Slovak border is three kilometers from the castle. Information and reservations are available at the Museum of Niedzica Castle, 34-411 Niedzica, tel. 0-187-59489.

EXCURSION IV

In the Steps of Early Settlers

The mountains have always fascinated people because of their inaccessibility and mysteriousness. Legendary happenings and tales about gods, spirits and great treasures were spun about the mountain regions. From the Greek Olympus, the Himalayan peaks, to our native Lysa Gora and the Tatras—human fantasy populated all of these places with supernatural creatures. That is why they were the last to be settled. Penetration of the primeval forests and mountains on the southern outskirts of the land of the Wislans came from two directions after the X century: from the south, the terrain of present-day Slovakia, and from the northern regions of Cracow-Sandomierz along the rivers and streams which flowed from the south.

As mentioned earlier, two ancient communication routes from southern Europe to the Baltic Sea ran along the east and west sides of the Tatras. The western route, leading from the Czech Lands through Brama Morawska (Moravian Gate), and specifically its offshoot along the valley of Wag and

Orawa, reached the river called Czarny Dunajec (Black Dunajec) skirting the peatbogs along the river. Where the Moravian trail crossed the river, a settlement named for the river was established. Further down the trail led along the Czarny Dunajec to the settlement of Nowy Targ (earlier called Nowe Clo). Close to this fortified center were the first settlements which depended on it for defense or refuge in case of invasion. From historical documents we know that one of the oldest was the settlement of LUDZMIERZ. In 1234 Polish Prince Henryk the Bearded granted the Cracow Voivode Teodor the privilege of installing the abbey of the Cistertian order in this settlement, building a church and conducting the activity of settling the Tatra region. The mission of the Cistertians lasted less than 10 years, probably due to difficult climatic and soil conditions, but Ludzmierz and nearby settlements of Krauszow and Rogoznik continued to exist, sharing the fate of the whole territory, later called the district of Nowy Targ.

Present-day Ludzmierz is laid out on both sides of the Czarny Dunajec; houses on the left bank almost reach the next settlement of Krauszow; the right-bank, called Zamoscie, reaches the Nowy Targ-Czarny Dunajec road in the region of an estuary of the Wielki Rogoznik stream. Ludzmierz is known beyond the boundaries of the Tatra highlands as the center of the religious cult of the Virgin Mary. A statue of the Virgin Mary some 600 years old, known as the Ludzmierz Madonna, was housed in the larchwood Cistertian church until 1824, when it was replaced by a new brick church in 1809-1877. Every year in the middle of August the residents of the highlands and other places gather in Ludzmierz for a church fair. On June 8, 1979, John Paul II visited Ludzmierz after he became pope. A tablet bearing the papal seal is embedded at the entrance: "Totus tuus—in memory of the pilgrimage of His Holiness John Paul II to the Ludzmierz Madonna, the Queen of the highlands—VI.8.1979."

There is a field altar built on a high podium behind the church where mass is celebrated when the crowd of pilgrims cannot fit inside the church. During such a celebration on August 15, 1994, two bells from the Highlanders' Foundation in Chicago were blessed and installed in the church steeple. One bell has John Paul II as its patron, and the other the Archangel Gabriel. The first reads: "To the Glory of God for His choice of a son of the Polish soil, our pastor at the Capital of St. Peter, and for the Sanctuary of the Virgin Mary, Queen of the highlands in Ludzmierz, this bell is funded by Jan and Aniela Kwak Bachnica and family from Chicago in the Year of the Lord 1994."

And the second reads: "To the Glory of God and in gratitude for the 600th anniversary of the reign of Maria Farm-Mistress of the highlands—for the Sanctuary of the Virgin Mary, Queen of the highlands in Ludzmierz, this bell is funded by the Club of the Ludzmierz Parish in Chicago in the Year of the Lord 1994."

Another structure whose significance reaches beyond Ludzmierz itself is the highland house named for Kazimierz Przerwa-Tetmajer and Wladyslaw Orkan. Opened in 1975, it is a creation of the members of the Highlanders' Association which holds its conventions and local functions there. One of the patrons of this house—Kazimierz Przerwa-Tetmajer— was born in Ludzmierz. (The readers of this guidebook have already been introduced to this personality in Excursion II). In 1966, on the 100th anniversary of his birth, a granite boulder was brought down from the mountains and placed in the center of Ludzmierz with an inscription in honor of this man whose writings glorified the area. Because of the many visitors who come to the village, it has a number of restaurants and shops, as well as rooms for rent.

Travelers on a walking tour will surely be interested in a tourist trail named for Tetmajer leading from Ludzmierz to the north-west through Krauszow, Dzial, between Pieniazkowice and Odrowaz to the Zelenica Mountain (912 meters over sea level). This trek, round-trip, takes some four hours, with a short rest at the destination. Numerous emigrants from Ludzmierz form Circle No. 38 of the Highlanders' Association in North America.

From Ludzmierz the way leads up-river to the locality of Czarny Dunajec, along the now abandoned railway line, which until 1918 linked Nowy Targ with Kralovany in the Wag region, near the important Bohumin-Koszyce route. As late as 1945 a section of this rail line was used for local traffic to Podczerwone; then all service was suspended. In 1994 this line and, what is more important, the territories belonging to it were sold at auction.

Beyond Ludzmierz and before the next village of Rogoznik there stretch the famous peatbogs of the Czarny Dunajec River, the first of which is called Przymiarki Peatbog. It is often exploited by the local population in a manner that may not be the best for the ecology of the region. There is a project in the works to create two sanctuaries there, called "Przymiarki" and "Na Grelu," because of the unique nature of the flora covering this terrain. It must be mentioned that much larger peatbogs can be found between the village of Czarny Dunajec and Piekielnik, already in Orawa.

The village of ROGOZNIK, located at 620-630 meters above sea level on the banks of the Wielki Rogoznik stream, gets its name from the stream, which was named back in the days of the Wislans. A part of the village, on the other side of the road, is referred to as "Za Goscincem" (On the Other Side of the Road), and is chronologically younger than the rest. There the last houses of Rogoznik blend in with the first houses of the village Stare Bystre Dolne, also served by the Rogoznik church.

The Rogoznik Rock, with a small surrounding area, some two kilometers from the village, comprises a nature preserve. The summit of the rock is made of limestone in which fossilized fragments of fauna from the Jurassic Period (about 150 million years ago) have been preserved.

The original setlement on the Rogoznik stream dates to the XIII century, and formed part of the property of the Cistertian order. Most of the present-day houses are new; old architecture with two-columned porches—influenced by the example of Nowy Targ and Czarny Dunajec—are hard to find.

The peatbogs stretching between the highway and the Czarny Dunajec River make it impossible to cross from Rogoznik to two villages lying on the bank of the Dunajec—Wroblowka and Dlugopole. Therefore it is necessary to travel in the direction of the town of Czarny Dunajec and, before reaching it, to turn right in the direction of buildings visible from afar. WROBLOWKA was settled at the beginning of the XVII century (1601). Its first *soltys* (village administrator) was Stanislaw Kielbasa, who later passed his duties on to the brothers Stanislaw and Jan Wroblewski. They are the source of the name of the village. The beginning and the end of this village are marked by two old chapels. Difficult conditions for farming in an area dominated by swamps and peatbogs induced many residents of Wroblowka to emigrate to North America. They form the energetic Chicago #41 Circle of the Highland Association in North America.

Continuing on the road in the northeastern direction, you reach DLUGOPOLE after some three kilometers. Dlugopole was established in the first half of the XIV century along the ancient trade route from Orawa to Cracow. Some scholars assign an earlier beginning to this settlement, linking it to the name of Longi Campi mentioned in documents from the XIII century. Most certainly the Cistertian monks, who again undertook their mission,were the first proprietors of Dlugopole, and in the XV century the village belonged to Nowy Targ *starost* Marek Radult. Today the residents of Dlugopole live partly from work on the land, and partly from jobs in Nowy Targ, which is accessible by bus. There is a noteworthy old church in the village and a school. It is hard to find traces of the old building style in the modern housing of Dlu-gopole. Everything is uniformly contemporary. On the way back to the main road you may observe the Wydzirowki peatbog (from the word *wydzierac*—rip out by force) and a somewhat larger peatbog called Puscizna (from *pustka*—emptiness), with such characteristic marshy dwarf mountain pine (pinus Pumilio), cranberry (oxycoceos Oudripetala), sedge (carex), insectivorous sundew (drosera) and marshy fenberry (vaccimium uliginosum).

Soon the main road from Nowy Targ appears again; a turn to the right and you find yourself in CZARNY DUNAJEC, a village with a small-town atmosphere. Like many other places in the highlands, it took its name from the river. Its founding is attributed to Cracow Voivode Cedro about 1230, close to the place where the trade route crossed the river. A documented mention of the village, in a royal decision, came in 1605, when King Zygmunt III confirmed the location of the village to the couple Zofia and Jan Pieniazek. Its first *soltys* (village administrator) was Tomasz Mietus, and its first parish priest Szymon Bukowinski. From 1720 Czarny Duna-jec was entitled to hold six fairs per year, which contributed to the small-town atmosphere of this village. It lies at the crossroads of routes leading in four directions: to the Tatras in the south and Zakopane and Spisz, in the west to Orawa, to the east and Nowy Targ, and to the north in the direction of Chabowka and Cracow. It is situated near the watershed dividing the catchment of the Baltic Sea and the Black Sea, which until 1918 constituted the border between Galicia and Hungary. The fact that Czarny Dunajec had the right to hold fairs (later extended to weekly affairs), influenced the growth of craftsmanship supplying nearby settlements in the highlands and Orawa.

On the night of April 22, 1859, the village was nearly destroyed by fire, an event commemorated by a stone cross bearing a bas-relief of St. Florian. When it was rebuilt, most houses were constructed of bricks, with characteristic porches and small pillared roofs.

In the center of Czarny Dunajec stands a brick church erected in place of the one destroyed by fire. It is the third place of worship in this spot. The first was built in 1595 in the time of *soltys* Mietus and survived until the fire of 1787. As was customary at the time, it was made of wood. A parish school was attached to the church in 1750. Initially the Czarny Dunajec parish covered half of the highlands, while the other half was serviced by the Szaflary parish. Now this parish only encompasses a few neighboring villages. At present Czarny Dunajec is the seat of the community government. It has a post office, pharmacy, several restaurants, shops and tourist beds. It is possible to rent rooms in private houses for extended periods. Many regional functions are held in the local House of Culture, such as the meetings of the Association of Highlanders, and every year, in January and February, traditional regional festivals are held in memory of the famous highland musician, composer and folk poet and teacher—born in nearby Ciche in 1886—Andrzej Knapczyk-Duch.

As in other highland localities, people emigrated from Czarny Dunajec in search of work. The town's residents now living in Chicago are organized in Circle No. 21 of the Highland Association.

Traveling south about four kilometers, one arrives at the next village on the settlement trail—PODCZERWONE. On the basis of the privilege granted by King Zygmunt III on July 4, 1604, Szymon and Barbara Podczerwinski were the founders of this village. Their sons inherited the rights to this property, but Nowy Targ *starost* Adam Kazanowski induced them to sell their *soltys* rights. After Kazanowski, the *soltys* function was taken over by the Lej family. To this day the houses in the northern part of the village are called Lejowka, while the valley where they grazed their sheep, by the stream bearing their name, is officially called Lej Valley.

The village of Podczerwone was built a little differently from most highland villages: the houses are concentrated on both sides of the road over a small area, extending in the direction of the fields. A chapel was built in 1908, at which the priest from the Czarny Dunajec parish held services on Sundays and holidays. Now the soaring roof of the new church, built in Podczerwone a short time ago, is attracting attention, with its blend of highland style and modern architectural style.

Further to the south, beyond the bridge crossing the river, lies the small village of KONIOWKA, renowned for its venerable period belfry. Belfries were common in the highlands, and their character was sacral as well as utilitarian, at a time when churches were a rarity. Every day at noon the bells sounded proclaiming the time and summoning the faithful for the Angelus (Agnus Dei). The belfries served as alarm centers, from which the bells warned the inhabitants of approaching danger. Such a "scourge of God" could be a fire or approaching storm. It was a common belief in the old days that the sound of the bells could deflect lightning from inhabited areas.

Another few kilometers south on the highway visitors find the village of CHOCHOLOW, a locality interesting from both the historical and monumental point of view. Chocholow was founded by the honest Bartlomiej Kluska-Chocholowski. "Honest" was the designation used to describe a peasant, while the title of "born" was given to noblemen. This was the beginning of the XVI century, and Bartlomiej received his privilege to found a village for his services during a Moscow expedition with King Stefan Batory. A later ruler, Zygmunt III, extended this privilege to hereditary *soltys* status. The village was part of the Czarny Dunajec parish, but the distance was so great that the villagers built a chapel in their own settlement in 1660, which was run by Dominicans. In time the chapel was enlarged to become part of the central nave of a church, and a steeple was added. In

1802 the Chocholow church became a branch of the Czarny Dunajec parish, then fifteen years later an independent parish covering Ciche, Dzianisz, Koniowka, Witow, Koscielisko and part of Zakopane.

The construction of the present church was begun in 1853 and completed in 1873. It was consecrated on June 14, 1874. The moving force behind the construction, securing the financial and material sources, was a native of Chocholow (although a parish priest in Sidzin), Father Wojciech Blaszynski. He died tragically at the church building site on August 11, 1866, struck by a beam from the scaffolding. His task was completed after his death, and the Chocholow parish became the fifth in the highlands, after Nowy Targ, Ludzmierz, Czarny Dunajec and Szaflary.

Chocholow became famous in 1846, when emissaries of the uprising being prepared in Cracow against the Austrians organized an armed demonstration of the peasants from Chocholow and neighboring villages, led by organist Jan Kanty Andrusikiewicz and Father Jozef Leopold Kmietowicz. On the night of February 21, 1846, the peasants marched against Austrian border outposts in Chocholow, Sucha Hora and Witow, disarmed them and destroyed the border stone bearing the image of the imperial eagle. Like the Cracow rebellion, this one was put down and its participants suffered serious repression. The incident is commemorated by a boulder placed at the church gate with the inscription: "To the insurgents of Chocholow—the people of the highlands." The other side of the boulder reads: "February 21, 1846—the boulder was placed and the plaque attached in 1966, on the 120th Anniversary of the Chocholow Uprising." Two paintings by the main altar done by Wojciech Eliasz (father) and the frescoes of Walery Eliasz (son) also deserve attention. On the wall to the right of the entrance hangs a painting depicting the swearing-in of the insurgents on February 21, 1846.

The historic and patriotic traditions of their forefathers

lived on in their descendants during the German occupation. An outpost of the Union of Armed Struggle was formed in January 1940 and from then on the village became an important center of conspiratorial transfer of Polish officers to Hungary and a base of Tatra couriers. Among them was Marshal Edward Rydz-Smigly, who was guided back to the occupied fatherland from Hungary by Stanislaw Fraczysty on October 24, 1941. On the night of February 20, 1942, the Germans surrounded the village and arrested both men and women en masse. Most of them later perished in concentration camps. But this did not stop the underground activities of the Chocholow inhabitants.

The spatial configuration of Chocholow has been included in the No. I group of the relics of highland architecture and as such is under protection. The old part of the village is wooden, with the roofs of the one-story cottages facing the road, while their front walls are turned to the sun. Shading the cottages and shielding them from the mountain winds are massive ash trees. The thickness of the beams used to build the framework for the walls is quite impressive. These beams, which are tree trunks cut lengthwise, are called *plazy*. The widest *plazy* can be seen in house No. 24, called "the house from one fir tree." To reach this house you have to walk behind house No. 23, between the houses to the right, pass the farm buildings and come upon an old highlander cottage considered a Class II relic of the past. The cottage is small—one room and a vestibule, two windows. The width of the shaped beams in the walls indicates that the fir tree cut down more than one hundred and forty years ago on the Ostrysz hill measured more than one meter in diameter at the base and thus had about thirty meters of usable height. Very little had to be added to this fir tree to make a highlander house. The house stands empty today; its last individual owner, Anna Stryczula, has died, and it is only a bother to her heirs—as a historical building, it cannot be taken down, and it is too primitive to live in.

Building No. 75 houses a branch of the Tatra Museum—the Museum of the Chocholow Uprising is open from 10am to 2pm Wednesday to Sunday. A house just as old, No. 28, holds the sculpture workshop of Jan Zieder. It is worth a visit not only because of the lovely wood figurines made there, among them Bethlehem creches of linden wood—each one a unique creation. The sculptor is a hobbyist-collector of implements and furnishings of old-time highland houses and farms. He has gathered many valuable exhibits of folk handicraft of a hundred and more years ago in his small vestibule and room, among them hand-mills, spinning wheels for wool, wooden kitchen utensils, dishes, glass paintings, etc.

There are bus connections between Chocholow and Nowy Targ and Zakopane, along with a commune council headquarters, post office, restaurants and numerous shops. A border crossing to Slovakia is located close to Chocholow. As in many other localities in the highlands, comfortable over-night accommodations are easy to find.

The southern border of Chocholow is marked by a bridge over the Czarny Dunajec River. Just before the bridge, a road forks to the left to the village of DZIANISZ. This is the only way to approach Dzianisz by car, since in the higher part of the village, after passing the hamlet of Gruszki, the road turns into a country lane, accessible only by foot or horse-drawn carriage. Dzianisz is typically built *w snurecku* over an area of seven kilometers (*w snurecku* means house after house like on a string). The village lies on the right bank of the Dzianisz Stream, from which it took its name. On July 17, 1619 Stanislaw Witowski from Popow, governor of the Cracow castle and Nowy Targ *starost*, granted a privilege to one Walenty Pietrzykowski to found a village by the Dzianisz Stream, which was confirmed by King Zygmunt III in Warsaw on January 30, 1630. This same Pietrzykowski received the office of Dzianisz village administrator (*soltys*), the necessary area of land and the right to run the mill, fullery and inn. In the XIX century Dzianisz came into the possession of Baron Borowski. A mansion house with its farm buildings was erected in the middle of the village. As early as 1746 twenty serfs worked on the estate and the landowner held the post of *wojt* (chief officer of a group of villages). Remnants of the foundations of the manor house and its park remain to this day.

Today most of the houses in Dzianisz are new, attesting to the fact that former residents of Dzianisz now in North America, whether members of Circle No. 33 of the Highlanders' Association in Chicago or not, care about the growth of their village. There still remain a number of older houses preceding World War II or more. Two belfries and a few small chapels bear witness to the village's past.

An independent parish was installed in Dzianisz in 1949. The church in Dzianisz was built in the highlander style and placed on a gentle hill above the road. Lower, on the left side of the road, stands the fire station which also serves as a cultural center.

There is a bus connection to Zakopane through Witow. The village has a post office, along with two schools and a medical facility. What is more, it is possible to find peace and rest in Dzianisz after the hubbub of the city and to revel in pure, unpolluted air. There is easy access to Zakopane and the Tatra's most beautiful valleys.

Past the upper limits of Dzianisz, beyond the hamlets of Gruszki and Kule, on the northern side of the Butorowy Wierch descending to a stream, lies the settlement of SLODY-CZKI. Concealed in a gully, its houses served as a convenient refuge for partisans. The inhabitants of this small settlement were touched by the bestiality of the occupiers as well. On July 6, 1943, the Germans executed fifteen or more residents of Slodyczki rounded up during a raid. A modest cross with a plaque makes it impossible to forget this crime.

Now it is time to return to the car left on the upper end of Dzianisz and, as you descend, once again look at the village, this time from the other side. This new look offers many new observations about the structure of the village and its old and new housing.

After returning to the main road, one must drive left over a bridge, beyond which the next locality, called WITOW, can be seen. The settlement plans of the Nowy Targ *starost* Stanislaw Witowski included the creation of a town here, to be called Zygmuntowo in honor of the king. However, there were not enough settlers to form a town, so a village grew up instead, bearing the name of the *starost*. The date of the village's foundation is given as 1606. As the village located most closely to the medieval metal ore mines in the Chocholowska and Koscieliska valleys, it enjoyed occasional opportunities for extra work and earnings, which contributed to its expansion. In the northern part of the village the houses are close together, while in the south there are mostly free-standing farms. There are many new houses, showing that Witow natives now living in Chicago and organized in circle No. 27 of the Association of Highlanders are investing in the prosperity of their village.

Among the houses of central Witow, on a tree-lined hill, stands a lovely wooden church, a branch chapel of the Chocholow parish since 1912.

Beyond the village, is pasture land merging into forest on both sides of the road. This is a glade called Pod Jaworki, an old pasture from the early days of Tatra shepherding still in use for this purpose. On the left side of the road, at the edge of the forest, is a primitive *bacowka* (flock-master's hut), where you can try *zentyca* (a drink from goat's milk) and fresh goat cheese. A bit further, on the right side of the road, there is a modern motel with a restaurant and all conveniences. There is also a forester's lodge and to the right of the highway a road leading to one of the longest Tatra valleys— DOLINA CHOCHOLOWSKA. At first it is wide, with the forest pushed back to ever steeper hills on both sides; to the left of the road, cutting through the middle of the valley, are three old highland farms. They bear the characteristics of ancient holdings of the Polans built on fields cleared of woods and meadows in the depths of the forest. They are still inhabited. Some five kilometers down the road you come to the Huciska Glade, which is as far as cars can go. The rest of the way to Dolina Chocholowska must be made on foot, first paying a fee to the Tatra National Park. Usually a couple of horse-drawn carriages can be found at the Huciska Glade parking. These carriages may be hired for the ride to the shelter-home on the Polana. If traveling on foot, the trip takes about 50 minutes to the gamekeeper's lodge—a former shelter home run by the Blaszynski family from Chocholow. The road runs along a stream as the valley becomes increasingly narrow; at its narrowest point, between two towering crags, it measures only 50 meters in width. After leaving the woods, you come upon a view of the treeless slope of the Chocholow Valley. Its special attraction are shepherds' sheds which are examples of the old building style, some of them still in use, as is the whole valley for the grazing of cows and sheep. One of these sheds has a crudely executed wooden tablet at its entrance informing visitors that on June 23, 1983, Pope John Paul II rested there. This was in connection with John Paul II's first visit to Poland since becoming pope and his meeting with Lech Walesa, then the head of Solidarity, which took place in the Dolina Chocholowska. A stone has been placed near the chapel at the top of the valley, bearing the words of the Pope: "On this day I could gaze at the Tatras close up and breathe the air of my youth."

In the southern part of the Valley, there stands a hospice on an elevated spot with food and lodging available. Hotel rooms may be reserved by writing to: Schronisko "Polana Chocholowska" Dolina Chocholowska 34-511 Koscielisko, tel. (0-165) 70-510.

Walking through the Starobocianska Valley from the gamekeeper's cottage, you come to Siwa Przelecz (Gray

Mountain Pass), which is 1,812 meters above sea level (abbreviation m. asl)—difference in altitude about 550 meters—and from there turning right to the Starobocianski Wierch (Peak), which is 2,002 m. asl, you can descend over the Jarzabcza Valley to the hospice on the Polana. This excursion should take about seven hours.

Another route leads up the Dolina Jarzabcza to the Konczysty Wierch, from there to the right to Jarzabczy Wierch (2,137 m. asl), then Wolowiec (2,064 m. asl), descending by the Dolina Wyznia Chocholowska or by Rakon (1,879 m. asl), and over Grzes (1,653 m. asl) back to the hospice. Total time of excursion about eight hours.

Going from the gamekeeper's house over Iwanicka Przelecz, one can reach the hospice of Hala Ornak in the Dolina Koscieliska in about three hours. For variety, it is possible to return by a path under Regle. The whole trip should take about five hours, not counting any time spent in Ornak.

In past centuries, iron, copper and silver ores were mined in Dolina Chocholowska and the neighboring Dolina Koscieliska, although these ores were never especially plentiful. The cost of processing these raw materials, particularly the cost of importing mining and metallurgic equipment necessary for the exploitation of these mines from great distances rendered this activity unprofitable. People who searched for useful minerals in the mountains were guided by traditional wisdom which indicated to them, by signs visible in the brooks and streams, what ores might be concealed in the mountainsides. Judging by the traditional names of the surroundings of Polana Chocholowska, such as Stara Robota (Old Work) and Dolina Starobocianska (Old Stork Valley), one can draw conclusions about at least two stages of mining-metallurgic work: the first in the XV century, and the second after 1765. Resuming work in the later period, the miners found old, abandoned tunnels with traces of the minerals sought in what was later called Stara Robota. Seven such tunnels were also discovered in Ornak. A mining settlement cropped up at the mouth of the valley, with processing plants and a little church, from which Dolina Koscieliska took its name. This second stage lasted for only three years, since the work came to a halt when the king stopped investing in the project. The operation was run by Germans from Spisz.

The passage of time has erased all traces of human endeavor of past centuries; what remains is the names passed on from generation to generation of highlanders, and these names later became official. Besides Stara Robota and similar names, the Polana Huciska draws its name from *Huta* (smelting works), which once stood there, Baniska Dolina—from the Hungarian name for a mine (*bania*), and Polana Smytnia from the forge active in the region (*Schmiede*—forge). In a clearing called Na Kunsztach (On the Masterly Skill) there must have once stood a masterly installation for processing ore.

EXCURSION V

Bialka Valley and Rybi Potok

Just as the stipulated western border of the Tatra highlands, connecting this land with neighboring Orawa, is defined by the Czarny Dunajec River, so from the east the highlands and Szepes are separated by the Bialka River. Although it is all the same region, the landscape of the valleys of these two rivers is diverse. It is pleasant to walk or ride over the valley of the Bialka and immerse yourself in the silence of the Bialka plains and hills, and to find yourself at last at the head of the river, in the heart of the Tatras, and to arrive alongside Rybi Potok, its source—the largest Tatra lake—Morskie Oko (The Eye of the Sea).

The final segment of the Bialka, about six kilometers to the estuary of the river flowing into the Dunajec, is uninhabited. Marshy meadows and trees line both sides of the river, while the wide stony riverbed cut through by several arms of the stream make one realize how the Bialka must look during springtime floods. It is only after this segment that two villages, somewhat set back from the river and connected by a bridge, come into view. On the left, highlands side, lies the village Nowa Biala, and on the right the Szepes village of Krempachy.

NOWA BIALA is reached most easily (by car) from the side of Lopuszna (see Excursion II), only 4 kilometers distant. Its houses are built close together, in small-town style, and there is a primitive market square with a brick church. A parish house stands next door—and here is the first surprise: the sign providing information about the office and its working hours is written in both Polish and Slovak. The second surprise is a sign near the church entrance in both languages as well, announcing that services are held both in Polish and in Slovak. And since the village lies on the left bank of the Bialka, it is very much in the highlands. The history of this region, which for centuries was the border area between the Polish and Hungarian kingdoms, accounts for this. Until 1918 the border between Hungary and Galicia (during the Austro-Hungarian Empire) ran west from Cislowa Skala and Nowa Biala was considered a Szepes village. Today Polish authorities respect these historical ties with the Slovak language and culture. In the local school, where the language of instruction is Polish, lessons are also taught in Slovak.

The beginning of the village was a XIII century settlement, located at the crossing of the trade trail over the river to nearby Nowy Targ. Some historians connect this settlement with the name Antiquum Theloneum (Stare Clo), but it is not certain which locality in the Nowy Targ region this name actually refers to. Like other settlements in the border area, Nowa Biala several times fell victim to fires accompanying successive wars. The beginning of the XVI century brought certain stabilization to the settlement process, and the village grew and prospered. A wooden church was built, only to be consumed by fire. Historical mentions of it remain. The present brick house of worship was consecrated in 1748. Its venerable interior, although somewhat mixed in style, is worth seeing.

After leaving Nowa Biala by the road leading south, you must watch the left side of the road where a wooded elevation will appear after about two kilometers. This is Oblazowa (670 m. asl)—at the left side of the Bialka Gorge, descending in a bare limestone wall to the east and south. You can park your car on one of the nearby dirt roads and walk to the crag, continuing to the bank of the river over a path along the crag's bottom. The Kramnica Crag (688 m.asl) will appear on the other side of the Gorge. Both of these elevations are elements of the mountain range of Jurassic limestone. On the western side not far away can be seen their "sister"—Cislowa Skalka (686 m. asl), and continuing to the west similar crags are encountered in the vicinity of the village of Szaflary and further on in Skalka Rogoznicka. The Bialka Gorge and the Oblazowa and Kramnica elevations form part of a strictly protected nature preserve. Between them, the river divides into several streams, forming shallow fanciful meanderings between the granite boulders. They may be crossed (during times when the water level is low), to arrive at the foot of the northern slope of Kramnica where the path leading to the top of the elevation begins. Here slight exertion will be rewarded by a magnificent view of the riverbed, Gorce to the north, the Tatras to the south and the tree-covered massifs stretching to the southeast all the way to Babia Mountain in Orawa. Some tourists, enchanted by the beauty of this remote corner of the highlands, refer to the Bialka Gorge between Oblawa and Kramnica as "The Tatra Highlands Paradise."

In 1985 archeologists became interested in a small cave on the southern wall of Oblazowa. Preliminary studies of the immediate vicinity of the cave confirmed the hypothesis that there had been a pre-historic settlement at the spot. The research carried on inside the cave itself consisted of system- atic removal of successive layers and thorough sifting of the earth. Valuable archeological material was obtained in this way, including fragments of undoubtedly honed stone tools and—most interesting—a worked mammoth tooth in the shape of a boomerang. Another important find was a human bone—fragment of a man's index finger—whose age moves back the dating of human remains on Polish land by several thousand years. All the items discovered were further studied at scientific institutes.

The route continues to the south, arriving at a crossroads: to the east over the bridge leading to Trybsz, and to the west to Gron. The road in the direction of the Tatras leads to the first houses in the village of BIALKA TATRZANSKA (there are three large villages named Bialka in Poland).

This is one of the most extensive villages in the highlands, drawn out over seven kilometers "in stringlike fashion." The northern periphery of the village—the hamlet of Grapa—is located by the river, far from the road. Further on, the road, the houses and river all converge. Soon you come to the end of the line for the Zakopane-Bialka Dolna bus route. The central part of the village begins. It is dated 1637, during the reign of King Wladyslaw IV, who gave Wojciech Nowobilski—the founder of the family—the right to settle a village by the River Bialka, "on a raw root," with the life-time designation of *soltys*. In 1669 King Michal Korybut Wisniowiecki confirmed these rights to the founder's son and made them hereditary.

A small digression is needed here, since it might seem surprising that the right to settle or found a village in the highlands, with the lands and privileges going to the founder, were granted at the highest level of power—by the king himself. The explanation lies in the fact that this area was under the king's care as so-called Crown Lands, meaning lands that supplied funds to the royal court either directly or through appointed *starost*s.

The Nowobilski *soltys* clan from Bialka used a large area of Tatra clearings for their flocks, practically the whole Bialka valley, along with terrains by Rybi Potok including Morskie Oko. The land was also cultivated on open glades and clearings. According to folk tales, highland robbers were also recruited from among the Nowobilskis—and they were the scourge of Szepes estate owners and innkeepers.

The central part of Bialka should be covered by foot for a better view of the sights. Near the bus stop Bialka-Kosciol, on the right side of the road there is a group of two fenced-in buildings. The building on the left is a wooden structure— seemingly the older of the two—and the other a new brick house. This is the House of Social Assistance in which the Seraphite Sisters take care of mentally retarded boys suffering from various diseases. This is hard work which demands a love of God and a generosity of spirit. As you pass by, consider making a donation to the work that the nuns are doing. Their address is: Home of Social Assistance for Children of the Seraphite Sisters, 34-405 Bialka Tatrzanska.

About 100 meters further is a clump of stately linden trees, and among them a little old wooden church built about 1700 by Jedrzej Topor and Jan Chlipalski. An earlier church, built some 80 years prior, stood at the spot until it burned down. Fortunately, this historic building was saved when a new brick church was built in the village. There had been plans to tear it down. Not used as a church for a long time, it now serves the function of regional museum. The surrounding area near the church with an old cemetery is also under protection as a historic site. Nearby, on the other side of the highway, stands a new brick church built after world War I by architect Franciszek Maczynski. It houses a beautiful baroque altar cross from the old church. Reconstruction of its steeple was completed in 1993, with the generous help of former Bialka residents now organized in Circle 42 of the Polish Highlanders Alliance in Chicago.

Owing to the lively interest of the local authorities and the commitment of the population, Bialka has become a resort known throughout the country. A lot of new houses with modern accommodations for tourists have been built. The village also has restaurants, stores and a gas station. A modern motel named Szalas is located in the upper section of Bialka, by the bridge over the river leading to the village of Czarna Gora. Easily accessible skiing terrains may be found on the northern slope of Glodowski Wierch, with a ski lift and small luncheonette. When you make your headquarters in Bialka, you can take several interesting excursions over the mountainsides and peaks of the Pogorze Gliczarowskie and visit the Szepes villages located on the banks of the river, such as Czarna Gora, Jurgow and Rzepiska. An exotic sight is provided by the Gypsies who have permanent camps set up across the river.

The highway begins to rise, curving up higher and higher, leaving the Bialka River below on the left and to the right after Odewsianski Potok can be seen beautifully situated new houses on a parallel hill. The old low part of BUKOW-INA TATRZANSKA is near the highway. After you pass its center on Kramarski Wierch, the road rises gently up to the crossroads known as Klin. It is interesting that Bukowina has a different look from the rest of the area, since its houses are built not in valleys near streams, but on the ridges of long, sloping mountainsides. It is more difficult to supply water for the farms in this situation, and there are only some 120 days per year without wind. But this is the location that the original settlers chose for reasons unknown. The first woodcutters began to clear the land here in the XVII century, and the first official royal document for the *soltys* position in Bukowina is dated September 20, 1636. Tomasz Zamoyski, the Nowy Targ *starost*, granted the royal privilege on behalf of the king to *soltys*, honest Kasper Bukowinski. Until the middle of the XIX century, Bukowina's villages were not easily accessible. Steep and muddy roads through forest over which horses were barely able to pull carts were the only way to go. The road to Morskie Oko over the upper edge of the village, the already mentioned Klin, was built quite early, but the road through the village itself was barely passable. It was not until 1897 that the first guests appeared in Bukowina seeking peace and quiet, without regard for the difficulty of access or the primitive living conditions in the highland cottages. The first house designed for tourists—the villa of Father Gadowski—was built in 1900.

As you stroll in the center of the village, you see from afar the tall, garlanded cross of the new church. The modern silhouette of the new edifice seems architecturally foreign in the Bukowina setting. Dedicated in 1983, this church still deserves attention for its beautiful, original interior. It is executed in wood, and the wonderful wood textures enhance the simplicity of design. It creates an atmosphere of peace conducive to fruitful contemplation. Directly behind the new church stands the small old church—the creation of virtually one man. Jedrzej Kramarz, a highlander from Bukowina, devoted more than a dozen years to its construction. He was self-taught, but managed to plan and execute his life's dream. He produced the bricks himself, laid them into a wall, did the carpentry and furnished the interior, down to the altars and holy figures. The work was completed in 1887. A wooden steeple was added a few years later, but Bukowina did not get its own parish-priest until 1902. It is worthwhile to visit the local cemetery, where the builder of the church, along with people who distinguished themselves in service to Bukowina and those who fell during the last war are buried.

Continuing to climb up the road, you come to a wooden two-story building near the top of the slope. It is covered with a natural brown patina often seen on the walls of old highland buildings. This is the Community Center whose history is tied to the person of the head of the new elementary school opened in Bukowina in 1923—Franciszek Cwizewicz, 32-years-old at the time. He initiated lively cultural activity around the school, organizing a peasant theater and choir, and founding the Community Center.

Work begun in 1928 was finally completed in 1934, and from that time the Center became the heart of the social life of Bukowina. It has an auditorium, a club room, a rehearsal and game room and a hall devoted to regional mementos. It houses the Amateur Theater which stages productions in highland dialect depicting the life of the region and its inhabitants. Two important events are organized each year by the Community Center: the first in the beginning of the year, the Highland Carnival, includes performances by regional troupes, sledging cavalcades and contests of highland sleigh riding, called *kumoterka* (two-seater sleigh) and review of horse equipment. The second event, held at the beginning of August, is called Sabalowe Bajania (Sabala's Tales), and is a contest of highland story-tellers, singers and instrumentalists. These contests keep alive the memory of Jan Krzeptowski-Sabala, the famous highland story-teller and musician who died one hundred years ago.

New buildings for community use have been localized in the central part of Bukowina; they include the post office built in highland style and designed to serve the large number of visitors, a department store, bakery, many shops and restaurants and—as in every village—a sizable Volunteer Fire Station.

Finally the last climb brings you to Klin—with crossroads leading in all directions: Morskie Oko through Lysa Polana, Poronin and from there to Zakopane or Nowy Targ, Gliczarow and from there to Bialy Dunajec and beyond, through Bukowina and Bialka to Nowy Targ and Nowy Sacz.

It must be added that a short distance beyond Klin, down the road to Morskie Oko, a road branches off leading to the village of Brzegi, from which it is possible to go through to Jurgow and the other Szepes villages.

There is a large parking area at Klin, as well as a taxi stand, two restaurants and a nearby bus stop. Neighboring hills are peppered with private homes and boarding-houses which give this village a touristy look.

Only when you reach the top of Klin can you see Bukowina in all of its architectural loveliness, panoramically displayed on the Kramarski Wierch. Skiing enthusiasts will probably note the eastern slope of this Wierch descending below the houses to the Podgorzanski Potok. There is another similar slope on the western side. Bukowina is an ideal spot for both downhill and cross-country skiing. There are many ski-lifts on the western, eastern and northern slopes with seasonal snack stands. The ski season in Bukowina begins in the middle of December and lasts until March. There is still skiing in April on some of the northern slopes.

Twelve thousand or more vacationers and tourists pass through Bukowina every year. An added attraction is its location as the point from which tourist excursions can be made in many directions with varying degrees of difficulty, while the views from Bukowina on the nearby Tatras to the south and the distant panorama of the highlands to the north will take your breath away.

And a couple of other bits of information: the Tatra part of the village's name was added because there is another village in Lower Silesia by the same name, with the addition of "Sycowska." And, the expression of "in Bukowina" and "to Bukowina" are used in literature, but the highlanders, when speaking in their dialect, say "on Bukowina." This is due to the fact that the village is located on the ridge of the *wierch* (or mountain).

The harsh living conditions which existed on Kramarski Wierch forced an increasing part of the Bukowina population to seek employment away from their native village. Some went to work in the Tarnow and Cracow provinces in the lowlands, and others emigrated to the southern side of the Tatras. The first emigrants from Bukowina left for North America in 1885. This emigration increased at the turn of the century, before the outbreak of World War I. Many Bukowina natives sought their living across "The Great Water," as the highlanders call the Atlantic Ocean, after World War II. There were large numbers of highlanders in Pennsylvania, but now most of them can be found in Chicago, forming Circle No. 57 of the Polish Highlanders Alliance in North America.

The way along the chosen trail continues to the south, increasingly close to the Tatra peaks. A few minutes after you leave Klin, a road branches off to the left, descending to the village of BRZEGI. It is worthwhile to spend a little time to see this village situated half-way down the slope descending to Brzegowianski Potok. The road continues downhill, with mostly "neo-highland" buildings on both sides and the panorama of Szepes villages off in the distance to the north. First mention of Brzegi as a separate settlement can be found in a 1692 document describing a survey of royal lands. But it seems certain that the beginning of settlement on the shores of the Brzegowianski Potok should be placed at the middle of the XVII century. All that is left standing today is one residential house with farm buildings dated 1826, which is considered a relic of the past. On a hillside to the left, in the middle of the village, appears the silhouette of a wooden church. It is not old—built in 1949-1950—but it is in the style of old highland architecture. Inside there is a statue of St. Anthony and side altars executed by folk artist Boleslaw Sztokfisz of Bukowina. The church presbytery is adorned with beautiful metal highland pins created by one of the folk artists belonging to the Circle at the Community Center in Bukowina, a native of Brzegi named Jozef Bigos. The road through Brzegi continues to descend until it reaches the bridge over the Bialka River. It would be pleasant to pause a little and take a stroll along the river or even wade in to eperience the temperature of mountain rivers in summer. There are two ways back to Klin: the same way you came, but going up-hill, or crossing the bridge to Jurgow and, after a few kilometers, again over the bridge to the left, returning by the already familiar way of Bialka-Bukowina.

A few kilometers past Klin, on the way to Morskie Oko, there is Polana Glodowka. On sunny days this meadow offers one of the most spectacular views of the whole panorama of the Tatras. It can now be seen that the Tatras are not terribly huge mountains. They cover an area of about 750 square kilometers. Four-fifths of the Tatras lie in Slovakia. The Tatra massif is divided into three segments: (from the east) Tatry Bielskie, Tatry Wysokie and Tatry Zachodnie. Looking north, they are all visible from Glodowka. The Glade itself is sparsely populated, with the beautifully situated Hotel Rysy as the largest edifice. There is a ski trail with lifts on the right side of the road, and a small snackbar by the bus stop.

After about two kilometers, the steadily climbing road brings you to the wooded ridge of the Poroniec Wierch (1,105 m. asl). This is where the road from Bukowina joins the road leading to Morskie Oko from Zakopane. The road through Bukowina is relatively new; before its completion you could reach Morskie Oko from Zakopane by way of Jaszczurowka, Cyrhla and Brzesiny. Until 1806 this was a narrow trail used by cattle and sheep on the way to pasture. The Nowy Targ Imperial-Royal Administration undertook the project of building a beaten track over it, completing it in 1811. It is a good idea to leave the road to the right at this point. After about two kilometers you will arrive at a sign showing a side road to Polana Zgorzelisko. There is a luxurious boarding house there built as a rest home for members of the Polish government. After 1989, it was opened to all. It offers wonderful views of the mountains and the southern part of Dolina Nowotarska, peace, clean air, woods all around, with ski trails, lifts and ample parking. Of course, full board and recreational facilities are available. Reservations can be made through the central office in Zakopane: tel. (0-165 120 51).

Now you must return to Poroniec Wierch to continue your trip to Morskie Oko. The road climbs steadily as it winds among the thick greenery of spruces lining the way. After about five kilometers the forest opens up, with receding woods on the right and the riverbed of the Bialka on the left.

Straight ahead is the border crossing to Slovakia—Lysa Polana. For centuries, this was one of the trails connecting Galicia with Hungary, and now it is one of the most busy tourist crossings. There is a gas station and restaurant open 24 hours at the border.

After less than two kilometers of travel by car you reach the next glade—Polana Palenica which is actually a huge parking lot. A 1954 decree of the Tatra National Park restricted the access of combustion-engine vehicles to Tatra valleys and thus arrested the ecological threat to the immediate vicinity of Morskie Oko. It must be noted that several thousand cars and buses travel toward this lake daily. The final part of the journey (some ten kilometers) must be made on foot, or ...by horse trolley. There are long benches along the platform of the carriage which rides on wheels with tires, pulled by a pair of good horses with a highlander at the reins. Naturally, such a ride costs money, so it is usually taken only by those who are not fit enough to make the trip on foot. The horse carriage is also available for the ride back.

There is a regular stopping place about three kilometers later past the bridge linking the two steep banks of the Roztoka Potok. To the right of the bridge the Roztoka Potok descends precipitously between tremendous boulders, making its last run before joining up with the Bialka River. There is an imposing view of the middle water course attacking a protruding boulder. There are two other waterfalls nearby, each eight to ten meters tall. The resounding roar of the pounding water induced the highlanders to call these waterfalls Wodogrzmoty (Water Thunder). After Adam Mickiewicz's ashes were returned to Poland in 1890 and placed in the Wawel Royal Castle, the waterfalls were renamed Wodogrzmoty of Mickiewicz in 1891. Less than two kilometers along the way, near the Na Wancie forester's lodge, the road imperceptibly goes over from the Bialka Dolina to the Dolina of Rybi Potok. It is here that Biela Woda, flowing from the Slovak part of the Tatras, joins up with Rybi

Potok, giving a start to the Bialka River. Now we are not far, just a climb to the shore separating us from the lake, and there is Morskie Oko in all of its glory. It must be said that you can only enjoy the view of this mountain lake fully on a sunny day, when the mountain peaks form a magnificent amphitheater over the limpid water. This most beautiful Tatra lake is also the largest (34.54 hectares surface) and the fifth deepest (50.8 meters). Because of the clarity of the water, the bottom is visible even at great depth. The surface of the water is 1,393 m. asl. Trout inhabit the lake, despite difficult living conditions. Highlanders called it Fish Lake in the past. The name Morskie Oko (Eye of the Sea) is connected with the legend about this lake's subterranean link with the sea. On a steep post-glacial moraine at the northern end of the lake is a hostel with a restaurant and tourist-class hotel. The hostel offers an imposing view of the peaks and the whole amphitheater rising above the water. Looking from the left: the peaks of Zabie Rysy, the massif of Mieguszewickie Szczyty, Cubryna and on the right Mnich, a steep separate peak resembling a monk's hood. The precipitous, almost perpendicular walls of these elevations are a wonderful terrain for advanced alpine mountain climbing. Often, if you view the mountains through binoculars or even with the naked eye, from the hostel on a sunny day, you can see climbers on the rocks.

There has been a dispute lasting many years between Hungary and Poland, later Galicia, over Morskie Oko and this corner of the Tatras. It began at the end of the XVI century, when Niedzica owner Olbracht Laski (see Excursion III) illegally seized a part of the Nowy Targ *starost*ship south-east of the Lesnica Stream, with the localities of Lesnica, Bialka, Bukowina and Brzegi, including the region of Rybie Jezioro and Rybi Potok belonging to the Bialka inhabitants. Laski then sold his property to Hungarian magnate George Horvath, including the plundered territories. Nowy Targ *starost* Mikolaj Komorowski took them back at the

163

beginning of the XVII century. At the end of the XIX century the whole Bialka-Bukowina estate was owned by Count Wladyslaw Zamoyski within Galicia, and the old lands of the owners of Niedzica were bought by Prussian Prince Christian Hohenlohe. These were Hungarian lands. A period of intense disputes over the Rybi Potok Valley and Morskie Oko followed. Hungarian gendarmes and the Prince's forest guards drove away the highlanders who tended their sheep in this region, and the highlanders paid them back in kind by destroying border posts, warning signs and huts. Finally, the Galician Parliament turned to the Emperor in Vienna to resolve the dispute, and the Emperor passed the dispute on to international arbitration. After numerous meetings and an on-site visit, Dr. Jan Winkler, the president of the Swiss Union Court announced his verdict: the border was to run through Rysow, Zabie and Siedem Granatow to Rybi Potok. Thus Morskie Oko remained a Polish lake. This was mainly due to Dr. Oswald Balcer, the representative of the Galician (i.e. Polish) side. His erudition and the historic documentation he presented persuaded the judicial panel.

The hostel at Morskie Oko is an excellent starting point for many excursions within the capabilities of the average tourist. First you have to visit Czarny Staw (Black Pond) near Morskie Oko. It is located in the depression under the Rysy massif, about 200 meters above the waters of Morskie Oko. From the hostel you can only see the dividing moraine. To get to it you first have to circle the lake by a path on the left to the opposite shore, from which you can climb up to the pond. This will take about one hour, with stops along the way to contemplate the receding view of the surface and surroundings of the lake, until you reach the murky Czarny Staw. Its depth, 76.4 meters, makes it the second deepest body of water in the Tatras. It is 20.4 hectares in size. Rays of the sun seldom penetrate this pond, which of course is why the highlanders gave it the name Black Pond. In the early days of interest stirred up by the Tatras, there was a raft taking visitors to the far end of the lake to facilitate visits to Czarny Staw.

The next two excursions have to be started rather early in the morning. The first excursion is a walk over Swistowka and Opalony to the Dolina Pieciu Stawow Polskich (The Valley of Five Polish Ponds). From the hostel the trail leads to the right over a wooded mountainside. After walking for three hours over a marked trail, you reach the ridge of the elevation called Opalony Wierch descending to the north. Following is a two-hour descent down the slope of Swistowka Roztocka until you come to the unfolding view below of ponds of various sizes. From the south the valley is bound by the crest of Liptowski Mur, to the right Orla Perc towers over the Valley, and to the left the ridges of Miedziany. The end of the Dolina Pieciu Stawow is followed by the beginning of the Dolina Roztoki, which is blocked off by a nearly 300-meter rocky wall. The water flowing out of Wielki Staw forms the highest waterfall in the Tatras—the c.70 meter-high Wielka Siklawa.

The first hostel in this valley was built in 1876. It was primitive, only a little better equipped than the shepherds' huts. Two larger hostels were built later, the second of which burned down in 1945. The present hostel was erected over the years 1949-1953. It is the least accessible hostel in all of the Tatras, since there is no vehicle access to it, only travel by pack horses. A commercial lift was also installed for getting provisions to the place.

After resting at the hostel you descend by a marked trail near Wielka Siklawa to the Dolina Roztoki. It is an easy road to walk, hard and even, continuing at the side of the forest and the Potok Roztoka, taking you in less than three hours to the Wodogrzmoty Mickiewicza and the road toward the parking on Palenica.

Another interesting excursion from Morskie Oko leads you to the highest peak in the Tatras—Rysy (2,499 m. asl). The first stage of the journey brings you to Czarny Staw over the way you already know, which will take about one hour from the hostel. Then there follows a climb to the top, rather perilous at times. You have to stay on the marked trail and make use of the ancillary devices (such as chains and metal railings) and be constantly on your guard, which is a must anyway in the mountains. We are not providing details on the various portions of the trails since it must be assumed that the excursion will be made under the leadership of a professional guide or an experienced person who is very familiar with the trail. The time for the climb from Czarny Staw is about three hours. After a rest, which will give you an opportunity to view the panorama of the Polish and Slovak Tatras, you will come back the same way to the hostel at Morskie Oko and from there either on foot or by horse trolley to the parking at Palenica.

This is the end of the trail over Dolina Bialki and Rybi Potok. For hundreds of years the ancestors of today's highlanders settled the territories by the river and its environs, cleared the land, sowed the fields, and built houses, in a constant struggle with the harsh climacte and soil conditions. When they ran short of land on lower ground, they drove their sheep up stream, over the steep rocky slopes to the green expanses of the mountain pastures. Then they led the first tourists longing for contact with nature over the roads that had been beaten down by driven livestock.

EXCURSION VI

To the Headwaters of White Dunajec

As the title above indicates, White Dunajec, one of the three main rivers of the highlands, does not have any one definite source. This is because its start appears at the confluence of the Zakopianka and Poroniec streams. Before coming together, these two streams collect a dozen or more smaller streams and brooks into their courses as they lead water out of the central massif of the Polish Tatras and the foothills of the Tatras from Czerwone Wierchy to the west, and to Woloszyn to the east.

At the beginning of the XIII century, when the Cistertian monks settled in Ludzmierz, the whole river-basin of the White Dunajec was covered by primeval forests intersected by stream beds turned to peatbogs in places. Although it was not a settled area at the time, this does not mean that it was not familiar to man. The oldest documents, such as those listing privileges granted to the Cistertians, mention names of rivers and streams which are undoubtedly Slavic in origin. It is not clear what tribes gave the territory its names. People who lived outside of the law found refuge in the forests, and although there were not many of them, they managed to make a nuisance of themselves to the monks as they tried to organize a new life in the Ludzmierz region. About 1240, the abbot of the Cistertians built a small fortified castle some six kilometers southeast of Ludzmierz and south of Nowy Targ, in a place with natural defense potential—a rocky hill fifty or more meters high. The castle, along with the settlement that arose around it by the river, appears in old records as Schefflary. Historians disagree over the actual meaning and ancestry of this name. It might come from the German term Scheffel, which means a measurement (half a bushel) of grain, or perhaps from the word Schaf, meaning sheep. It actually does not matter, so long as we recall that in time the first settlement on the trail to the Tatras received the polonized name of SZAFLARY. This is undoubtedly one of the oldest settlements in the highlands, and its history deserves attention.

Church sources report that the first church in Szaflary was built about 1340. It was actually more of a chapel, since the population of the fortress and borough around it was quite small. In 1380 the Cistertian abbot rented the Fortress on a Cliff (*skalka*) out to a neophyte, a converted Jew, to cover the costs of its upkeep. As it later turned out, the neophyte needed this secluded spot for use as a mint for counterfeit money. When this became public, the Ludzmierz abbot showed leniency toward the counterfeiter, since he derived a sizable income from him. But soon, on orders from the king, Knight Sedziwoj from Szubin captured Skalka, burned the couterfeiter at the stake, and the king withdrew the privileges and titles of ownership from the Cistertian monks. Intercession by the abbot with the king in Hungary (Louis the Hungarian, Polish king in the years 1370-1382) returned only Ludzmierz and Krauszow to the monks, while the fortress in Szaflary became a border watchtower of the Polish kingdom. It grew less important with time, so that in 1456 it was not mentioned as a provider of horses and archers for the defense of Cracow. Plans were made in 1505 to rebuild it, but they were never realized. The first survey of the crown lands made in 1564 shows, in place of the fortress borough, a farm belonging to *starost* Mark Ratuld, as independent of the village of Szaflary, which housed eighteen resident farmers. The village had been incorporated into the Nowy Targ parish since 1519. It expanded in size on both sides of Bialy Dunajec, but more to the east in the direction of Dluga Gora, since the river caused damage every year in the area immediately on its shores. The center of the village is now about two kilometers from the farm near Skalka. The highlanders have given the name of Podmajyrz to the Skalka farm based on the German name Maierhof. The present church in Szaflary was built in the years 1799-1810, becoming the parish church for the whole area of the central highlands all the way to the Tatras. This was already after the partitions of Poland, in the time of the rule of the Austro-Hungarian Empire, which put the whole Nowy Targ area up for auction, dividing it into four sections (dominions).

The section including Szaflary, Zaskale, Banska, Bialy Dunajec, Poronin, Gliczarow, Skrzypne, Mur and Zasihle was purchased on May 27, 1819, by Polish nobleman Tomasz Uznanski from Olwita. According to the listing of 1880, his property under Majyrze in Szaflary ran to 162 morgs of land (one morg measures 5,600 square meters), with a sawmill, mill, brewery, two inns, and eleven residential houses, not counting the estate buildings. During the same year, the peasants' property consisted of 1,610 morgs of arable land, 492 morgs of grass and pasture lands, forest and 230 houses. This will give you an idea of the dynamics of the village's expansion. Over a period of about 300 years, between 1564 and 1880, the number of farms in Szaflary grew thirteen-fold.

As from other villages in the highlands, the Szaflary residents emigrated to America before World War I and later. A large group of them settled in Canada, but some also went to Chicago, where they formed Circle No. 24 of the Polish Highlanders Alliance in North America.

During the German occupation Szaflary native Augustyn Suski was one of the co-creators of an underground organization known as the Tatra Confederation. He perished in a concentration camp, along with 24 other members of this organization.

Today SZAFLARY is the seat of a rich community numbering seven villages and more than 9,000 residents, whose source of income is still farming, supplemented by jobs in Nowy Targ and cottage-work. The village has a school, post office, milk plant, volunteer fire station, health center and wholesale building material establishment. The largest ski-making factory in Poland was located here, but because of the changing economic conditions and foreign competition, the production profile and the production itself has changed greatly. An experimental geothermal plant has been established at the edge of the village, designed to utilize the subterranean hot springs, which underlie most of the Nowy Targ valley. This is the future of this region from the economic point of view, and it will protect the environment. The first residential buildings in the village of Banska Niznia are already utilizing this underground heat source. There is a great opportunity for investment here.

In Szaflary, where residential construction is visible at every step, it is easy to rent private rooms with all comforts. A modern motel named Krokus offering rooms for rent, a restaurant, SAT television and private indoor parking 24-hours a day, is located at 21 Zakopianska Street. A Center for Hippotherapy and Movement Rehabilitation for children and adults can be found at 20 Kolejowa Street.

A descendant of the former owners of the farm in Szaflary, Antoni Uznanski, who is living permanently abroad, has in the past five years repossessed his rights to the territory around Skalka, has fixed up this area and built a stylish summer and winter residence at the top of the hill. The roof of this rather small residence is visible from the highway, and the limestone boulder on which it perches is also prominent. The house may be better seen from the road Zaskale—Szaflary, that is, from the western side. The whole property is fenced in, private, with no right of entry, which is announced on a sign on the enclosure surrounding Skalka.

Directly behind Skalka, the highway from Nowy Targ in the direction of Zakopane divides, leading to the village buildings on the left, while the right fork continues south, bypassing the village and runing alongside the railway tracks. The road bypassing Szaflary was built before the war, so that the old road used for local traffic is in a sorry state beyond the village structures. That is why it is easier to go to the next locality by way of the bypass to the place the roads join and then, after a sharp turn to the left, you arrive at a good road with buildings of the village, next to Szaflary, which is BIALY DUNAJEC.

Chronologically, it is younger than Szaflary, because the settlement process proceeded from the north toward the Tatras. An archival document states that on February 23, 1579, the leaseholder of Nowy Targ and Szaflary properties, Jan Pieniazek from Kruzlowa, gave permission to Szaflary resident Jedrzej Pawlik to found a village in the woods beyond Szaflary on the River Bialy Dunajec. Together with the location privilege for the village, which took its name from the river, the founder received a plot of land (about 25 hectares) to clear and provide free access to mountain pastures for his flocks by the Poronin River. This privilege, together with other rights, was later confirmed by the king as hereditary, and, for wartime service in the so-called conscript or recruit infantry, Pawlik's heirs were granted nobility and the right to use the name Pawlikowski.

Documents preserved in the archives of the lustration of the Nowy Targ *starostship* contain information about the further development of the village. In 1635 Bialy Dunajec already housed 119 families and in 1769 246 families. The cultivation of the wilderness moved primarily in the southern direction, since there were other villages already in existence to the east and west of Bialy Dunajec. Bialy Dunajec is a good example of the social structure of the highland village of the XVIII century. The basic, economically strongest group was composed of peasants who owned arable land in the village and grazing territories in the mountains. In 1769 there were 30 such families in the village. The second group were the *zarebnicy*, semi-farmers, who had not yet completely cleared the land for cultivation. The third group were the *zagrodnicy*, who already had their cottages and had begun the clearing of the woods; and finally the fourth group, called *komornicy* (tenants), did not own cottages, but lived with their families or others who employed them. All peasants were obliged to render service, either in work or in goods (later in cash) to the *starosts*—the royal leaseholders— for the use of the land and for living in the village. One of the duties of the *soltys* was to see to it that these obligations were met.

As the more accessible tracts of land for cultivation grew scarce, some villagers, particularly the young, were forced to move outside the village proper. And so by the Poronin River a settlement called MUR (later called Poroniec) was formed by *soltys*es from Bialy Dunajec along with a setlement called MALE CICHE on Cicha Polana. Residents of Bialy Dunajec also began to emigrate to America in the 1880's, primarily due to lack of prospects to have a farm of their own. There are sizable groups of descendants of the first emigrants along with new emigrants from Bialy Dunajec in both Canada and the United States. In Chicago they are organized in Circle 40 of the Polish Highlanders Alliance in North America. They have not broken off ties with their native village, financially participating in all civic endeavors taking place there. A second school was built in the upper section of Bialy Dunajec in 1910, and in 1921 work was undertaken to build a church ot their own, since the northern part of the village belonged to the Szaflary parish, and the southern to the Poronin parish. Bialy Dunajec became an independent parish in August 1938, although the upper part of the village remained in the Poronin parish. Only in recent years, owing in part to help from countrymen in the U.S.A., have the villagers been able to build a chapel in the upper part for use on Sundays and holidays. An attempt to create light industry was made with the construction of a cardboard factory, but other enterprises did not follow. The village was electrified, the local mill was modernized, but other projects were interrupted by the war.

The period of German occupation cost the village a great deal in human and material sacrifices. From among dozens of people arrested for conspiratory activities, sixteen perished in concentration camps. Several hundred residents were deported for forced labor in Germany. The constant forced requisitions of grain, potatoes and livestock exhausted the assets of the village.

At the war's end, Bialy Dunajec again began to develop on the basis of cottage industries—handicrafts were the people's only salvation during the occupation. In the ravaged country after the war, everything useful found a buyer, so that highland articles of wool and woolen materials, or things made of wood, from the simplest to the most intricate, were very popular. The highlanders were skillful in bypassing the restrictions placed on private initiative which were the doctrine of the post-war authorities, even if their methods bordered on illegality. New housing with big-city facilities sprang up, helping the burgeoning post-war tourist boom. Roads were repaired and lighted. An imposing fire station with an auditorium and a District Cultural Center, the heart of the civic life of the village, were built. The Center is home to the regional song and dance troupe Bialodunajcanie which has been active for years and often performs all over the country and abroad, as well as on television and during festivals. At the beginning of every year there are parades and races of highland horse carriages in the snow, as well as youth sports competitions. More than twenty boarding houses offer rooms for rent year round, and there is a restaurant and six snackbars. Andrzej Gandera's Auto Mechanical and Electromechanical Enterprise located in the middle of the village on the road to Zakopane offers a wide variety of auto services.

The Bialy Dunajec community is composed of the villages of Gliczarow, Sierockie and Leszczyny. The latter two are located on the gentle hills sloping toward the Dunajec River on the right side of the highway. They lie on the banks of streams which flow into the Bialy Dunajec River. Leszczyny is especially well situated, far from communication routes, with a beautiful view of the Tatras and the valley of Bialy Dunajec. Most of its houses are new. To get to Leszczyny, you have to stay right from the area of the church over a narrow but straight road, climbing all the way to the village. From there, after passing Leszczyny, you arrive at Sierockie. You could also use the approach by Krajowa Street (to the right from the highway under the viaduct), which in the village of Banska Niznia will lead to the road to Sierockie and then left downhill to Leszczyny. Both places have overnight accommodations with full board. They are ideal for rest, far from the civilization of the contemporary world and yet not completely isolated because of their accessibility.

GLICZAROW is a village about as old as Bialy Dunajec. In the beginning of the XVII century, it grew on the right bank of the Gliczarowski Potok, which enters the Bialy Dunajec River from the right side. The *soltys* rights in this village were granted to the Bafij family. The lustration of 1636 confirms the presence of several farmers recetnly settled there. But in 1765 there were already 12 farms in Gliczarow. The road to Gliczarow leaves the highway about one kilometer from the church in Bialy Dunajec to the left, and then over the bridge it climbs until the first houses of Gliczarow Dolny appear, all the way along the 4-kilometer long Gliczarowski Potok. The road rises in hairpin bends ever more steeply, to finally reach Gliczarow Gorny and the highest part of the village—the settlement of Knapy (965 m. asl). Before the war, this region was uninhabited because of its inaccessibility. After a road link with Bukowina over Klin was built, the area became more attractive for tourism, housing was built, along with a school and a lovely modern church. The special charm of Gliczarow Gorny is its location on the ridge of a mountain with views below. The panorama of the Tatras can only be compared with the view from Polana Glodowka on the way to Morskie Oko. Also, the scenery of the hills, valleys and highland settlements is unique. To fully enjoy the grandeur of Gliczarow Gorny, you must go there on a sunny day, if only for a few hours. You can have a rest in Bozena Jasinska's Kunc bar or enjoy a more serious meal a few kilometers lower in Bukowina Tatrzanska over Klin. Bukowina may be observed in all its glory from the settlement of Knapy.

You have to go back to the trail leading to the sources of Bialy Dunajec, continuing past the upper part of the village named for the river. The highway crosses over an old reinforced concrete bridge called Cudzichowianski. This is a relic of road building, since it was the only one to survive the great flood of 1934. To the right past the bridge can be seen the buildings of the cardboard factory. About a kilometer down the road, you come to a crossroads: the road continues straight between houses, and then off to the right into a bypass of the next village. To see the relics of the old building style, it is necessary to go down the so-called "old" road. After a small bridge over the barely visible Skupniowy Potok, the roads leads you to the left where the next village— PORONIN—begins.

Taking this route in 1839, traveler Ludwik Zajszner wrote in his diary that "if there had not been a big sign announcing a new village, no one would be able to tell where Bialy Dunajec ends and Poronin, whose northern section is called

Bankowka (actually Bankowki), begins." Today there is an plaque with information near the bypass which runs between the river and the railway tracks, with a railway station nearby. The old name of the village, or rather its rudimentary beginnings—Bankowki—was in use until the names were changed, when the Wierch and the river were named Poroniec and the village was given the name of Poronin. Until then, crowded by mountains, the valley opens up, the oval shape of the elevation to the left, called Galicowa Grapa, veers to the east, revealing a view of the already close peaks of the Tatras. On the right is the long eminence of Losiowek, which turns into the Gubalowski Wierch over Zakopane to the south. This is where two mountain streams join together—Poroniec which comes from the east under Galicowa Grapa, and Zakopianka which is rushing down from the south. Together, the two form Bialy Dunajec.

This open space at the confluence of the two mountain streams, the damp, unforested terrain under Galicowa Grapa, made settlement most inviting. The residents of Szaflary began to use this area from the time when economic considerations first forced them to seek pasture land in the Tatras. Bankowki (the origin of the name is not clear) was their usual place to stay overnight on their way from Szaflary and surrounding villages to the mountain pastures. From there the sheepherding trails went in two directions—alongside Poroniec and along Cicha Woda, as Zakopianka was then called. In time the seasonal tents were replaced by permanent huts, and a settlement was born. A document dated June 26, 1624, is the first to mention Poronin as a separate settlement unit paying tribute to the *starost*. Before this date, the *zarebniks* who settled under Galicowa Grapa paid their dues to the *starost* together with the residents of neighboring Bialy Dunajec. Old documents show that the Galicias of Szaflary were the first to settle there permanently, later becoming the most prolific Poronin clan. Poronin belonged to the Szaflary parish, where the first registry entries are dated 1659-1669, but we must remember that during these times registering births, marriages and deaths was something unusual. The parish church was more than fifteen kilometers distant over poor roads. A survey of 1765 revealed that there were eleven farmers on land in Poronin, five yeomen and three mills, but thirty years later there were already 125 houses and 734 residents of the village. A chapel was built in 1806, adjoined by a cemetery. This was followed by a wooden church, and on September 7, 1833, Poronin became a separate parish.

Poronin developed in two directions on the road which ran alongside the Poroniec Stream to Bukowina Tatrzanska and along the stream flowing to Zakopane. The way to Bukowina had been used for a long time as a sheepherding trail and as a connection between the Nowy Targ region and Szepes through Czarna Gora and Jaworzyna. The houses were built some distance from the river, which dug a new bed for itself every spring. When land along the river was taken, the housing increasingly "climbed" up the slope of Galicowa Grapa. After a Szaflary-Poronin estate was bought by the Uznanski family, a manor house was built at a crossroads in Poronin and about a kilometer away a sort of guest house as well. Some three kilometers further, in the direction of Bukowina, stood the Old Manor House, with a residence, farm buildings, a sawmill and most importantly a smithy. This is where iron ore brought from the steelworks in the Hrabusice region of Szepes was processed. The smithy products from Poronin enjoyed a good reputation in Galicia; scythes forged in *hamry* (the Germanized name of the smithy), which gave the name to this factory and later to the settlement beside the estate—Kosne Hamry—which is used even now—were in special demand. Besides the natural exploitation of water to run the mechanisms of the sawmill and smithy, there was extensive use of timber for the production of charcoal. Just after the bridge over Poroniec, the settlement of MUR, the property of the *soltys* clan of Bialy, climbed the banks of the river. Since Mur's expansion was limited only to the east, houses were situated along the road to Bukowina, sometimes straying beyond the bounds of the village. That is how the village STASIKOWKA, to which Mur administratively belongs, came into being. Both villages are in the community of Poronin. The river climbs up the slope where the southern part of Bukowina (Klin) is and turns south, or actually flows from the southern side down the northern slope of the Poroniec Wierch. There is a pasture meadow of the same name on this slope as well. And thus you come to the first sources of the Bialy Dunajec. A stream called Cichowianska Woda formed from the confluence of two other streams—Filipczanski Potok and Sucha Woda—enters Poroniec near Kosne Hamry.

The settlement of Male Ciche, already mentioned in the section about Bialy Dunajec, is located on the banks of Cichowianska Woda. The clearing of the forests was conducted over the slopes in the easterly direction, and this is how the wide arable tracts of Tarasowka and Pod Zgorzeliskiem came into being. MALE CICHE became a popular vacation spot because it was off the beaten path and yet had good connections with Poronin and Zakopane. Many houses were built there after the war, equipped with all conveniences, and a lot of children's camps are located in Male Ciche. After a few kilometers, the road leading south through the village reaches the Zakopane-Morskie Oko highway through Poroniec Wierch. This is the region of the Za Zadnia forester's lodge. Leaving your car by the lodge, it is worthwhile to take a stroll on foot to Wiktorowki and Rusinowa Polana. Wiktorowka is a place in the forest near the above-mentioned Polana, where there is a shrine of the cult of the Virgin Mary, frequented by pilgrims and tourists. According to the legends told by the highlanders, a lady in a long blue gown appeared to a little shepherd girl there. A small chapel was placed on a tree there at first, then a statue of the Blessed Virgin, and finally a small wooden church under the care of the Dominican Fathers was built in Wiktorowki after the war. The owner of this area, a highlander originally from Dzianisz, built a tourist hall under the church where those in need can find shelter and even overnight accommodations and food. Nearby is a glade called Rusinowa, which is still in use as pasture land, to the extent that its status as part of the Tatra National Park will allow. The time necessary for the excursion from Za Zadnia to Rusinowa Polana is about two hours at a leisurely pace, all the way through the woods and uphill. There are three other glades in the vicinity of Rusinowa Polana—Jaworzyna, Filipka and Kopy Soltysie. They are all within a radius of five kilometers and thus an hour's walk. These glades are noteworthy because they contain the sources of springs which later form Filipczanski Potok which flows through Male Ciche.

The traveler Ludwik Zajszner mentioned above noted the peat deposits in this area when he visited the smithy, seeing in it a possible substitute for the disappearing supplies of timber. A settlement called "bor" or siyhla (from the Valachian *silha*) was situated behind these peatbogs, and came to be called Za Siyhla. It is built along the road leading south, gently inching upward, on one side by the Sichlanski Potok and on the other by Wyzacki Potok. On top, in the settlement of Capowka, the road reaches a parallel route, which crosses the neighboring village of Budzow Wierch. Merging together, the roads feed into the Zakopane—Morskie Oko highway by the Brzeziny forester's lodge. During the Austrian occupation, the settlements of Mur and Za Siyhla were joined administratively, creating an odd name—MURZASICHLE. This actually only refers to Za Siyhla, since Mur is located four kilometers from the setlement of Za Siyhla and also, as was already mentioned, Mur is called Stasikowka at present. Now Murzasichle is a popular resort, with good facilities, recreation and an easy bus link with Zakopane. We recommend Murzasichle as a home base for excursions into the Tatras. After a three-kilometer walk beyond the last houses of Capowka, you find yourself on the highway Zakopane—Morskie Oko. From there, after a one kilometer walk from the Brzeziny forester's lodge, you arrive at the rocky road leading to Dolina Gasienicowa. At a distance of about six kilometers, the walk should take less than two hours. In the valley of Hala Gasienicowa can be found a large tourist hostel where you can rest. After you recover from your walk, take the tourist trail to Czarny Staw Gasienicowy (Gasienica Black Pond) located at 1,622 m. asl. The round trip should require one hour. Returning by the same route to the Brzeziny forester's lodge, you should take note of the stream flowing alongside the road. This is the so-called Sucha Woda (Dry Water) which, after absorbing the waters of Czarny Potok coming from Czarny Staw Gasienicowy and Zolty Potok, feeds into Cichowianska Woda and with it to Poroniec past the village of Male Ciche. Thus additional sources of Bialy Dunajec can be found in Dolina Gasienicowa. Hala Gasienicowa is one of the most important tourist junctions in the Tatras and a starting point for interesting excursions with varying degrees of difficulty. We will have to return to this place, but by another route.

After examining the vicinity of one of the main streams creating Bialy Dunajec, let us return to the starting point—Poronin. Its development was tied to its proximity to Zakopane, since to some degree Poronin formed a backup for this increasingly popular resort. By the end of the XIX century, Zakopane was already "too loud" for a certain category of vacationers, who sought a peaceful stay in a not too distant neighborhood. They found it in Poronin, only six kilometers away, where summer rentals were available as early as 1900. A 1918 guidebook of the Zakopane region contains the information that Poronin then had about 50 houses for summer rental and 30 for the winter. Some 455 tourists visited Poronin in 1908. The village had four restaurants, a railway station, a post office and two shops. Poronin has grown a great deal since then, and by 1939 was a resort known throughout Poland, with a dozen or more boarding houses open during the summer. Now this number has greatly increased, and the new houses built since the war all have modern facilities. The informational booklet published on the occasion of the *Spartakiada* listed more than 50 addresses in Poronin offering lodging. Accommodations of the highest category are represented by Jozef Pawlikowski's motel Bulcyka situated by the bridge near the highway to Zakopane, the Matuska boarding house at 3B Tatrzanska Street, and the Paryzanka boarding house located at Stasiowka 1D.

There is a Peasant Cultural Center in Poronin, where you can amuse yourself, listen to highland music and watch highland dances. For the past decade, every July brings a spectacle called Poroninskie Lato (A Poronin Summer), in which many singing and dancing troupes invited from the highlands and Slovakia participate. The village church, which replaced the wooden structure destroyed by fire in 1915, has interesting regional elements in its interior, such as a sculpted "rainbow" with a cross over the altar, period pews, and frescoes depicting motifs from highlander life.

A ski lift runs on Galicowa Grapa during the winter, with easy access to other more numerous lifts in the Bukowina Tatrzanska region.

Just as they did from other highland villages, some of the Poronin natives emigrated to the United States. One of them—Stanislaw Galica-Pisarzow—became famous in 1911 wne he made the whole journey from Poronin to Chicago in full highland garb. His outfit created much interest in the U.S.A.; the press wrote about him, many of his pictures were published. When asked why he did this, he said his father had ordered him to. The Poronin emigrants form circle No. 45 of the Polish Highlanders Alliance in North America.

After visiting Poronin, it is time to set out to see additional sources of Bialy Dunajec. The road leads in the direction of

Zakopane and again separates after the bridge. The new section of the road, completed after the war, is straight, but the old road meanders among the houses of old Poronin, now interspersed with new construction. After about one kilometer you come to a bridge over the old riverbed of the Olczanski Potok, which is the administrative border between Poronin and Zakopane. The settlement of Ustup appears after the bridge and beyond it a large gas station and repair shop open twenty-four hours. The new riverbed of Olczanski Potok, which is the main tributary of Zakopianka, runs through Ustop. The road to OLCZA, a beautifully situated mountain settlement, spins off from the highway in this area. The village is composed of several groups of houses called by the names of the families which settled there during the XVIII century, such as Stachonie, Walkosze, Mrowce, Gawlaki, etc. Chronologically, the process of settling the land by the Olszanski Potok was earlier than in Zakopane. That is why, when the decision was taken in 1845 to make a parish in Zakopane, Olcza (some 10 kilometers distant), refused to participate in building the church. Like the northern part of Zakopane, it belonged to the Poronin parish at the time. Eventually, these animosities simmered down, since the distance to Poronin was about the same as to Zakopane, but they pushed the Olcza residents to try for an independent parish. First, in May 1914, they formed an independent clerical outpost in the building of the St. Vincent a Paulo Missionaries, where the monks have a rest and retreat house. Then in 1919 a chapel was built, followed by the consecration of a newly built church in Zakopane-Olcza on July 30, 1988. The energy behind this undertaking, unique in the highlands, is architect J.T. Gawlowski. The church, with its soaring roofs akin to the mountains outside, and its sunlit interior with its traditional highlan decoration, is worth seeing. The parish has about 1,700 members, who care for their village and spare no effort to improve it. The regional

Artistic Troupe "Giewont" from Olcza has many successes to its credit.

After climbing the road along Olczyski Potok for two kilometers, you reach the settlement of JASZCZUROWKA and the road between Zakopane and Morskie Oko. There is a small parking area on one side of the road and on the other—a hillside pearl of the highland building style, the chapel in Jaszczurowka. It was funded in 1908 by the sons of the proprietor of Szaflary, Uznanski, who owned this property as well. Stanislaw Witkiewicz, a champion of the Zakopane style in architecture and decoration, planned the whole project. The building of the chapel stands on a granite foundation, with its slanted main roof and belfry dome kept in the style of other old highland structures. The interior, also designed by Witkiewicz in the Zakopane style, is striking in its simplicity, reminiscent of the interior of a highland peasant cottage. The chapel's colorful stained-glass windows depict Our Lady of Czestochowa and the crest of Poland on one side, and on the other Our Lady of Ostra Brama and the crest of Lithuania, from where the Uznanski family originated. During the period between the two world wars, the warm springs which come to the surface in Jaszczurowka were utilized, but now the thermal baths have been moved to the area of the railway station in Zakopane.

You can walk further from Jaszczurowka up along Olczynski Potok to Dolina Olczyska (about 2 kilometers), and then to Hala Olczysko where a *wywierzysko* (brook flowing from limestone rocks) and a small stream arriving from the foot of the Wysokie elevation form additional sources of Bialy Dunajec.

In order to continue along the trail by the Zakopianka Stream, it is necessary to go back to the gas station on Ustup. Going right from the old road over a bridge across this stream, you will reach the settlement of HARENDA on the left bank. In the midst of the old as well as new housing of the settlement, you will find a building concealed in a cluster of ancient trees—this is the Museum of Jan Kasprowicz. It is more clearly visible from the side of the river, which it faces, and you can get there by crossing a footbridge then climbing up stairs leading to a high buttress which forms the foundation of the house. The poet bought this house in 1924 and died there in 1926. The dining room, living room and bedroom, filled with mementos, books, paintings and portraits done by friends, are open to the public. Born in Kujawy, Jan Kasprowicz loved the highlands. He came to Poronin often, bringing other people distinguished in Polish culture with him. He was a professor and rector of the Jan Kazimierz University in Lwow. After his death he was buried in the Cemetery of Meritorious Persons in Zakopane and on August 1, 1933, his ashes were transported to a mausoleum built next to his house in Harenda. His wife Maria was buried in the mausoleum in 1968. The museum is open daily, except for Mondays, from 10am to 2pm.

A wooden church from the XVIII century stands fifty or so meters from Kasprowicz's house, moved there in 1947 from Zakrzow near Kalwaria, where it had stood empty after a new church was built in that village. Various styles are represented in the interior of this church, but the 1717 wall-paintings deserve special attention.

Traveling south on the road through Harenda, soon again over the bridge on Zakopianka and then returning to the old road to Zakopane, you reach the main highway betwen Cracow and Zakopane. There is a gas station and carwash where these roads converge. And then you are in Spyrkowka—a district of Zakopane. Near there, Zakopianka Stream loses its name after it is joined by Bystry Stream. Further uphill, it becomes Cicha Woda, gathering into its fold many streams flowing from the valleys on the northern slopes of the Tatras. You will get to know them when the time comes to discuss the paths of the most popular excursions, for which ZAKOPANE will be the starting point.

Lesnica Stream

Next to the church in Ostrowsko, which is located at the edge of the village (see Chapter II), a road leads to GRONKOW, less than two kilometers distant. This is the first locality you come to at the beginning of the nearly 20 kilometer valley through which the Lesnica Potok flows. The name (referring to "forest") comes from the fact that as late as the XVI century the stream ambled in the midst of forests covering both of its banks and the slopes above them which spread to the east and west of the stream until it reached the Dunajec past Ostrowsko.

Historical sources indicate that supposedly in the place where the old trading route from Szepes to Nowy Targ crossed the Lesnica Stream there was a settlement referred to as "Clo." It must be mentioned that this name of the stream is contained in the oldest known document from the beginning of the XIII century, so that the name is probably a leftover from the previous inhabitants of these lands—the Wislans. Documents connected with the emergence of Nowy Targ speak about a settlement with a similar name—Stare Clo—which does not exclude the possibility that Clo also existed on the route leading from Czech lands through

Orawa. In one of the documents founding Nowy Targ in 1346, King Kazimierz the Great confirmed the *soltys* status in Clo of one Dytrych, at the same time incorporating Clo into the Nowy Targ lands. Maciej, the parish priest of Clo, is mentioned in a document from 1327 written in Nowy Targ, which indicates that the settlement must have had at least a small church. It is most likely that the settlement was completely destroyed during border wars, since it is no longer mentioned in later historical writings. It was not until the years 1580-1591 that a new settlement was established in the location of the old Clo by *starost* Jan Sienienski, which initiated a centuries-long dispute between the Sienienskis and the Nowy Targ burghers over the rights to this land.

Today's Gronkow is built on both sides of the road from Ostrowsko, on the left bank of the Lesnica Stream. Two small streams flow into Lesnica in the lower part of the village. The larger of them—Czerwony Potok—runs through the hamlet of Bor and then to two villages parallel to each other on the banks of the same stream—GRON on the left side and LESNICA on the right. The road was built in the way that was most suitable to the terrain and the incline of the stream banks, so that it goes back and forth from one side to the other, once through Gron and then in a moment through Lesnica. This is because the two villages were established at different times, while the road was laid out later. The Lesnica Stream was the border of both places.

The founder of Gron, originally called Groniec, was Adam Gronski-Belzyk (or perhaps Belczyk) who on July 7, 1628, was granted the proper privileges by King Zygmunt III and the right to clear two *soltys* fiefs for himself on the right side of Lesnica Potok all the way to the Bialka River. He had the right to settle yeomen on this terrain. Within the framework of the privileges he was granted, Gronski came into possession of pasture fields known as Lesnica, Karpencina and Jaworzno. His son inherited the privileges held by his father, but nevertheless on November 14, 1749, these *soltys* rights were transferred to the brothers Wojciech and Bartlomiej Rusin by royal decree. The Rusins were probably Valachians. To this day the peak rising above Upper Gron is called Rusinski Wierch and in time the Jaworzy Glade came to be known as Rusinowa Glade. According to a survey made in 1869, still under Austrian rule, Gron continued to grow and then numbered 173 houses and 768 inhabitants.

The expansion of the village of Lesnica developed in a rather different way, as can be observed from the arrangement of the farm buildings. Only the lower part of the village is built in an organized manner along streets, while in the central and upper part one can see signs of scattered groups of houses—probably relics of the Polanie era. Usually forming family groups, individual settlers established their domiciles a certain distance from others in order to have cleared land for their use near their homes. The territory of villages settled earlier than Gron, such as Szaflary and Bialy Dunajec, were located a little further to the west. Walking around the central and upper part of the village, you encounter a group of farms with names such as Makowie, Stasiki, Stefany, Czubiaki, Galowie, Wojtusie and Losie. Similar groups of family farms can be seen in Upper Gron as well. There are two elementary schools, one in Lesnica and the other in Gron, a post office (in Lesnica), a health center (in Gron) and a common Center of Rest-House Vacations offering rooms and board year round. Former residents of Gron and Lesnica coexist harmoniously in Circle 37 of the Polish Highlanders Alliance in North America in Chicago.

After 1945 the residents of both villages undertook the initiative to build a church. Until that time, there were only two small chapels there. An old legend was connected with the chapel dating from 1776—claiming that the chapel was moving on its own in the direction of the Szepes locality of Trybsz beyond the Bialka River. By the time the chapel drifted to Trybsz—the world was supposed to end. The new church was built on the right bank, and thus in Gron. It is just beyond the bridge over the Lesnica Stream. Although the church was built only 40 years ago, it is made of wood, with beamed walls tied in the highland fashion, and a shingled covering of the roof and steeple. These shingles, called *gonty*, are boards measuring about 70 centimeters in length and 12 centimeters in width, with the necessary notches and projections to make them tight-fitting on the long side and overlapping on the short side.

The road continues to climb steadily until finally, by the last bus stop, the asphalt ends. A small chapel stands in the field nearby. There is one more settlement called Szewcy before you come to the slopes of Bachledowy Wierch and Dziadowka, below which can be seen several small streams. These are the sources of the Lesnica Stream. After arriving at the ridge of the mountainside, you again find a good road leading left to Bukowina and Klin and right to Gliczarow.

While you are staying in one of the three places by the Lesnica Stream, it would be worthwhile to make an excursion over the nearby Bialka River in order to to gain at least a rudimentary acquaintance with Polish Spisz (Szepes). Over the road from Nowy Targ which crosses Gronkow, you come to the village of Bialka and then over a bridge you reach the first Szepes village—Czarna Gora. The first striking sight you encounter is the Grapa decline by the Bialka, which reveals the geological structure of the subsoil risen up in a heap. Right after the bridge there is another attraction—a Gypsy settlement belonging to Czarna Gora. You can leave the car with them for a few hours if you did not come to Bialka by bus, in order to continue your excursion on foot. A tourist trail marked in red leads east from the Gypsy camp, bringing you to an old chapel at the beginning of the Rzepisko hamlet. From there the trail leads north through Bryjow Potok and Sarnowska Grapa (936 m. asl), where you come upon a trail marked in blue leading to Trybsz. You may wish to rest there before continuing on your way, which will be a southern route to Czarna Gora. If time and your physical condition allow, you might wish to make another two-kilometer walk south to Jurgow, which is referred to as "the most Szepes of all villages." Over the whole course of the excursion, and especialy in Jurgow, you should concentrate your attention on the old architecture which clearly indicates that Szepes was under different influences than the highlands. White-washed structures made of brick, never encountered in the highlands, prevail in the old housing. This is a result of the efforts of the Hungarian authorities in the middle of the XIX century to lessen the danger of fires. Despite similar external shapes, the Szepes houses differed from those in the highlands in their interior configuration. Under the Giewont Peak, the typical set-up was two rooms with a vestibule and, occasionally a hallway. In Szepes the house was arranged in railroad fashion. The side entrance into the house led to a hall, then to a kitchen (called *izbecka*), which had a stove, benches, shelves and other kitchen accessories. The kitchen led to a chamber, also equipped with a stove and benches, but also beds and a table, which was the most important piece of furniture. From the chamber there was an entrance to the hall, where food and clothing were stored. The windows of all lodgings faced east, and only the chamber had an additional window on the western side for the purpose of observing the property. Today's architectural unification is making the houses of the highlands and Szepes similar both on the outside and the inside, particularly when it comes to the "comforts" provided in them. No one builds houses today without a bathroom and toilet.

When you are in Jurgow you should visit the old parish church, built at the turn of the XVIII century. It stands inside a brick wall with an equally old gate. The church is of wood, with shingle-covered walls and under the roof a turret with a spherical dome for a small bell—an ave bell. An 1811 free-standing belfry is nearby, with bells dating back to 1699 and 1785, apparently brought to Jurgow from an older church.

You now have to return to Czarna Gora and then back to your starting point through Bialka. The time required for the excursion, counting rest periods on the way, is not more than five hours.

EXCURSION VIII

The Mining Trail

We find the following notation in a survey document of 1564: "The new village called Banska on the road over which people went to New Banie in the Tatras, which was first built by Mr. Lubomirski and then Mr. Pieniazek and Mr. Karsperbar—10 serfs." *Bania* means mine in Hungarian and this name became generally accepted first in Moravia and Szepes, along with the miners imported from the other side of the Tatras, and then spread to the Nowy Targ region in the highlands. The search for precious metals in the Tatras went back very far. As chronicler Miechowita wrote in 1502, in the times of King Aleksander Jagiellonczyk, "when silver and copper were discovered three miles from Nowy Targ," Voivode Lubomirski took care by royal decree of building a new road to the mines more convenient than the old roads running alongside the two Dunajec rivers. This time the course of the road designed to carry heavy equipment was set for higher elevations over lightly forested hillsides along the ridges running from south to north, far from the rivers which tended to change their course with every spring's floods. The new road began in Szaflary. A short section went west, and then along the foot of an elevation which looked like a pyramid covered with woods—called Raniszberg (678 m. asl) in earlier centuries. Then it turned south and kept this direction to the end. The peasants working on the road's construction (or perhaps war prisoners, since Lubomirski often engaged in wars) built cottages along the road and so in time a new village came into being. It was called Banska because it lay on the road to Banias. Its building style is typical for most of highland villages—"in string style," but it was only later, when the number of houses grew, that individual farms joined in a continuous line along the road. Banska stretches out for over six kilometers and is divided into a Niznia (lower) and Wyznia (upper) part. Niznia Banska is built along both sides of the road on a gently rising hillside; you can view its whole panorama from the Szaflary-Zakopane road. The village looks like coral beads strung among green and gold fields spreading on both sides of the village. In the middle of this part of Banska stands a church and parish buildings. Despite its "young" age, the church already has its history, which is worth exploring.

Banska belongs to the Szaflary parish, so that its inhabitants had to travel five to ten kilometers to church. This was tiresome, especially for the older generation in the fall and winter seasons, so that a move was started to build their own church "on" Banska, as the highlanders are say. But this was a period when the authorities were strongly opposed to erecting sacral structures, and were not inclined to grant permission for such projects. In this situation, two brothers named Bafij petitioned the building authorities to let them erect a sheepfold on their property which would be large enough to serve as a temporary chapel, to which the priest from Szaflary commuted on Sundays and holidays. Later, a residence was built on the same principle, in time housing the priest and the parish office. In the meantime the political situation changed to the extent that the authorities gave permission for the building of a church. This was a tremendous effort for the village population numbering about 1,100 souls. They gave the priest donations for the construction—as much as they could—and the villagers themselves did all the work on the structure except for the highly specialized tasks. In the meantime, fire broke out in the chapel, almost completely destroying it. The Banska residents went into action again: the chapel was rebuilt within a month, of course made of beams and boards provided by the villagers. The building of the church was greatly aided by former Banska residents and other Szaflary parishoners living in North America. They are organized in Circle No. 24 of the Polish Highlanders Alliance in North America. Along with group donations, there also came many individual and family gifts.

Past the church, the road climbs up the hill to the other part of the village, BANSKA WYZNIA. Here settlers built their houses on a mountain ridge called Swierkowy Wierch. The houses are similar to those in the lower village, but they are built further apart, and not right by the road. Two buildings nearing completion—a church and an elementary school—are noteworthy. Here the effort to build a church must have been even greater, since the village numbers fewer than one thousand inhabitants. At about the same time, the old school burned down. While it is true that it was a relic of the past, one of the two oldest in the highlands, with especially difficult learning conditions, still it was there. According to people familiar with the affairs of the village, two students decided to burn up compromising records of their scholastic achievement. They ended up burning down the whole school. Residents of the neighboring village of Sierockie "envied" the Banska people their fire. Their own school was even older. Schoolwork continued in substitute schoolrooms, while a delegation of highlanders from Banska, in their original highland costumes, traveled to Warsaw to ask the Ministry of Education for help. They returned with the first donation of 500 million zlotys (about $3,000). Work was begun on the new school, with the residents contributin money and labor; other sponsors were found and in less than two years an impressive school building was completed in Banska Wyzna.

Continuing further up the hill, the road arrives at the settlement of SIEROCKIE, (see Excursion VI). You will see a belfry characteristic for this area on the side of the road, with a little chapel under it. Near the school the local road leads left over a hill dropping down toward Bialy Dunajec to the settlement of LESZCZYNY which lies on a mountain ridge. Only a kilometer more uphill, and the road becomes level after reaching an elevation called Rolow Wierch (1,013 m. asl). One and a half kilometers later comes a road goes off to the right leading to the village of Czerwienne, stretching out nearly nine kilometers over the lovely hillsides. A little further, a local road branches off to the left between houses to the village of BUSTRYK. This village is located on a hillside, near the Bustrycki Potok flowing toward the Bialy Dunajec. Looking south from this village, you see a magnificent panorama of the Tatras without any obstructions. Dr. Franciszek Lukaszczyk, the first director of the Maria Curie-Sklodowska Radium Institute in Warsaw, and the father of Polish oncology, is a native highlander born and bred in Bustryk. During the German occupation, he worked to save the Institute's radium from the Germans, hiding its supplies in various places. Insufficient protection from radiation caused him to develop radiotoxemia, from which he died in 1956 at the age of 59.

Bustryk belongs to the community and parish of nearby ZAB; it has a school, historic chapel, and links to a state bus route. A Center of Highland Alliance with its own youth regional troupe is active there.

The local road to Bustryk leaves the main Banska road in the village of Zab, earlier called Zubow. The location document for the village of Zubow has been preserved. On April 25, 1620, Nowy Targ *starost* Stanislaw Witowski issued a privilege to Wiktor Zdanowski and his wife Anna to found two villages—Zubow and Jastrzebiec on "unused lands from the village of Banska all the way to the Tatras, on the other side up to the river called Ustup (now Zakopianka), from the third side to the territory of the village of Ratulow, from the fourth side to the lands of the village of Skrzypna and on the fifth side to the Bialy Dunajec." The entire grant covered 45 franconian fiefs (about 1,100 hectares), of which 3 fiefs (about 70 hectares) were destined for a future parish. This document indicates the degree of settlement in the area, especially that the terrains from the village of Banska all the way to the Tatras were unpopulated. The village of Zubow began to develop, but there were not enough settlers to inhabit the second village of Jastrzebiec. It was only ten years later that the first cottages of a settlement called SUCHE (after the stream) began to appear in the Suchy Potok valley east of Zubow. The use of the name of Jastrzebiec was abandoned. Like Bustryk, Suche became a hamlet of Zab, which had its own *wojt* (officer of a group of villages) in the Austrian times. It was then that Zab and Suche were joined administratively, creating the onomastic oddity of Zubsuche. This name is somehow always associated with Suche, and never with Zab. From 1834, both villages belonged to the parish of Poronin. When the wooden church in Poronin was destroyed by fire on November 30, 1915, the Zab residents saw this as an opportunity to form their own parish. A wooden church was built through the efforts of the Zab inhabitants, and it is still in use to this day. It is worthy of attention not only because of its age, but also because it is a classic example of sacral architecture dominant in the highlands years ago, with its interior decoration strictly conforming to old highland traditions. Other public buildings in Zab are the post office, health center and school, built on one of the highest elevations in Poland. Highlanders from Zab have formed Circle No. 58 of the Polish Highlanders Alliance in North America headquartered in Chicago.

A road to Poronin through Suche and later to Zakopane

or Nowy Targ leads east from the crossroads in Zab, and to the left another road goes down to Nowe Bystre and further to Ratulow. The Banska road, however, turns to the south-west, soon reaching the village of FURMANOWA. It is composed of fifty or more houses forming a link between Zab and Gubalowka. A lovely highland-style chapel with a soaring roof and a small belfry tower can be seen behind the village houses. After about two kilometers you will see a high radio-television tower at an elevation of 1,120 m. asl, and behind it the settlement of GUBALOWKA. On the left side of the road stands a group of buildings of the upper cable-car railway linking Zakopane with Gubalowka. It was built in a short period of five months in 1938 in preparation for the FIS world ski competition. The technical documentation, driving gears and cars were provided by the Swiss firm of Ludwik de Rolle. The line is 1,338 meters long, with the difference of 300 meters in altitude between the upper and lower stations. The cars attached to either end of the line travel on tracks, each one capable of holding about 80 passengers. By means of the rotary motion of an electrically-powered drum, the line is wound around; when one car goes up, another one goes down. In mid-span, the tracks separate, making it possible for the cars to pass each other. The trip takes about five minutes. The upper station is next to a large scenic terrace on several levels, offering a magnificent view on sunny days—of Giewont and other rocky peaks on either side, with Zakopane spread out below. A sculpture of a woman holding a dove, done by Stanislaw Kaniak and called Polonia Restituta, stands in front of the terrace building. It had adorned the Polish pavilion at the Paris world exhibition in 1937. The area around the station and the restaurant building is described as the largest "frying pan" in Poland, on which hundreds of tourists bask in the sun, even in the early spring when the mountains are still covered with snow. There are pedestrian paths along the tracky leading to and from Zakopane. Ski lifts are also available, although in 1997

196

their owners are locked in a dispute with the proprietors of pastures on Gubalowka, which always makes skiing down an "iffy" proposition. And that is a shame, because this terrain is especially suitable for less advanced skiers. But now there is a new attraction in Gubalowka—the only one in Poland so far—in the form of a chute down which you ride in special carts. A metal chute set a cement base slithers down serpentine turns a restaurant below, providing a thrill-filled ride. The passenger carts descend by means of natural gravitational pull, without mechanical power.

After enjoying these attractions, you must return to the Banska road, which now leads west, always over mountain ridges, offering lovely views of the Tatras on the left and the area beyond Gubalowka on the right. Houses of the Gubalowka settlement on the side of the road are mainly new, since here, as in Gliczarow Gorny, building expansion only began in earnest after the mountain road over the peaks was brought to a car-worthy state. A chapel funded in 1962 by the Bachledns stands on the right side of the road not far from the cable car station. A plaque inside the chapel gives a detailed account of its history. Less than a kilometer beyond, a local road on the edge of the forest takes you to Dzianisz next door to the settlement Slodyczki. A little further along the road, you will find Polana Palkowka with buildings notable for their size and placement in the shape of a horseshoe. To the left is the highest elevation in the Gubalowka range—Palenica Koscieliska (1,198 m. asl) with a triangulation tower at its peak. The road then reaches the settlement of BUTOROW where you see the upper station of the cable-car station. The distance between the upper and lower stations is 1,660 meters, with an altitude difference of 277 meters. The perpetually moving cable has two-person seats. The maximum capacity of the lift is 720 passengers per hour. There are two choice for a downhill run for skiers from Butorowy Wierch to the southern part of Zakopane. About a hundred meters to the west, located on the northern slope, you will find an easy trail with a mechanical lift, which is a great place for learning to ski.

There is a beautiful view below south from Butorow of the village of KOSCIELISKO. Despite the growing size of this village, you can still see from above how far from each other people settled on secluded cleared glades. For a long time they were referred to as *Polaniarze* (glade people). To this day, individual regions of the village bear names derived from the first settlers who cleared the forest and farmed there. The origins of the village go back to the time when attempts at exploitation of ores in the valley named for the little church located at its entrance—Dolina Koscieliska— were abandoned. The little church was one of the buildings of a whole mining-metallurgic complex. When the mining work was abandoned, former miners began to settle on the slopes north of the Dolina. They brought the name of Koscielisko with them, adding Nowe (new) to it. According to a document from 1799, there were only ten cottages on the glades at the time, but the village continued to develop on the basis of Vallachian law covering shepherding villages. For this reason Koscielisko, like Olcza, did not want to unite with nearby Zakopane, because Vallachian law was more to their advantage. Upon the liquidation of the settlement in Dolina Koscieliska, the little church was torn down as well, and the parish church in Chocholow inherited its appointments. When Koscielisko received the right to elect a *wojt*, an official seal was made bearing an outline of the church. Those studying the history of Koscielisko may encounter the opinion that the name of Dolina Koscieliska comes from the bones of the Tartar invaders, whose large contingent was wiped out by the highlanders in this valley. This is nothing but a legend, since at the time of the last Tartar invasion of region, at the start of the XIII century, there were no highlanders there yet. The area was covered with primeval forests.

In 1836 the Koscielisko *wojt* and village officials sent a

petition to the National Council in Lwow asking that a parish be established in their village. The nearest church (in Chocholow) was some 15 kilometers away. In the meantime, however, a parish was formed in Zakopane (in 1848), and Koscielisko was incorporated into it. But this did not dampen the enthusiasm of the villagers, who built their own church after receiving the necessary permission from the sacral and secular authorities. Its inauguration, together with the beginning of parish activities, took place February 2, 1916. Four years earlier, February 5, 1912, a country school named for Wladyslaw Jagiello started.

Past the church and the school, the road continues south through a separate group of houses called Budzowka (from Budz) and Rysulowka (from Rysula). After crossing through a wooded area, you arrive at the Zakopane-Witow road, in a place called KIRY, at the entrance to Dolina Koscieliska. This is the end of the "Banska Way" which centuries ago led to Nowe Banie in the Tatras.

DOLINA KOSCIELISKA is one of the loveliest valleys in the Tatras, with very diverse features and surroundings. This is why hundreds of tourists visit this valley, especially since a road suitable for cars runs nearby, making for easy access, and the crossing of the valley itself is quite easy for even the least adventurous tourists. Dolina Koscieliska also has an interesting history, although unfortunately it is not of much interest to those visiting it today and the material relics of this history are few. But it seems worthwhile to recall what this place witnessed 300 years and even 150 years ago before you take the stroll along its paths.

Iron, copper and silver ores were mined in Dolina Koscieliska, as well as in neighboring Dolina Chocholowska, while the processing plant for these ores was located in Dolina Koscieliska. In a settlement later called Stare Koscielisko and on the glade of the same name, there was a small hamlet with cottages for the miners and metallurgy workers, along with an administration building called "the manor," a mill for grinding the ore, flotation fixtures, a great oven for melting down the iron and a sawmill. And, of course, there had to be an inn. It was decided to locate the processing plant here by the *wywierzysko* (brook flowing from limistone rocks) to make use of the water power available to drive the mechanical installations. The rapid stream, called Lodowe Zrodlo, was an outflow of underground waters from the whole masiff of Czerwone Wierchy. Koscielicki Potok also ran through parts of the valley. The temperature of the water was constant winter and summer—4.3 degrees Celsius. Tourists visiting Dolina Koscieliska in the 1860's encountered remnants of the old manor, the forester's lodge, the inn and the smithy (still active in 1841). Besides the old names, what has remained in the valley is the millstone for the ore mill about two kilometers away. An iron cross has been set into this stone, first in 1852 and replaced in 1948.

An excursion into Dolina Koscieliska begins at the settlement of Kiry. This name has remained from old times and hear it in other places in the Tatras as well. It comes from the German name *die Kehre*, meaning curve in the road. A rest house with a restaurant is located near the road, next to it an inn and shops with souvenirs and drinks. There is also a large parking field, since no cars are allowed in the valley. Dolina Koscieliska is a territory of the Tatra National Park and there is a small entrance fee used for upkeep of trails and tourist places in the Tatras.

On the left side, near the entrance to the valley, there is a limestone slump called Jarcowa Skala (barley rock; barley is *jarzec* in highland dialect) composed of calcified protozoan shells similar to barley seeds. Half a kilometer later is a narrowing of the valley, carved out by a stream in rosy limestone. It is called Brama Kantaka (Kantak's Gate) in honor of the great Polish leader, defender of Polish interests in the Prussian parliament (Kazimierz Kantak 1824-1886). The valley widens beyond the gate, forming a glade called Wyznia Kira Mietusia by the turn to the Mietusia Valley, and after 30 minutes you reach the Stare Koscieliska glade. This was once the center of metallurgy; all that remains is an old chapel called "robbers' chapel," although it is undoubtedly a remnant of the mining and forging settlement. There is a little bridge over the stream at the southern edge of the glade and beyond it a steep path up the wooded slope, which after 20 minutes brings you to the entrance to the underground Jaskinia Mrozna (Frosty Cave). This cave, whose name comes from the cold always prevailing there, is about 500 meters long and extends parallel to the Koscieliska Dolina at about 1,100 m. asl. It is composed of corridors (low in some places) and chambers of varying sizes with limestone dripstone above and below. The trip through the cave, which is lit throughout, takes about 45 minutes. The exit is also on a slope, leading to a steep path with railings that takes you back to the road across the valley. Below Jaskinia Mrozna, some half a kilometer down the road, there again is a narrowing of the valley walls, about 500 meters long, called Brama Jozefa Ignacego Kraszewskiego. In 1879, on the fiftieth anniversary of Kraszewski's literary work, a memorial plaque was placed on this rock.

About an hour after your entrance to the valley, not counting the time spent in visiting the Jaskinia Mrozna, the road reaches Hala Pisana, above which tower the limestone peaks called Stoly, Organy, Saturn and Raptowickie Turnie. Rich iron ore (40—70% Fe) was once mined on the slope of Stoly, in a gully called Zelezniak, but it turned out that the lode was not a rich one.

Some 150 meters beyond Hala Pisana, the Cracow Ravine extends to the left. It can be reached by a 150-meter-long path through a wooded area. This ravine is an example of perpendicular erosion of limestone rocks, and made the highlanders think of the tall houses on Cracow streets—thus the name. For reasons of safety, visits to the ravine are confined to its lower part. A round-trip stroll through the gorge takes about an hour's time, counting a look at a shallow cave called, like the one in Cracow, the Dragon's Den. Skala Pisana can be found along the path leading to the ravine, at the foot of the Zbojeckie Turnie crag. It is a perpendicular plate of rock covered with carved autographs of tourists. Koscieliski Potok flows out of the rocks of Jaskinia Pisana. A path goes off to the right leading to Jaskinia Mylna and a little further on there is one to Jaskinia Raptowicka. Jaskinia Mylna is one of the longest underground passages in the Tatras, with about 1,300 meters in corridors, but only a 300-meter section may be visited, and only then with a good flashlight.

About a half kilometer from Skala Pisana, the Valley widens, turning into Hala Smytnia. There has to have been a forge here at one time, leaving behind a distorted form of the German word *schmieden* (meaning "forging"). At the end of this mountain pasture stands a cross placed on the wheel of an old metal mill. After a small bridge over the stream, the road passes Stara Polana and as you leave the woods, the regors of your journey are rewarded by a magnificent panorama of the Tatras where they close off Dolina Koscieliska. Hala Pyszna lies under the peaks and sub-alpine forests and below, bordered from the west by the Ornak slope, is Hala ORNAK. This is where Dolina Chocholowska and Dolina Koscieliska meet, since on the west side of the Ornak slope lies Stara Robota and Starorobocianska Dolina (see Excursion IV). There is a tourist hostel on Polana Ornaczanska situated on Mala Polanka. It has about 80 beds, a tourist restaurant with a large dining hall, and a community center housing a station of the Mountain Volunteer Fire Department.

After a rest at the hostel, you can still make a small excursion to Staw Smreczynski (Smreczynski Pond). A small path among boulders to the left of the shelter requires a steady climb. There is a 120 meter difference in elevation between the two places, and the trip should take about half an hour. Smreczynski Staw is a remnant of a morainal depression between two glaciers. Its surface measures about 0.8 hectares, and its average depth about 1.8 meters. Thanks to its sodden shoreline, the pond abounds in organic life, marshy vegetation and small reptiles and amphibians.

EXCURSION IX

East of Black Dunajec

Roughly speaking, "the Banska way to the Tatras" divides the highlands into eastern and western parts. This division is dictated by streams feeding the Czarny Dunajec River from the western areas, namely Skrzypny, Czerwony, Bystry, Cichy, Dzianiski and many smaller streams and brooks.

Skrzypny Potok, also known as "Rogozniczek" in old documents, rises under Wierch Rolow where the village of Zab begins. It bears this name until today, but only to the end section of the stream, while in its upper part it is called Skrzypny. The village of SKRZYPNE is nestled on two gently sloping hills above it. Its settlement began at the start of the XVII century. A survey of the Nowy Targ royal lands conducted in 1636 listed 14 early woods-clearing farmers in Skrzypne. Twenty-five years later, there were already six farms with partially cleared land and nine cottagers. A survey of 1765 showed 12 farms and a mill. Today Skrzypne is densely built up, extending to both the eastern hill of Upper Skrzypne and the western hill called Lower Skrzypne.

Most of the housing is modern, but here and there you can spy traditional, small highland houses among the ancient trees. There is a new brick church in the upper village, consecrated in 1976, which replaced the chapel that had served the inhabitants since 1934. The roads leading through both parts of the village join below where you find a road to Sierocki, Zab and Zakopane. After three kilometers you come to a crossroads again, near which, on the right, is the tree-covered Raniszberg hill. If time permits, you may wish to climb this hill to see, concealed by the trees from below, a cross placed there in 1914 to honor the 500th anniversary of the Battle of Grunwald. The cross was made by a local highlander, Maciej Lukaszczyk, a smith and mechanic, resident of the settlement Pod Lubelkami on the right side of the Dunajec in Szaflary. A similar cross may be seen on Galicowa Grapa in Poronin.

A turn left at the fork leads you to the village of MARUSZYNA. On the right side you will see the Zdzar elevation (773 m. asl), which faces the beginning of the village, composed of sparsely built houses, most of them old. The village was founded at the turn of the XVI century. A 1636 survey noted 22 settlers in Maruszyna. By 1765 there were 22 farms along with a number of wood-clearing peasants, and in 1777, 153 houses and 786 inhabitants. To this day the mainstay of the population is farming and animal husbandry (cows and sheep). After World War II some Maruszyna people began to seek work in Szaflary and Nowy Targ, while many others tried their luck "beyond the Great Water." In Chicago they are organized in Circle No. 35 of the Polish Highlanders Alliance in North America. They were instrumental in the construction of the recently built primary school and church. A local road turns left above the church to the village of Czerwienne, visible on a neighboring hill. You can also take a local road to the village of Stare Bystre.

Skrzypny Potok passes Raniszberg on the left side and in its final run flows by the settlement of ZASKALE. This is a village located behind the Szaflarska Skalka, thus its name (*skala* means rock). A small settlement in the beginning, it first appeared in tax records of the Nowy Targ *starostship* in 1674. Two hundred years later it had 54 houses and 276 inhabitants. Despite the fact that Ludzmierz is only a few kilometers away, a church was built in Zaskale during the past few years, and consecrated in 1987. The cornerstone of this church was blessed by Pope John Paul II. You can reach Zaskale either from the Szaflary side, near the train station, or from Ludzmierz by the road branching off from the highway from Nowy Targ.

After seeing Zaskale, its church and new housing, take the tourist trail upstream along the Wielki Rogoznik. It joins Czarny Dunajec beyond Ludzmierz, so you have to drive to the crossroads near this village and turn in the direction of the village of Rogoznik, which has one of the oldest pedigrees in the highlands (see Excursion IV). By the first cross along the road you have to turn left to an old road leading among the houses of the village to reach the church located at the edge of the settlement, where the houses come close to the banks of the stream. It is there that Rogoznik ends in an imperceptible way and STARE BYSTRE begins as its extention on the shore of the stream. This is a stream which flows from the south and is called Bystry higher up, becoming Wielki Rogoznik after joining with Cichy stream at the high end of the village. The village of Stare Bystre was founded at the beginning of the XVII century on the banks of the stream from which it took its name. The brothers Wojciech and Krzysztof Cubala were granted the privilege for its foundation on July 7, 1617. In 1636 there were 12 farmers on the land, seven cottagers and two mills. The position of *soltys* of this village was granted to the brothers Jan and Tadeusz Gadowski on the basis of a privilege issued by King Jan Kazimierz on August 7, 1650. The adjective "Old" appeared with the Bystre name from 1777 because of the emergence of a settlement called "New" Bystre upstream from the original village.

Stare Bystre is situated on a hillside mostly on the left bank of the stream, near the road below which the stream has its run. This village also has an upper and a lower part. The border between them is considerd to be Skalka, a limestone wall rising a dozen or more meters above the road. Stare Bystre belonged to the Rogoznik parish in the past, but a church has been built here recently. It was placed in such a way that the residents of the upper part of the village did not have too long a walk to it. With its soaring roof and steeple, its architecture is a reflection of the regional style. The Bystry and Cichy streams come together above Skalka. From this spot the upper section of Stare Bystre seems to separate into two parts because of the by-pass that circles the village at this point, going around the old part of the village. New houses, build in accordance with modern standards, line the thoroughfare. To see the XIX century part of the village, you must walk to the old road over a path winding among the buildings or drive around to where the old and new roads meet. Then there is a turn to the left on the narrow old road lined with typical old highland housing. There are a few new houses here as well, but this part of the village has still retained its period character. For example, there is a house at number 15, built of unusually wide planks, up to 70 centimeters. This house, like others down the road, are no longer inhabited—it is awaiting its fate. But houses built 50-60 years ago seem to be holding up well. This road, lined with old houses, comes to a sudden end, blocked off by a building. The rest of it was liquidated when the bypass was built. Only the stream bank remains. Return to the highway, where the next village—MIETUSTWO—begins. It is a place rich in tradition tied to the name of its founder. It was founded "on a raw root"—a place covered with woods—by Tomasz Mietus in accordance with the privilege granted by King Zygmunt III Waza on July 26, 1595. Tomasz

Mietus was a very busy man, since he had also served as the first *soltys* in Chocholow (see Chapter IV) upon his nomination by *starost* Pieniazek. The Mietus name made its presence felt in the highlands in a big way. Besides Mietustwo at the confluence of the Bystry and Cichy streams, there is also Mietusia Rola, by a peatbog called Bory Mietusie at the source of Czarny Potok at the start of Dolina Koscieliska; Dolina Mietusia goes off to the left from the upper and lower Kira Mietusia and above it there is the Przyslop Mietusi mountainpass near Zawiesista Turnia. Today Mietustwo forms something of a central point for three villages, since the roads from Stare Bystre, Ratulow and Ciche converge here. There is an old church with an adjoining cemetery in the village and on its peripheries, already considered Ratulow, there stands a modern Health Center for the whole area. There are also bus stops on the Zakopane-Ratulow and Nowy Targ-Ciche lines.

The church is worth seeing because of its interior decoration. One of its niches holds a life-size nativity scene unique in this region. Some of the village houses also deserve a look. At Number 14, for instance, the downstairs porch is adorned with an old sculpted wooden screen.

Right outside of Mietustwo, after you pass a crossroads, begin the first houses of the next village on the banks of Bystry Potok, RATULOW.

The original name of this locality was Radultow, in honor of the Nowy Targ *starost* Marek Radlut. A man known as "honest Maciej" was granted the *soltys* position of the village on July 17, 1643 on the basis of the privilege granted by King Zygmunt III. His last name was entered in the documents as Ratulowski, and from that time the village has borne the name of Ratulow. A survey of 1660 showed 15 cottagers on the land. Ratulow developed uphill on the sides of Bystry Potok, and in time it was divided into the upper and lower village. Its houses were built in accordance with the vagaries of the terrain—on the left and right side of the stream. This gives the place a great deal of charm, especially since the road continues to climb up the hillside.

In 1751 the *soltys* status of Maciej's descendants—Antoni and Marcin Ratulowski—was confirmed by King August III. A 1765 survey indicated 18 farms with arable land and three mills. The village school is situated in upper Ratulow, near a small highland-style church, or rather a chapel open on Sundays and holidays. Ratulow natives now living in North America and organized in Circle No. 55 of the Polish Highland Alliance in Chicago contributed generously to its construction. The village boasts a Volunteer Fire Department Station. The people of Ratulow have been known in the highlands for a long time as specialists in metal engraving. Ratulow highland pipes, whose tobacco holders were richly carved, metal pins and belt clasps, and finally highland sticks with metal handles have been in great demand at fairs for more than a hundred years.

And again imperceptibly Ratulow ends and the next village by Bystry Potok—NOWE BYSTRE—begins. This is the youngest village along the stream, dating back to the XIX century. The wooden village church and little chapels along the road, along with the few farms that remain, date from this period. But new construction has encroached on the area as well, as exemplified by the building housing the Volunteer Fire Department. You can climb a walking path to Gubalowka from the southern end of the village, or take another path leading to Furmanowa. A road veers off to the left, one kilometer before Noski and then climbs in a serpentine fashion to a crossroads in the village of Zab. From there, you may go through Suche or Poronin to Zakopane or Nowy Targ.

The hill on which the village of CZERWIENNE is situated is visible from Zab, Ratulow and Skrzypne. In the old days, it was referred to as Miedzyczerwone or Miedzyczerwienne. Czerwony Potok emerges from a small peatbog at the foot of a hill in the lower part of the village. The rust-color of its substratum indicates the presence of soddy ore with iron compounds as evidenced by the red color of rocks protruding from the surface in places. They have given the "red" name to the village. The locality's origin goes back to the start of the XVII century. No location document has been preserved, and there may never have been one, since lands suitable for farming were often settled spontaneously, together with the exploitation of territories in legally established neighboring villages. A survey taken in the highlands listed seventeen woods-clearing farmers in Miedzyczerwone in 1636. By 1765 there were ten full, established farms in the village. At that time, people worked mostly in farming, keeping sheep, and some also transported ore from the mountains to the smelting works in Kuznice.

It would be best to begin a visit to Czerwienne by the "Banska" road. A road though Czerwienne which ends in Mietustwo breaks off to the right about one and a half kilometers beyond the Rolowy Wierch. An original highland "tablet" stands where the road forks, reading: HERMITAGE OF PAULINE FATHERS dedicated to Jaworzynska Virgin Mother and PATH OF PRIMATE OF THE MILLENIUM.

There are several noteworthy things to see during the four kilometer ride to the hermitage. One is an old belfry surrounded by equally aged spruce trees on the right side of the road. A bit further, also on the right, is one of the oldest buildings in the village, a primary school perched on a stony foundation. This school bears the name of its teacher and a musician renowned throughout the highlands, Andrzej Knapczyk-Duch, who was born in 1886 in the nearby village of Ciche. Continuing down the road, which follows up and down in serpentine fashion, you cannot miss another old little chapel shaded by towering ash trees. The size of the trees reveals the age of this relic. Beyond the chapel there is a fork in the road: the right continues to wind among the houses of the village, while the left goes up to Bachledowka hill visible from afar. You can also see a church on this hill with a large highland-style residence at its side. This is the Pauline Fathers' Hermitage mentioned in the tablet above. This building has an interesting history. After the World War I a legionnaire officer named Kowieski bought a few acres of land on Bachledowka and built himself a house there. He was seeking peace and quiet in a secluded corner of the highlands after his wartime travails. This is where he died before World War II. In time his widow married a local highlander named Wladyslaw Jarzabek-Chrapek. This marriage, like her first, remained childless. During the German occupation, Jarzabek was engaged in underground work, which drew the attention of the Gestapo. Seeing from a distance that a car was approaching his property, Jarzabek went into hiding so successfully that the Gestapo men left empty-handed. As he recounted later, he secretly swore to himself that if he survived be would leave his house and all his property to the Church. He did live through the war and, together with his wife, willed everything to the Pauline Fathers from Czestochowa. The Fathers founded a hermitage on the spot, first with a chapl in the residence, attended by the people of Czerwienne on Sundays and holidays. Years later, the Paulines built a church, filling a need in a village. There is a cemetery nearby. The church has an interesting silhouette, rising as it does from the hillside in the form of a Tatra crag. Cardinal Stefan Wyszynski, referred to as the Cardinal of the Millenium, spent a lot of time in the hermitage. He grew very fond of the place, with its magnificent view of the whole panorama of the Tatras and the western part of the highlands, finding an atmosphere conducive to work and rest there. There are lovely walking trails in the vicinity of Bachledowka. Czerwienne highlanders now living in North America and organized in Circle No. 52 of the Polish Highlanders Alliance have contributed generously to the construction of the church on Bachledowka.

The road curves downhill in a westerly direction, with houses all around, ever closer to Czerwony Potok running by on the left. Just a few more houses of the Podogrod settlement, and after one kilometer you find yourself in Mietustwo.

At the crossroads you are already familiar with, you must choose a new way, this time to the left, to CICHE. After a turn in the road, it will continue to the south for nearly 14 kilometers, steadily climbing slightly uphill. Because of the village's length, it has informally been divided into a lower, middle and upper part. The whole locality is sometimes called Wielkie Ciche, to differentiate it from Male Ciche on the banks of Cichy Potok and Filipczanski Potok (see Excursion VI). The southern outskirts of Ciche reach Zawierszki at the foot of Tominowy Wierch, with Szeligowski Wierch rising in the east. This upper part of the village once bore the name of Wierchciche, and is probably its oldest part. It boasts an old belfry. The settlement of Cichy began at the end of the XVI century. The lowest outskirts of the village lie on the foothills of Domanski Wierch and the difference in altitude between the top and bottom of the village's 14-kilometer stretch is about 300 meters. An elongated slope called Nad Gorkami rises above the western side of the stream, and thus of the village, while to the east ploughed fields stretch over a gentle elevation in the direction of Stare Bystre and Ratulow. The village has good connections to its neighbors. There are several buses a day from Nowy Targ, and nearby Mietustwo has a bus to Zakopane. A road starting in the center of the village leads to Chocholow, and another would take you from Dolne Ciche to Czarny Dunajec, four kilometers away.

Not far from the intersection in Dolne Ciche stands the Westerplatte Heroes' primary school. Inside there are many displays with photographs and descriptions of the heroic defense of this scrap of Polish seashore in September 1939. A well-equipped sports field adjoins the school. Continuing uphill alongside Cichy Potok, you soon cross a bridge and shortly past it on the right side you will see number 185, which is the family home of the Czerwienny teacher mentioned above, the patron of its school. After finishing his teachers' college, Andrzej Knapczyk-Duch first taught in Radziechowe near Zywiec, then in Za Sihla, and finally in Czerwienne, where he remained for 22 years. Deprived of work during the German occupation, ravaged by disease, he died on July 16, 1946, at his family home in Ciche. He formed the musical group called Duchowie, which was famous before the war. You can see the aged highlander cottage where the premier musician spent his childhood and final years in back of the new house built by the road.

Settlement on the banks of Cichy Potok began at the end of the XVI century; good conditions for cultivating the land on the eastern part of the stream favored the influx of settlers. By 1888, there were already 376 houses and 2,067 inhabitants. Some of them belonged to the Czarny Dunajec parish, and others to the parish in Chocholow. A chapel where services could be held on Sundays and holidays was built in the village in 1875 by special permission from the bishop of Tarnow. This permission was granted for ten years, with the expectation that a church would be built in Ciche by that time. But this did not happen for a hundred years or more. When a church was built, it was situated on a square near the stream, more or less in the center of the village. A concrete retaining wall, which forms a kind of riverside embankment, protects the church from the vagaries of the stream. At the entrance to the church a tablet proclaims that the cornerstone of this sanctuary was laid by Pope John Paul II on March 9, 1980. Ciche residents now living in North America, who form Circle No. 30 of the Polish Highlanders' Alliance in Chicago, contributed generously to the construction. There is a Center of Folk Art in Ciche promoting wood carving, toy production, embroidery and artistic iron work. A song and dance troupe, organized in 1952, has performed to great success not only in the highlands but also at national and international festivals. As you continue uphill in the village, you come upon more old residential and farm housing; pass the last bus stop and find yourself on a road that is only passable by horse carriage, and of course by pedestrians. One of these trails leads to Dzianisz and another to Butorow and Gubalowka. From these elevations you have a beautiful panorama of the Tatras with nearly all of Zakopane and Koscielisko at your feet.

An excursion through the western part of the highlands, since this is what we may call this part, extending between the Gubalowka-Zab elevation and the Czarny Dunajec River, should not be confined to driving through the villages discussed. You can find excellent conditions for rest and relaxation in each and every one of these places. The newly-built housing visible everywhere offers guest rooms with full board and all conveniences. It is easy to shop for incidentals anywhere, and two towns—Nowy Targ and Zakopane—offer many tourist attractions, from art exhibitions to regional taprooms, performances by regional troupes, and exclusive nightclubs within a 20-kilometer radius. As to Zakopane and what it offers—this will be discussed in the next chapter.

EXCURSION X

Zakopane

"A village called Zakopane is located at the foot of the Carpathian Mountains. Its inhabitants belonged to the Czarny Dunajec parish at first. This was part of the Szaflary church, which was a branch of the one in Nowy Targ. In time the part belonging to Czarny Dunajec was incorporated into the parish established in Chocholow, and the other part merged with the parish in Poronin." This is how the first parish priest of Zakopane, Father Jozef Stolarczyk, installed on January 6, 1846 at the new parish in the Tatra highlands, began his chronicle.

To recount the beginnings of Zakopane as a settlement, however, we must go back at least three hundred years, when the residents of Szaflary and other villages in the vicinity of Nowy Targ began to drive their sheep and cattle for summer pasture to the glades among the primeval forests under the Tatra mountainsides. As usual in those times, primitive shacks needed to protect the shepherds from inclement weather began to crop up on the glades. Later, there were those first brave men who dared to spend the winter in the glades as well. When this worked, they tried to sow or rather plant oats or barley. "Plant" is the proper expression, since in the early times and as late as the end of the XIX century, grain in the highlands was planted in small cultivated patches of land "under the hoe," or simply buried in the soil. Some claim that this way of "planting" gave Zakopane (buried) its name, although this name, or something similar to it, is encountered outside the highlands as well. It is not impossible that this is the origin of the name, but it is more likely to be just a legend. Another version of the name's origin claims that the name comes from *kop*, a word used to describe gently sloping, grassy hills. The village beyond the *kops*, well, maybe. ...Many places in the highlands draw their names from the names of streams whose appellations go back many centuries. Zakopane is not one of them. Its genesis may be compared to the genesis of highland surnames. Not those officially recorded, but names given to every inhabitant by the village community. By the second or surely the third generation, those who inherited a name from their father or mother cannot say where these names came from.

It is a similar story with the registered name of one of the oldest highland families—Gasienica. Here human fantasy dressed the first settler under the Giewont Mountain in a striped suit which made him look like a caterpillar. But this name is also sometimes encountered on the other side of the Tatras, in Slovakia, but there our Gasienica is called Husenica, which undoubtedly indicates its derivation from the name of a domestic bird—the goose (in Czech and Slovak—*hus*). In the highlands and beyond, the names of peasant families were derived from the names of birds, fish and animals, such as: *Cap* (*Capek*), *Gawron, Gil, Gudzia, Jarzabek, Kocor, Zajac*, etc.

A few documents preserved from the beginning of the XVII century show that the users and owners of some Zakopane fields were highlanders from villages such as Maruszyna and Banska, which were situated at a lower altitude than Zakopane. A 1624 survey of the Nowy Targ *starostship* mentions a settlement called Nowa Osada in the location of Zakopane. Its further development was influenced by the exploitation of the Tatras' deposits of iron, copper and silver, which were processed in forges (called *hamry* in a German way and *Kuznice* in Polish) at the outlet of Dolina Bystra. This opened up opportunities for the residents of the village of Zakopane to earn money by digging and transporting this ore and by making charcoal for the blast-furnaces. A manor house was built by the owners of Kuznice—the Homolacs family—near the forge, along with an inn. There were guest rooms at the manor house—a beginning of the tourist-resort future of Zakopane. In time the arriving guests began to rent so-called "white rooms" in highland homes. The new summer vacation spot in the Tatras was recognized in Warsaw, Cracow and Lwow, but the greatest obstacle to visiting Zakopane was the difficulty in getting there. The closest rail station was in Cracow—more than 100 kilometers north. From there was only a primitive roadway to the Tatras which necessitated wading through streams. So the highlanders traveled to Cracow and brought the visitors to Zakopane with an overnight stop on the way. The situation improved when the rail line was brought up from Cracow to Chabowka, some 40 kilometers distant from Zakopane, in 1884. The way became much easier when the rail line was brought all the way up to Zakopane in 1899, greatly increasing the number of summer visitors. Records show that in 1888 there were fewer than 4,000 visitors, and in 1900—8,000. This number grew year by year, causing rapid development in the building of boarding houses and public facilities.

The greatest credit for popularizing Zakopane (and thus for its development) must go to Tytus Chalubinski, a professor of the Warsaw Medical-Surgical Academy. He came to know the Tatras in the years 1852 and 1858, and twenty years later lived in Zakopane for an extended period. Already enjoying great renown in Warsaw as a physician, Chalubinski promoted the cause of Zakopane among the Polish intelligentsia, singing the praises of its virtues in curing respiratory diseases. Over the years Zakopane became popular, and the liberal policies of the Austrian government with regard to nationalities, vastly different from the repressive policies of Russia and Prussia, made an oasis out of Zakopane for the Polish intelligentsia from all three occupied territories. Such luminaries of Polish culture as Sienkiewicz, Konopnicka, Witkiewicz, Paderewski, Modrzejewska, Brzozowski, Sklodowska-Curie, Pawlikowski, Boy-Zelenski, Staff, Kasprowicz and many others congregated in Zakopane. Before World War I, there were summer-long lectures, theatrical performances, concerts and art exhibitions organized in Zakopane. It became a true center of Polish art.

This growth in Zakopane's rank was also influenced by the existence of the Tatra Society, founded in 1873, which watched over the condition of the streets, proper living facilities for the visitors, and the construction of tourist trails and hostels in the mountains. In 1886, Zakopane was granted the status of a climatic station. Warm springs in Jaszczurowka were utilized. Curative sanatoria were constructed: two private ones and several belonging to civic organizations. These sanatoria treated mainly respiratory ailments, heart problems, neuroses and anemia.

The central point in Zakopane was a group of houses called Nowies (Nowa Wies), the spot where the road to the east led along Mlynski Potok over glades and woods belonging to the Krup family (the present Krupowki) after separating from the road leading from Nowy Targ futher to Dolina Koscieliska. The original housing was concentrated along the road to Koscielisko (Koscieliska Street), and this is where the first church in Zakopane was built. Because of its history, this spot deserves to be the starting point for sightseeing in present-day Zakopane. Several old buildings preserved from the end of the XIX century are worth seeing. But to get a general view of an even older Zakopane and the fauna and flora of the Tatras, you must first visit the Dr. Tytus Chalu-binski Tatra Museum at 10 Krupowki Street. The idea of assembling exhibits connected with the Tatras and the high-lands was born as early as 1875 in the Tatra Society and bore fruit in the at first modest exposition, in time enlarged by contributions from amateur collectors. The year 1888 saw the birth of the Society of the Dr. Chalubinski Tatra Museum, which was instrumental in building a museum in its present site. The construction was finished in 1920, and the museum was opened on July 22, 1922. Its first designer was Stanislaw Witkiewicz, and its first director was ethnographer Juliusz Zborowski (1888-1965). He fulfilled this function, together with the post of custodian of the ethnographic section, for more than 30 years. In 1966 a tablet in his honor was embedded into the wall on the main floor of the museum.

There are plaster models of Dr. Chalubinski and Jan Krzeptowski-Sabala facing the entrance in the same hall. The original of Sabala's statue stands on the road to Kuznice, at the intersection of Chalubinski and Zamoyski Streets. Por-traits of people distinguished for their efforts on behalf of Zakopane and drawings depicting the history of the region are displayed in the entrance hall. Another exhibit shows an original interior of an old highland cottage moved to the museum from Koscielisko in 1922 and built into its new home. The exposed upper part of the front wall of the house reveals the interiors of the black and white rooms separated by a hallway. You can see here how Zakopane highlanders lived in past centuries, how their homes were furnished and what utensils they used every day. As you observe the room to the left of the hallway, you have to use your imagination to realize how its name came about. This is the room containing the source of heat, a kitchen stove with a fire in it, exuding smoke into the room, until it made its way to the attic through a hole in the ceiling. For this reason, as the years went by the ceiling and the upper part of the walls became blackened from the smoke, giving the chamber the name "black room." Meals were prepared in three-legged pots on the stove. There is no stove in the "white room" to the right of the hallway, so it could be used for storing Sunday clothes, feather beds, pillows and other valuables in painted wooden trunks. The "black room" had a dirt floor, while the "white room" had a floor of wooden planks. On frigid winter nights, baby lambs and calves were brought into the "black room" out of the cold. The "sosreb" (a wide carved beam laid across the ceiling beams, usually containing the date the house was built) in the "white room" is especially noteworthy.

The exhibition in the next room of the museum contains everything connected with Tatra sheepherding. Please note the decorations on the utensils and equipment, usually simple on the older exhibits and more elaborate on the more recent examples. Next comes an exhibit of regional costumes from the Rocky Highlands, Spisz and Orawa, which demonstrates the differences in the cut and decoration of the costumes worn by neighboring highlanders. There are also paintings on glass from the second half of the XVIII century, usually of religious subjects, which were sold by itinerant painters, mostly from Slovakia.

The second floor of the museum holds mineral exhibits illustrating the geological structure of the Tatras, a short history of mining in this area, and examples of the flora and fauna of the Tatras and the Tatra foothills. This is an interesting and instructive scientific collection, with ample explanations.

The Tatra Museum has branches in Zakopane and neighboring areas, such as:

- St. Witkiewicz Museum of Zakopane Style in "Koliba" at 18 Koscieliska St.
- Wladyslaw Hasior Gallery at 18b Jagiellonska St.
- Wlodzimierz and Jerzy Kulczycki Art Gallery at 8 Koziniec St.
- Kornel Makuszynski Museum at 15 Tetmajer St.

- Chamber Honoring the Memory of Bronislaw Czech at 4 Plac Niepodleglosci.
- Museum of Chocholow Uprising in Chocholow 75
- Soltys Farm in Jurgow, house no. 215
- Karkoszka Farm in Czarna Gora, Za Gora 86
- Lopuszno Courtly Troupe

The Mountain Botanical Gardens, with a collection of about 500 kinds of plants representing the present flora of the Tatras, is located behind the museum building.

The 1903 structure of the so-called "Tatra Station" stands next to the museum. Originally (since 1882), there was a wooden building in this spot housing an exhibition hall and ballroom, a library, reading room and a restaurant. Following a fire in 1900, it was replaced by a brick building with a glassed-in veranda (taken down in 1939), where artists famous before World War II used to meet. The building was also the headquarters of the Polish Touring Society, as well as the Tatra Group of the Mountain Volunteer Fire Department (GOPR). Both of these organizations have moved to other locations, but there remains a tablet at the entrance honoring the memory of a Tatra guide and rescue worker, Klimek (Klemens) Bachleda, who perished in the Tatras during an extremely perilous climb to try to rescue an injured tourist marooned on a precipice wall.

On the other side of the museum there is a more than 100-year-old building of the School of the Lumber Industry, erected in 1882 for the school which had already been in existence for six years. The school was founded on the initiative of the Tatra Society in 1876 with the purpose of instructing highland youth in the local crafts. The school went through its ups and downs, with various trends predominating, depending on whether the director was a Czech or a Hungarian (in Austrian times), or finally a Pole. Young people were educated at this school in construction, carpentry and ornamental carving. The school survived World War II as a technical school, and after the war a Construction

Technical School and Lycee of Fine Arts were organized there on the level of secondary school. In the years 1954-1959, Antoni Kenar was director of the Lycee. A former student at this school, he later graduated from the Warsaw Academy of Fine Arts, and became a renowned sculptor with close ties to Zakopane, where he died in 1959. His works adorn many Zakopane churches, hotels and restaurants. They are also exhibited at the Tatra Museum. The Lycee he headed is popularly referred to as "Kenarowka."

When you go down the narrow road leading from the school, you descend to the crossing over the stream and arrive at the starting point for sightseeing in Zakopane—the convergence of Koscieliska, Nowotarska and Krupowki Streets. Left of the bridge over the Mlynska Stream, at the spot which in the past century and beyond was the traditional place of the market square, there now stand two peasant cottages. One houses a regional restaurant called Redykolka (*redyk* means one who chases sheep to the mountain pastures), and in the other cottage there is a shop with highland handicrafts. You can buy a whole highland outfit here, both for men and women, as well as individual pieces of it, souvenirs of Zakopane carved in accordance with old designs, everything in good quality. On the other side, near Nowotarska Street, stretches the largest open-air market in Zakopane. You can find food there—always a lot of fruits and vegetables, household items and clothing. Along the road leading to the lower station of the lift to Gubalowka, there is a whole string of kiosks with folk art items in wood, wool and leather, among them many souvenirs.

Returning to Koscieliska Street and turning right, you enter an area of highland construction of many years ago. It has not been possible to preserve the uniform style in architecture entirely, but along Koscieliska Street the highland style definitely predominates. This peculiar *skansen* (historic village) begins with a small wooden church built through the efforts of Zakopane's first parish priest, Father

Jozef Stolarczyk (1816-1893), the owners of Zakopane territories named Homolacs and local highlanders almost 150 years ago. A little brick chapel from the same period stands at its side. It has one nave, with a steeple added after a free-standing belfry was taken down in 1863. There are three altars in the church executed by a highlander from Gliczarow, Wojciech Kulach, along with old paintings, statues of saints and simple benches. There is a balcony in the back of the church over the entrance, which fulfills the function of a choir loft, and also an organ from 1854. St. Klemens was the original patron of the church (from the name of the owner of the local estate—Klementyna Homolacs), but he has been replaced by the Black Madonna of Czestochowa.

There is a cemetery near the church dating back to the time it was built. The land for the cemetery was donated by Zakopane resident Jan Peksa. Situated on a hill above the shore of Cichy Potok, the cemetery is referred to as Na Peksowym Brzyzku (on Peksa's little corner). In 1908 this was the only burial place (not counting burial places from times of the plague), so it soon became too small and another cemetery was opened on Nowotarska Street. Now the old cemetery is considered the "Cemetery for Distinguished Persons," and this is true of the people buried there when there was no other cemetery in town. The following people lie there: Father Jozef Stolarczyk, Dr. Tytus Chalubinski, Jan Krzeptowski-Sabala, Wladyslaw Orkan, Kazimierz Przerwa-Tetmajer, Kornel Makuszynski, Kazimierz Dluski, Stanislaw Nedza-Kubiniec, Antoni Kenar and many other people who did a lot for the highlands. When the new cemetery was opened on Nowotarska, the Na Peksowym Brzyzku became a relic of the past. Permission for burying people there now requires special consent from the Provincial Preservation Conservator. At the side of the stone gate to the cemetery hangs a tablet placed there by a later parish priest, Father Tobolak. It reads: "The fatherland is land and graves. Losing their memory—nations lose their lives. Zakopane remembers."

The skansen continues along Koscieliska Street going to the right right from the church area. Relatively many highland houses (or rather cottages) 100 or more years old have been preserved here. Among the tall ash trees bearing witness to the time that has passed since these houses were built live the descendants of those who first built these houses: the Gasienicas, the Sobczaks, the Janiks, the Walczaks and others. It is evident that someone cares for these houses, and the Tatra Museum has provided the oldest of them with informational plaques on the year of construction and the names of the first owners. The dates run from 1850 to 1880. As you look at these relics of the past, you have to bear in mind the dilemmas connected with owning them. Preserving them in good condition takes a lot of money, and it is not possible to bring them up to modern standards, since they are "relics." If the house owner has a car, there is a problem with building a garage—where can he put it? Unfortunately, sometimes such problems solve themselves, as happened in the case of the old Walczak cottage: it burned down and what is left of it is awaiting the decision on what is to happen next.

Some houses bear plaques informing us that distinguished people lived there. For instance, Jozef Ignacy Kraszewski—noted historical writer—lived in the house of Jozef Sieczka in 1866, followed a year later by Helena Modrzejewska (Modjeska)—an actress renowned as far away as the U.S.A. Along a side road called Sobczakowka stands the house of the famous Tatra guide Maciej Sieczka. This house, No. 5, hosted well-known poets Adam Asnyk and Seweryn Goszczynski, in 1813 and 1879 respectively. Every old house along Koscieliska Street is worth looking at. Despite the similarity in their styles, each one has something different, something original about it, depending on the personal tastes of the highlander who built it. Not all the houses are open to tourists, since their owners are living in them, but you may and you should go inside two of them. They stand side by side.

The house at No. 42 is the Cicha villa, property of the Klosowski family. The progenitor of this clan, Karol Klosowski (1882-1971) was a student at the School of the Lumber Industry in Zakopane during his youth. He later studied sculpture at the Vienna Academy of Fine Arts and then painting at the Academy in Cracow. In 1907 he returned to Zakopane, settled in the house of the Gasienica-Sobczaks and married their daughter Katarzyna. He worked at the School of the Lumber Industry and at the Lace-Making School as a teacher and draftsman in the years 1909-1939. He exhibited his works in Poland and abroad, but his greatest passion was the home he lived in with his family. Systematically and skillfully, he transformed a highlander cabin into a two-story villa, at the same time retaining its regional style and enriching it both in the urban and artistic sense. Everything is worth seeing in the Cicha house—the Klosowski Gallery," as well as every room and corner richly decorated with highlander ornamentation. Even the utlity shed behind the house rests on pillars which are decorated with carvings and texts of highland songs (these are called *spiewki*, characteristic two-verse ditties).

The neighboring house at No. 44 belongs to Franciszek Mardula-Gala, born in Poronin in 1909. During his youth, he achieved the profession of carpenter, but was later drawn to violin making. He studied his second calling with Andrzej Bednarz, the premier violin maker in Zakopane. From 1953 he in turn taught violin making at the Professional School and Technical School for the Construction of Violin Instruments in Nowy Targ. He is a member of the Association of Polish Artistic Violin Makers and the laureate of many violin competitions in Poland and abroad. Despite his 85 years, he continues to work and demonstrares to guests how violins and lovely highland furniture made by him and his son are created. He can also be persuaded to talk about his sports career, since before the war he was a top competitor in cross-country, downhill and ski jumping and worked with young people in this field.

On your way back to the little church, you should have a good look at the houses a little further away from the street, in order not to miss the venerable house located near the stream at No. 18, called *Koliba* (this is a highland name of a primitive shanty—transcribed phonetically). It is the first house designed by Stanislaw Witkiewicz in the Zakopane style and built during the years 1892-1893. It now houses the Museum of Zakopane Style. At No. 12 you will see what is left of the old Walczak home after the fire mentioned above. It was built before 1850 as a farmstead of the Gasienica-Nawsiow family (from the name Nowa Wies). Dr. Chalubin-ski, Ferdynand Hoesik (writer and publisher) and Bronislaw Dembowski (attorney and ethnographer, author of the first dictionary of the highland dialect) all lived in this house.

A little further, under Number 8, you may wish to rest a bit before continuing your journey around the Zakopane Old Town. This is the regional inn called "U Wnuka." The house, built about 1870, was the first in Zakopane to incllude residential rooms upstairs in place of the traditional attic. At that time, it was whispered about that they had "built one house atop another." Its first owner was Jozef Krzeptowski— the brother of the famous raconteur and hunter Jan Krzep-towski-Sabala. This house has a special significance for Zakopane: it was there that the first shop was opened, the first restaurant, followed by a summer and then year-round post office. The Tatra Society had its casino and periodical reading room in this house. Obviously, the whole Zakopane intellectual-artistic elite passed through these rooms before World War I. It was also at U Wnuka that the founding meeting of the Highlanders Union Society, the first regional organization in the highlands, was held on March 4, 1904.

After a little rest, it would be a good idea to go over to a street parallel to Koscieliska, Kasprusie Street, leading slightly uphill. There is a house there under No. 15 with a tablet reading that Wladyslaw Matlakowski, a physician-surgeon, translator from the English language, and first of all a folklorist and specialist in highland lore, lived there in the years 1886-1895. He suffered from lung disease and he utilized his health-saving time in Zakopane to write such innovative works as "Folk Architecture in the Highlands." He is credited with inspiring painter Stanislaw Witkiewicz to study the highland style. The Group of Professional Schools of the Lumber Industry in Zakopane has been named for him.

A bit further, at No. 19, can be found the Museum of Karol Szymanowski, or "Atma." Karol Szymanowski (1882-1937) was one of Poland's greatest modern composers and musicians. He began visiting Zakopane for health reasons as early as 1894, but in time he became interested in highland music as well. He added fragments of this music into his famous ballet Harnasie. Several other works by this composer were born in Zakopane. He lived in Atma after 1930, dying in Lausanne (Switzerland) during one of his concert tours. The idea to make a Szymanowski museum in Atma came up in 1938, but was only realized in 1976, after the house was purchased by the Civic Committee and refurbished. The configuration of the residential rooms was left virtually unchanged, and the exhibition covers photographs and documents from various periods of the artist's life and likenesses of people he came in contact with. There are also pieces of furniture made especially for Szymanowski at the School of the Lumber Industry in Zakopane, and assorted souvenirs and personal objects. The composer's studio has been reconstructed in one of the rooms. Atma is a branch of the National Museum in Cracow. It is open to the public 10am to 4pm except Mondays.

The Jesuit church Na Gorce is also considered one of the venerable structures in the area of Koscieliska Street. While chronologically it is the third oldest church in Zakopane, the ties of the Jesuits with this locality go back to the middle of the XVIII century. They were the first missionaries in this remote corner of the highlands. According to local lore, it was at the urging of Jesuit Father Karol Fabiani that on April 1, 1759 the highlanders cut down the "holy spruce" by the Regle. This was a tree that the people customarily gathered under for prayers asking for clement weather and good crops. For the inhabitants of Zakopane and neighboring settlements, the holy spruce was simply a place for common prayers to God, but Father Fabiani saw a throw-back to pagan rituals in the practice. These old ties of the Jesuits with Zakopane caused them to settle there permanently on land purchased on a mountainside near the Gladczanski Potok, where they consecrated their monastery in 1899 and a church two years later. The interior decoration of the church, its sculptures and paintings, are works by Zakopane and Cracow artists. You can go to the Na Gorce church from Koscieliska Street by way of Father Kaszelewski's Street, uphill to the viaduct past the marketplace and then either up stone steps with a railing or by a road which turns left a little further, climbing to the square in front of the church.

A custom peculiar to Zakopane and surrounding villages is connected with this church. It is said that men who go to confession only once a year around Easter choose to go to Na Gorce (for reasons known only to themselves) with their "baggage of sins."

After descending on Koscieliska Street, it is worthwhile to walk about three kilometers to the right, up the old road, to the settlement of Krzeptowki. A Sanctuary of Our Lady of Fatima is there. The new church, situated on a hillside, harmonizes beautifully with the nearby Tatra peaks. The interior decoration of this church is especially fine, with the beauty of the natural wood skillfully enhanced with a rich display of highland ornamentation. A statue of Pope John Paul II decorates the square in front of the church.

Koscieliska Street sufficed during the last century and until World War II for the rather modest traffic in the direction of Koscielisko and Czarny Dunajec, as well as to the Chocholowska and Koscieliska Valleys. But when the number of visitors to Zakopane increased and motor vehicles increasingly replaced transportation by horse carriage, the need to build a bypass became urgent. The Galician Parliament discussed this problem as early as 1910, but it was not until 1938 that Youth Labor Brigades began earthworks under the Gubalowka mountainside. The war interrupted the realization of this project and it was not until December 29, 1976, that the first part of the palisade and highway connected Nowotarska Street with the new Hotel Kasprowy (opened in 1974 and about two kilometers distant from the Na Gorce church). Two years later, two sections of the palisade and highway were already open to the public. Its name was changed from the Droga Junakow (way of young labor brigadeers) to Droga Powstancow Slaskich (way of Slask insurgents).

Beautifully situated on Szymoszkowa Polana on the right side of the road, Kasprowy is the hotel built at the highest elevation in Poland (870 m. asl). The seven-story building has 600 beds in rooms with a bath and apartments. The guests have a restaurant, cafe, bars, indoor pool, bowling alley, tennis courts and in the winter a ski slope and lift at their disposal. Convention facilities can accommodate 500.

Walking or riding further up the road toward the mountains, you soon reach the lower station of the cable railway to Butorowy Wierch (see Excursion VIII) and three kilometers further you come upon the first houses of the settlement of Koscielisko. Turning left and downhill from the church, after two more kilometers the Koscielisko road joins the one from Zakopane to nearby Kiry at the start of Dolina Koscieliska.

The Zakopane Old Town is not only Koscieliska Street, but also includes Krupowki Street and Nowotarska Street uphill to the left, by the bridge over Potok Mlyniska. In old times this was one of two roads leading from Zakopane to the estates of the owners of Zakopane at the outlet of Dolina Bystra and to their foundries popularly referred to as Kuznice. At the beginning of Krupowki you will see atop a hill to the left a neo-Roman parish church built in 1877 and consecrated in 1899. Obtaining the land for this project and laying its foundations took place during the lifetime of Father Jozef Stolarczyk. It is said that despite its high elevation, the soil supporting the foundations of the church proved to be unstable and required special reinforcement. A great mass of stone had to be placed in with the earth, much of it hauled in from elsewhere. Supposedly, as penance for breaking the sixth commandment, "do not commit adultery," Father Stolarczyk made men bring a certain number of carriages filled with stones to stabilize the underground driftsand. This penance was facetiously referred to as "stallion dues" and until recently old highlanders joked that the Zakopane church is built on "stallion dues." Jozef Pius Dziekonski from Warsaw designed this church.

The construction of the church was completed during the time of the pastorship of Father Kazimierz Kaszelewski, who had the final word on the interior decoration of the church, which was a subject of heated discussion in Zakopane. Father Kaszelewski rejected the plans of Stanislaw Witkiewicz, along with two other plans which followed. Finally, the main altar was designed by Cracow sculptor Kazimierz Wakulski. The central three figures at the altar represent the Holy Family, who are the patrons of the church. Two side altars and the chapel are the work of Edgard Kovats, director of the School of the Lumber Industry at the time. The altar in the left section of the side chapel was executed following a design of Stanislaw Witkiewicz. The ornamentation of the church is mainly the work of local sculptor Wojciech Brzega, who did the side chapel of St. John the Baptist, the entrance doors, benches and confessionals in the Zakopane style, according to the concepts of Witkiewicz. The holy figures and some of the sculptures in the church are the work of Jan Nalborczyk and Jozef Gasienica-Kasprus. On the Krupowki side of the church, do not miss the huge wooden church with a proportionally large crown of thorns, erected in 1861 to commemorate Poles killed by Russian gendarmes during demonstrations in Warsaw and Wilno. Next to the cross is the largest group of yew trees (Taxus baccata) in Zakopane and a shepherds' hut concealing a life-sized Christmas creche. There is a stone chapel in the form of a grotto holding a statue of Our Lady of Lourdes built into the enclosure behind the church. Visitors to the church (when masses are not being held) may use the services of a professional guide (who also gives information in English) from the Zakopane section of the Polish Touristic-Sightseeing Society. The address is 12 Krupowki Street, tel. 124-29; there is another organization (Center of Tourist Information) at 2 Kosciuszki Street, tel. 122-11.

Continuing uphill on Krupowki, it is hard to miss another relic of the past—the stand of horse carriages. One hundred years ago, the universal form of transportation were the so-called *furki* (wagon with a canvas top open at the sides and suspended seats). In wet weather, the *furki* were covered by heavy linen cloth. Later, copying what they had seen in Cracow, the highlanders introduced one-horse hackney coaches and two-horse landaus for travel inside Zakopane and to nearby Tatra valleys and glades. They were also used for all-day excursions to Morskie Oko. Automobiles began to appear in Zakopane before World War II, and after the war the cars systematically edged out the horse carriages. Today they remain only as a regional attraction, with drivers decked out in highland gear, but the horse carriages still retain their monopoly in places where motorized vehicles are not allowed to go.

Passing the bridge leading to the Tatra Museum, you arrive among the brick houses on Krupowki. There was a fire there on January 21, 1899, which destroyed most of the wooden structures and farmsteads. Soon after the fire, investors appeared to buy up the parcels of land from the highlanders and build brick houses in their place, with commercial space on the ground floor. This corner of Krupowki Street and Kosciuszki Street leading from the left to the rail and bus terminals was considered the center of town. But time made changes here as well. At the corner of Krupowki and Kosciuszki (presently No. 1 Kosciuszki) was an establishment famous at the turn of the XIX century, the Zakopianska Cafe and Restaurant, where private concerts were held from time to time. After World War I, Cracow restaurateur Franciszek Trzaska bought the place, and from then on it was known as U Trzaski, renowned beyond the borders of Zakopane as well. There was dancing, large parties, and performances by the most famous musical groups. The place burned down in 1948, to be replaced by the Orbis Hotel Giewont, with 78 beds in 48 rooms, restaurant, cafe and a bar named Murowana Piwnica (the Brick Cellar).

Beyond the hotel, at No. 3, stands the several-story-high Granit department store, where you can buy anything you need for the home.

On the other side, at the corner of Krupowki and Kosciuszki, a large structure was built in 1922 to house the Highland Bank, successor to the Loan Society founded on the initiative of Dr. Chalubinski in 1882. The neighboring building at No. 4 is the property of the Highlanders' Union, Zakopane Division. Downstairs there is a regional-style restaurant, on the first floor a club room called Swarna, where various highland functions are held, primarily the weekly *posiady* (gatherings) which were discussed in earlier chapters, often accompanied by highland music.

The extension of Kosciuszki Street to the other side of Krupowki is called Mariusz Zaruski Street (1867-1941), after a man who as a sailor, skier, soldier, writer and painter distinguished himself for Zakopane and for Poland. He was the co-organizer of the Tatra Volunteer Ambulance Service (TOPR). The long structure housing the Hotel Gazda (highland equivalent of the word "householder") stands on the corner of this street and Krupowki, offering more than 100 beds in 63 rooms and a full variety of gastronomic offerings. On the opposite corner is the building of the Post-Telecommunications Bureau.

Further down Zaruski Street, at Number 5, stands the Tourist House of the Polish Tourist-Sightseeing Society (PTTK). A statue dedicated to Mountain Rescuers, the work of Zakopane sculptor Wladyslaw Hasior, stands in front of this building. You can get all necessary information about excursions into the Tatras at the Tourist House.

After returning to Krupowki, bearing right past the Post Office building, you pass a group of smaller houses and turn to the right into a narrow street which widens into a large square traditionally called the Market Square; from 1912 to 1927 the Zakopane Local Government Office was located here. The official name is Independence Square. Set back on the right side of the Square stands the local movie house called Giewont with the additional name of Sokol (falcon), since from 1929 it has been under the management of the Sokol Gymnastics Society. On the left side of the square, behind one-family houses, is the area of the town park. Inside the park you will see a Grunwald monument with the bust of Wladyslaw Jagiello on a high base, designed by Wojciech Brzega. This monument, honoring the 500th anniversary of the Battle of Grunwald, was funded by the people of Zakopane. From 1911 to 1941, it stood in the center of the square, from which it was removed on the orders of the German occupying powers. While it was being taken down, it was possible to throw off the vigilance of the Germans overseeing the project and to remove and hide the metal elements of the monument. Since after the war a statue honoring the soldiers of the Soviet Army was placed on the square (then called Victory Square), the Grunwald Monument was installed in the town park. It is there that patriotic demonstrations are held now, and there is no monument at all on the square. An inter-school sports stadium is located behind th movie house.

Buildings of two stories or more dominate the outskirts of Krupowki, among them the Morskie Oko Hotel. The original hotel of this name was erected in 1897, and was then rebuilt, after a fire in 1899, as the largest brick building in Zakopane at that time. Morskie Oko soon became the central point of the social life of visitors to Zakopane. The most famous artists, politicians and lecturing scholars, along with leading artistic troupes, passed over the stage of the 200-seat concert hall at Morskie Oko. This continued until 1978, when the Tatra wind ripped off part of the roof of the hotel and destroyed the ceiling of the concert hall. Now there is a restaurant, a cafe and a club in the rebuilt part, but the concert hall was never restored.

A little futher down, at No. 40, is a cocktail bar with a history back to the year 1900, tied to the person of Stanislaw Karpowicz (1869-1936), a renowned restaurateur. The artistic creme de la creme gathered at Karp's—Stefan Zeromski, Ludwik Solski, Stanislaw Witkiewicz and many, many others.

Immediately beyond the building of the historic Karp, a little street shaded by lofty trees goes off to the right toward the town park. You will find the town baths on the left. On a square formed by the crossroads there is a gas station, another stand of horse carriages and the headquarters of the town photophapher. You can view the north wall of the Giewont through a telescope there, have a picture of yourself taken in a highland hat, a *cucha* (short cloth coat) and with a highland sheepdog. Pilsudski Street, to the right, leads to the Sports Center and ski jumping team headquarters in Krokiew. To the left, the short Staszica Street joins the "old" Krupowki with the new, nearly parallel May 3 Street, popularly known as "New Krupowki." You will find a small parking lot on this street. One hundred meters further is an intersection, where Krupowki Street comes to an end. This is where the above-mentioned May 3 Street begins, leading through the so-called Rownie Krupowe, Kosciuszki Street, and Nowotarska Street. There is a large guarded parking lot on this street, between Staszica and Kosciuszki Streets, and a bus parking facility beyond Kosciuszki Street.

The next cross street is Tetmajer Street from which, as a sort of extension of Krupowki, Wladyslaw Zamoyski Street goes off in the direction of Kuznice. Wladyslaw Zamoyski (1853-1924), the owner of large properties in Wielkopolska, was forced to leave them because of the difficulties made for him by the Prussian authorities. He settled in Zakopane, where he became the initiator of many undertakings designed to further the economic development of this locality. In 1899 he bought Zakopane properties, whose forests were largely devastated by the previous owners, at an auction. He is credited with extending the rail line to Zakopane and to a great extent with winning the court case with the Hungarians over Morskie Oko. Before he died, he left his property to the Polish State.

The Kornel Makuszynski Museum is located at No. 15 Tetmajer Street, off to the right. The house, called Opolanka, may be visited, except on Sundays and Mondays, from 9am to 4pm. Kornel Makuszynski (1884-1953), a writer, publicist, known mostly for his books for children and young people, was a well-known personality in Zakopane before World War I. In 1931 he was granted honorary Zakopane citizenship. Keepsakes of the author, Polish and foreign editions of his books, along with many works of art belonging to the Makuszynski family are dispalyed in the four-room museum.

Witkiewicz Street, to the left, will lead you to the next intersection, which marks the beginning of Sienkiewicz, Chalubinski and Jagiellonska Streets. Stanislaw Ignacy Witkiewicz was a man of versatile talents, with ties to Zakopane since his youth. He was baptized there in 1891 with Helena Modrzejewska and Jan Krzeptowski-Sabala for godparents. "Witkacy," as he was popularly known, was a talented painter, playwright, novelist and art theoretician. He is considered the creator of the so-called "Zakopane style" in which he adapted old, traditional forms of highland architecture and decorative art to modern times and new building techniques.

Zamoyski Street, which is something of an extension of Krupowki, has rather dispersed housing. At one time, this was the territory of the mansion in Kuznice. On the left the houses stand surrounded by trees, remanants of the forest that once grew there and eatended all the way down to the present Kosciuszki Street as recently as 100 years ago. The great facade of the church of the Holy Cross, built in recent years on Zamoyski Street as a parish church for this part of town, is an attention-getting structure. After a few hundred meters, Zamoyski Street reaches Chalubinski Street at the point where we find, surrounded by a cluster of venerable trees, the statue of this physician who did so much for Zakopane. Chalubinski's bust is placed on Tatra stones, while at the foot of the column, in a sitting position, is the figure of Jan Krzeptowski-Sabala, the Zakopane highlander who was Chalubinski's close friend for many years.

Chalubinski Street leads to the so-called Rondo—an intersection of four streets: Chalubinski, Droga na Bystre, Avenue of Tatra Guides leading to Kuznice and Bronislaw Czech Street. Bronislaw Czech (1908-1944) was a famous skier and Olympian who was murdered by the Germans. Elementary School No. 2 in Zakopane and the Cracow Academy of Physical Education have taken his name. Thanks to the efforts of his sisters, a memorial room has been organized in the house he lived in from the age of seven—No. 4 Plac Niepodleglosci—and where he was arrested by the Gestapo. Many mementos, photographs, sports trophies and diplomas, as well newspaper clippings of his sports achievements are gathered there, along with records of annual competitions dedicated to the memory of Czech and Helena Marusarz, also a victim of Nazi terror. The house on Plac Niepodleglosci is occupied, but Bronislaw Czech's sisters gladly make the memorial chamber available to visitors. It is part of the Tatra Museum.

Bronislaw Czech Street leads to the nearby Central Sports Center and ski jump area. At the beginning of the street, at No. 2, is a tourist hotel named Sport-Zakopane. The corner plot (No. 42 Chalubinski Street) is occupied by the headquarters of the Tatra National Park (TPN) and the Natural Science Museum of this park, open every day from 9am to 2pm, except Monday. Bronislaw Czech Street leads to the main sports center named for him. Facing it, on a sub-alpine slope in the shape of an equilateral triangle ("Krokiew" in highland dialect), is a large ski-jumping installation, with a medium, small and low jump (for teaching children) nearby. Ski competitions including world championships are held on the large and medium jumps (FIS). Bleachers for twelve thousand spectators have been placed along the landing slopes, with standing room for others as well.

The last section of the several-kilometer-long tourist trail called Droga pod Reglami leads under the ski jump area. This trail follows the lower line of the forest, from Dolina Strazyska to the Avenue of Tatra Guides. You soon reach the Avenue by taking this trail and after crossing it find the beginnings of Mieczyslaw Karlowicz Street. He was a composer, musician and an avid mountainer. During a lonely ski excursion in the Tatras, he perished under a snow avalanche on February 8, 1909, at the age of 33. You reach the settlement of Bystre by taking Karlowicz Street. You will see a cottage called "Tea" on the right side. This cottage originally stood on Olczy-Janosowka, until it was moved to the banks of Potok Bystry when its owner began work at nearby Kuznice. Dr. Stefan Szymanski, an admirer of highland folklore, bought it in 1919 and called it by the first letters of his mother's name—Teodozja Anna. The doctor's brother inherited the cottage in time, and in 1951 gave it to the Tatra Museum. At present, the Stefan and Tadeusz Szymanski Folkloric Collection has found a home there. It may be seen on Tuesdays, Fridays and Sundays from 10am to 12 noon and 4pm to 6pm. The custodian of the museum lives nearby and makes the collection available at times other than the official ones upon request. This house is actually on Slowacki Boulevard which crosses Karlowicz Street.

A side street connecting Karlowicz Street and Slowacki Boulevard passes the St. Anthony Church of the Bernardine Fathers. This interesting wooden structure in the highland style was erected in 1950 atop the chapel which had been there earlier. Its interior decoration, also in highland style, is the work of local sculptors. In place of traditional stained-glass windows, paintings on glass by Bozena Romanowska and Maria Veltuzen-Nagrobecka are in the windows and entry.

Further on is a meeting of five streets: the first, leading right, is the Oswald Balzer Street to Jaszczurowka (see Excursion VI). Hotel Imperial stands along this street, with the Special Rehabilitation-Orthopedic Center for Children and Young People at No. 15. The Children's Sanatorium on Bystre (since that was its original name) dates back to the final years of World War I. The founder of the Center as it is now was Professor Emil Godlewski (1875-1944), and the construction was carried on under the auspices of the Princel-Bishop Committee for Rendering Aid to War Victims (KBK), which gave the name still popular today: Kabeka.

The second road at the crossroads leads to Olcza (see Excursion VI), the third to Koziniec. There, surrounded by old trees, stands the Dom pod Jedlami (the house under the firs). It was designed by Stanislaw Witkiewicz and is considered a model of the Witkiewicz Zakopane style. It took nine months to complete in 1897; the builders were highland carpenters—Wojciech Roj, Jan Obrochta and Maciej Gasienica-Jozkowy. Providing funding for the house was the outstanding writer and art historian Jan Gwadalbert Pawlikowski. The house is inhabited by the Pawlikowski family and you can only see it from the outside. The fourth road leads to the Rondo, and the fifth to Antalowka. This last one passes extensive ski slopes near Koziniec. Below the hillside, taking the street to the left, you pass the Hotel Bristol in the direction of the Chalubinski statue and continue down the street bearing his name. Kraszewski Street goes off to the left before you come to the already visible crossroads. On the right side of this street are residential blocks of a cooperative settlement. One of them, No. 7a is the tallest building in Zakopane—eight stories high. Next door, under No. 7, a little set back from the street, is the pre-war Palace boarding house, the Gestapo headquarters during the war. The character of this Hitler outpost is best described in the title of a book by Alfons Filer and Michal Leyko: "Palace—the Place of Torture in the Highlands." More than 1,100 people were tortured to death within its walls. At the present time it serves as a secondary school.

After the bridge over Potok Bystry and a turn to the left, Jagiellonska Street begins, along the foot of the Antalowka hill. Halfway down the street, on the right, there is a car parking facility and next to it the entrance uphill to the area of thermal bath pools and tennis courts. The swimming area is fed by two bore-holes with artesian effluence at 26.5 to 37 degrees Celsius from a depth of 1,009 to 1,600 meters. The complex covers a main pool measuring 25 x 12.5 meters, two small wading pools, and a 3.5 meter high waterfall, excellent for water massage. The water contains nuclear-carbonate, sultureous, calcic and magnesian ions. These are beneficial in the treatment of rheumatic disease and rehabilitation of motor skills. The baths are open from 6am to 10pm. The tennis courts are next to the baths, a little higher up the hill. When you return to the road, you must turn left, because there, under No. 18b, you will find the Wladyslaw Hasior Gallery. It is open to the public on Wednesdays, Saturdays and Sundays. It is part of the Tatra Museum. Wladyslaw Hasior, a painter born in 1928, has strong ties with Zakopane and "Kenarowka." He has had many exhibitions in Poland and abroad.

Jagiellonska Street ends by the Rondo next to the railroad station and not far from the bus station. Further, beyond the Rondo, it becomes Chramcowki Street, one of the oldest roads leading, in the old days, along the village of Zakopane to the manor house and the ironworks in Kuznice. Below, the road coming from Nowy Targ came to a fork: straight ahead it went in the direction of Koscielisko and left to Kuznice. The extension of the road leading toward Koscielisko was called Stara Polana, and Nowotarska Street only began after the bridge over Potok Bystry. Now this whole section, from the fork away from Chramcowki all the way to Potok Mlyniska is called Nowotarska Street.

The buildings of the rail station constructed together with the completion of the last rail link from Chabowka to Zakopane were located on Chramcowki. The first train arrived at the Zakopane rail station on October 25, 1899. The rail station building also provided lodgings for the first railway workers.

Chramcowki Street took its name from the Chramiec family, which owned the territories around it. The first highland physician, Andrzej Chramiec (1859-1939), came from this family. After finishing his medical studies at the Department of Medicine of Jagiellonian University and fulfilling his residency in Styria (Austria), he established a hydrotherapeutic center in Zakopane. After a fire which consumed the wooden buildings of the center in 1910, Dr. Chraniec rebuilt, this time in brick, but had to sell it in 1916 to the Galician Red Cross because of financial problems. Besides his duties as a doctor, he also held responsible positions in the management of the local government and the resort facilities. After selling the Center, Dr. Chramiec left Zakopane for Wadowice, then for the Wilno area and finally settled in Wielkopolska. He died while visiting his son in Katowice at the age of 80. In 1952 his ashes were moved to the Peksowy Brzyzek cemetery in Zakopane. A small chapel, fulfilling the function of a parish church, was built on the property of the center in 1892. A new church, built right next to it, took over this function in 1994. It was designed by Janusz Ingarden. The church was consecrated on October 1, 1994. It received its benches, tabernacle, confessionals and beautiful organs as gifts from a charitable organization in Holland.

You turn left to Nowotarska Street from Chramcowki Street. There are many old buildings there from the period after World War I. Sienkiewicz Street is left beyond the bridge over Potok Bystry. A hundred meters farther, on the right, stretches the territory of the new Zakopane cemetery. Although it dates back to 1908, it is called "new" to differentiate it from the "old" on Peksowy Brzyzek. This cemetery also plays host to people distinguished for their food works for Zakopane and for Poland, starting with Father Kaszelewski, Zakopane's second parish priest. Also buried there are: Bartlomiej Obrochta—famous highland musician, Klimek Bachleda—heroic Tatra rescuer, Mieczyslaw Swierz—outstanding mountaineer, Julia Tetmajer—the poet's mother, Tytus Chalubinski—grandson of the renowned doctor, and Helena Sikorska—the general's wife. There is also a Legionnaires' section, which is the resting place of the following Legion generals: Marian Januszajtis, Mieczyslaw Boruta-Spiechowicz, Michal Galazka and Andrzej Galica (the last born in nearby Bialy Dunajec). There is a stone obelisk by the graves of the founders of Polish Scouting (1911), Olga and Andrzej Malkowski, and a short distance away a monument to the victims of World War II. These are all surrounded by graves of famous highland families.

Past the cemetery on the left, a new street joins Nowotarska. It is May 3 Street, also referred to as "New Krupowki." In the distance, at 13 Kosciuszko Street, can be seen the structure of the Municipal Building in Zakopane. The road then turns slightly downhill, and a palisade goes off to the left above the market square; this is the start of the road of Bohaterow Slaskich (Silesian Heroes). On the right is the old wooden building of the primary school built in 1890. Until 1933, it was the only primary school in Zakopane before the completion of a second school on Orkan Street. Behind the school to the right, the road leads to the lower station of the cable cars to Gubalowka. The last historic houses on the route of your excursion are No. 4 on Nowotarska Street, built about 1870 for Father Jozef Stolarczyk, in which Henryk Sienkiewicz stayed on his first trip to Zakopane, and the neighboring house on the corner of Nowotarska and Krupowki (Nowotarska No. 2), which was the location of the first hotel in Zakopane. And here we are by the Potok Mlyniska—the beginning and the end of our trek through Zakopane.

The description of Zakopane in this guidebook and the trek through Zakopane described in it are not complete. The aim of the author was to show those streets and places where you could find the beginnings of this at first unknown village, then a town renowned in Poland and abroad—a town with less than 180 years of written history. Other guidebooks suggest a stay of seven to ten days to become thoroughly familiar with Zakopane and its close surroundings. A visitor from abroad, visiting his family in the highlands, does not always have so much time at his disposal, unless he goes to Zakopane for a longer stay, choosing from many side trips available, depending on his needs and his pocketbook.

EXCURSION XI

Off to the Mountains

Zakopane is the best, but that doesn't mean the only, starting point for excursions into the Tatras. The advantage of beginning there is the easy access it offers to the entries to the valleys where most of the tourist trails into the Tatras have their start.

Just as Zakopane is the starting point for the whole Tatra region, so KUZNICE, located at the outlet of Bystra Dolina (Bystra) serves the same purpose for most trips into the central part of the Tatras—from Czerwone Wierchy to Krzyzne Pass. Here we find further sources of Bialy Dunajec and thus brooks flowing from limestone rocks in the caves along the Giewont massif, brooks at the outlet of Dolina Jaworzynka, Goryczkowy Potok flowing out of the valley bearing the same name, and the periodically vanishing stream from Hala Kondratowa.

The settlement of KUZNICE, which took its name from the metallurgic and ironworks plants there from about 1700 to 1885, was called Hamry (Hammerswerk in German—Polish equivalent *kuznica*) by the highlanders. During the period of its peak prosperity (1830-1850), there was a huge blast furnace producing from 50 to 60 tons per month, four tremendous hammers to forge steel, three rolls and several other production workshops. The Bystra stream, which did not freeze during the winter in this sector because of the temperature of the flow from limestone rocks (4+ Celsius), provided the energy to run all of these installations. The furnaces were heated with charcoal produced locally, for which whole hectares of the best standing timber from near and far valleys and slopes were sacrificed. Near the Kuznice plants stood the manor house of the owners of the Zakopane estates (the Homolacs family from 1824), who played host to the first Tatra tourists and explorers, such as: Seweryn Goszczynski, Wintenty Pol, Oskar Kolberg and Ludwik Zajszner. In the years 1884-1905, there was a plant producing wood pulp in Kuznice. The first hydrotherapeutic establishment was founded a little lower downhill, but also by the Potok Bystra, in 1876. When Count Zamoyski was owner of the Zakopane estates, the School for Women's Housework, where about 200 girls studied at one time, was moved from Kornik in the Poznan region to Kuznice. The highlanders called these girls "cepcule" because of the uniform caps they wore. Today Kuznice is primarily the lower station of the lift to Kasprowy Wierch and the starting point for many excursion trails.

There are various ways to get from Zakopane to Kuznice:

- On foot—by the following streets:
  Krupowki-Zamoyski-Chalubinski, to the Rondo and then by the Road of Tatra Guides to your destination. The distance is about four kilometers; time needed, about one hour.
- By private car to the Rondo, and since past this point travel is restricted to only certain types of vehicles, you must leave your car in the parking lot on Bronislaw Czech Street and continue on foot on the Tatra Guides Road or take the municipal bus, which has its closest stop at the end of Chalubinski Street. Total time about 45 minutes. You can also go to the

Rondo by horse carriage with a highlander at the reins, making sure to ask ahead how much it will cost, since prices are negotiable.
• By bus or microbus, from the bus station located next to the railway station, directly to Kuznice. Trip lasts 15 minutes.

The cable railway to KASPROWY WIERCH is a great tourist attraction. Built in the years 1935-1936, it contributed greatly to the expansion of Tatra tourism. Thanks to this railway, persons who, because of their age or physical infirmity, had never been in the high Tatras, could now see from above the whole panorama of the Tatras and the Zakopane valley. The opportunity to ride to the principal crest of the Tatras did away with the tedious trudge there on foot. The cable railway also contributed to the development of skiing. Cable cars made it possible to ski down Kasprowy Wierch several times a day. There is only one railway, with limited capacity (see guidebook) and hundreds want to use it. Without an advance reservation, it is sometimes necessary to wait for hours to go up the mountain. Of course, this affects entire vacation plans. The lower station of the cable railway is located in a stone and concrete building (1,023 m. asl) containing the engine room, the waiting room with a ticket office and accommodations for the personnel. The intermediate station has been built on Na Myslenickich Turniach (1,352 m. asl), where you have to transfer to another cable car, and the end station is located under the peak of Kasprowy Wierch at an altitude of 1,959 m. asl. Each cable car holds 30 passengers; while one is going down on the cable, another is coming up. Between stations there are three supporting steel pillars about 30 meters high. The ride takes 20 minutes, and the cable car achieves a 933-meter change in altitude. The upper station is located in a large cement-stone building. Besides the equipment and quarters connected with the running of the railway, the building also has a restaurant and a tourist hotel with 20 beds. There is telephone communication with Zakopane and beyond. A large terrace attached to the building offers magnificent views and deck chairs for a fee. There is a building of the State Meteorological Observatory at the verytop of Kasprowy Wierch with an observation tower of granite built in 1937.

There is a wonderful view stretching out from the terrace on the Polish, western part of the Tatras and on the Slovak High Tatras. The Polish-Slovak border runs near the cable car station on the ridge of the mountains.

The continuation of the excursion depends on whether you have purchased a round-trip ticket for the ride back to Kuznice by cable car, or a one-way ticket, intending to walk down from Kasprowy Wierch. In the first case, depending on the time left until the return trip on your ticket, you may wish to sunbathe on the terrace, or to stroll on the trail on either side of the station. You can also walk up the mountain, to get a closer look at the Meteorological Observatory. Two of the major ski trails in the Tatras lead down from Kasprowy Wierch, one to Dolina Goryczkowa, and the other to Hala Gasienicowa, both with ski lifts.

If you bought only a one-way ticket for the cable car, the best route for walking down to Kuznice leads through Hala Gasienicowa. From the station on the cable railway, you walk down a wide path in an easterly direction toward Sucha Przelecz, and then over a gentle incline down to Kasprowy Kociol. The trail is marked. It continues downhill, passing the lower station of the ski lift, then beside two small ponds, and over a usually dry river bed of Sucha Woda to the "Murowaniec" shelter visible in the distance. The walk should take about 1½ hours. During your rest at "Murowaniec" you should establish whether you have enough time to go up to Czarny Staw Gasienicowy (the round trip takes an hour, plus the time spent at the pond), or to begin your walk to Kuznice. The way back leads from "Murowaniec" over a gently rising trail in a northeasterly direction to the

Kopa Magury mountain pass and then along the Skupniowy Uplaz. After about one hour of walking, during the last minutes zigzagging over a wooded slope, you arrive at the bridge over Bystra Stream by the lower station of the cable railway.

On sunny days in Zakopane, the tourist enjoys a constant view of an imposing granite wall growing out of the wooded sub-alpine hillsides. This is GIEWONT, which fantasy credits with the silhouette of a sleeping knight lying on his back. The long eastern section, descending in a sheer 600 meter wall, is separated from the main peak (1,909 m. asl) by a gap said to be the neck of the prone figure. A 15-meter high cross is set at a depth of two meters on the principal peak. Its binding agent is a metal alloy with a lead base. The cross was placed on the peak in 1901 when the highlanders hauled individual elements up the mountainside. Despite the threatening look of the northern wall, the climb to the top of the Giewont from another direction is one of the easier excursions in this area. There are two main trails to Giewont from Zakopane: one is through Dolina Strazynska and the other over Hala Kondratowa. Of course, you can get to the top of Giewont from other sides, for example over Czerwone Wierchy or from Kasprowe over the Liliowe pass. The trail over Hala Kondratowa begins beside the lower station of the cable railway. It leads over a rocky road slightly uphill near the cable lines hanging overhead. After about 15 minutes you see the wooden convent of the Albertine Sisters with a chapel built in 1898 in accordance with the design of Stanislaw Witkiewicz; next to it, also rebuilt after a fire, is the hermitage of Brother Albert, Adam Chmielowski (1846-1916), founder of the Albertine Monastery and canonized by John Paul II. Behind the convent the road turns left and, first going through a sparse forest (the result of a hurricane, called "fohn wind" here) arrives at the upper reaches of Kalatowki meadow. You will find a brick shelter there with guest rooms and sleeping accommodations for tourists, a restaurant, buffet and a community center. Continuing up-hill for another hour, you arrive at Hala Kondratowa (1,335 m. asl). There is a shelter here as well, even though it is only a small, wooden structure, similar to an ordinary highland cottage. An interesting item to see is a large boulder right beyond the south wall of the shelter. In 1953, several boulders broke off from the crest of Giewont as a result of the natural weathering of the limestone rockface and one of them, with a mass of about 50 tons, crashed to the side of the shelter, partly rolling inside it. It was necessary to break up a major part of the boulder by means of hand tools in order to rebuild the damaged wall of the shelter. The small part of the rock left in place serves as a reminder of this incident.

Beyond the shelter the trail leads up steeply; in places, it zigzags to facilitate the climb, and after about 1½ hours you reach Przelecz Kondracka (1,725 m. asl). After a rest, set out for the final part of the climb—to the Giewont peak "toward the Cross." A wonderful view stretches out before you—of Zakopane some 1,000 meters below, of the whole highlands all the way to Gorce, of Orawa on the western side in the distance, and of the Western Tatras closer by. The excursion to Giewont is one of the most popular in the Tatras, so you have to consider the possibility that you might have to wait in line for a while before you can cross from the Kondracka Przelecz to the summit. After a stay on top of the mountain, sometimes necessarily short if others are waiting, when you are finished taking pictures and admiring the view, you take a trail down back to Przelecz Kondracka. From there, you have two choices of routes to Zakopane—one is the same way you came, over Hala Kondratowa, the other over Dolina Strazyska. The time of return by the first route is about 2½ hours through Kuznice to the Droga pod Reglami; the second way is about one hour longer, but it is more varied and the trail a bit more diffiicult.

Along with Dolina Chocholowska and Dolina Koscieliska,

DOLINA STRAZYSKA is among the most visited valleys in the Tatras, because of the ease of its climb, the diversity of its surroundings and the sight of the 600-meter wall of Giewont rising above the valley which grows increasingly closer as you climb. An excursion to the Strazysks—as the highlanders say (using the name derived from *stragi*, which are enclosures for sheep)—begins with Kasprusie Street in Zakopane (see Excursion X). The street leads up a gentle hill, later changing into Strazyska Street, passing close to Potok Mlynski. When you get to a wooded subalpine slope, you cross Droga pod Reglami by the Roma bar, which usually offers music by a Gypsy band. The crossing of the valley, which is always accompanied by the ripple of the small Strazyski Potok, begins right there. It is a tributary of Mlynska Potok, so again here we find another source of Bialy Dunajec. The slopes of the valley are wooded, partly by a deciduous forest, with rocky crags appearing periodically between the trees. Particularly picturesque, and often photographed, are the Trzy Kominy (Three Chimneys), dolomite spires standing side by side. After less than an hour of a relatively good uphill road, you come to a fork in the tourist trails: Droga nad Reglami goes off to the left, Przelecz w Grzybowcu to the right, and the path straight ahead leads to a rocky fault over which a small waterfall emerging from a stream under Giewont cascades. Looking up, you see the imposing stone wall of this mountain. It is only from close that you can observe in its structure—full of crevices and hanging rocks. This wall has been conquered by mountaineers, but twenty persons have perished trying. The rocks forming this wall are not stable, as evidenced by the rock rubble at the foot of Giewont.

From the crossing of the trails, the path to the right leads to Przelecz Kondracka and to Giewont over Przelecz na Grzybowcu (about one hour uphill). First through forest land, then over terrain overgrown with dwarf mountain pine, you approach the slopes of Maly (Little) Giewont, with a beautiful view of the Mala Laka Valley on the right. The precipices of Wielka Turnia are especially picturesque there. The path continues under rock walls to the Siodlo Pass and, leading uphill under the slopes of Maly Giewont, enters Przelecz Kondracka under Giewont. The time needed to get there from Dolina Strazyska is 2½ hours. Now, all that is left to overcome is the last portion of the trail "toward the Cross." This trail is considered more taxing than the one leading over Hala Kondratowa.

In the sense of physical endurance, the succesful conquest of Giewont, along with a descent from Kasprowy Wierch through Hala Gasienicowa to Kuznice, qualifies you to undertake a greater effort—the conquest of a peak called SWINICA. It is distinguished from the chain of peaks visible from Zakopane by the pyramid shape of its western wall. The attack on Swinica can be undertaken from either of two sides: from Hala Gasienicowa, over which this mountain towers, or from the side of Kasprowy Wierch. From Hala Gasienicowa, to which you go over the trail by way of Skupniow Uplaz from Kuznice as described earlier, there is a fairly easy trail, which nevertheless involves a steep climb (time needed 1½ to 2 hours—difference in altitude 450 meters), to Swinicka Przelecz. From here, the ridge of Swinica rises between piles of stone, and as the tourist trail also rises, in passes over screes and piles of rock. The trail continues some 100 meters across a sloping gulley, followed by a difficult section made safer by climbing irons set into the stone, until it reaches a rocky sill. After you pass it and then get over another rocky formation, you climb over stones to the left to the main peak of Swinica. The climb should take about one hour, but you must wear appropriate shoes and protective gloves for the chains and climbing irons encountered on the way. Persons suffering from fear of heights should not undertake this excursion, since it takes you over extremely steep paths on occasion.

The trail to Swinica from the upper station of the cable

railway has the advantage of getting you to the starting point—climbing out to the rocky ledge under this mountain—by cable car without any wear and tear. After leaving the cable railway station, an easy path leads you to Sucha Przelecz (pass), followed by Liliowa Przelecz and then Swinicka Przelecz, without much effort. Further, a marked trail leads you to the top of Swinica by the same path as described above. The time needed to walk from Kosprowe to Swinica—is about 2½ hours. After enjoying the great view and having a little lunch, it is time to start back. And here again you have two possibilities: if you bought a round-trip ticket for the cable car, you have to return over the same trail from Swinica to Kasprowy Wierch, but if you only bought a one-way ticket, you may descend from Swinica by another way, over Zawracka Przelecz, commonly referred to as ZAWRAT. Below the peak of Swinica you encounter a rocky ridge over Dolina Pieciu Stawow Polskich and there a trail marked in red leads downhill to the crest between Swinica and Gasienicowa Turnia. From there, over a steep slope which is covered partly in rocks and partly in grass, you go down under Gasienicowa Turnia, over several rocky ridges secured with climbing irons and chains. Below you will see Zadni Staw in Dolina Pieciu Stawow Polskich. In a series of steep terraces, the path continues downhill, until you come to a shallow slanting crevasse where you continue down over smooth rock plates (again protected by climbing irons and chains). After traversing the rocky wall downward (proper gear necessary), you descend to a scree-covered gully dropping down below Niebieska Turnia, which from the left side looks like a cracked stone wall. Zigzagging over easy terrain, you traverse the gully and continue by a steep trail marked in red until you reach Przelecz Zawrat (2,159 m. asl). The descent from the peak of Swinica to Zawrat takes about one hour. Although it is not considered one of the most dangerous trails, a fairly experienced tourist can still suffer from anxiety along the way, and wonder whether he should go on or go back to the trails he knows. That is why you should only make this excursion in the company of an experienced person, always bearing in mind that you should never take the mountains lightly.

The Zawrat Pass has the form of a saddle between Zawratowa Turnia and Maly Kozi Wierch. South of Zawrat, a relatively comfortable path leads to the Dolina Pieciu Stawow Polskich (see Excursion V) visible from above, but the 1½-hour walk, always downhill, can be very tiring for the inexperienced. On the northern side of the pass, the scree-covered Zawratowy Zleb descends steeply toward Zmarzly Staw, with Czarny Staw visible below. The northern wall descent from Zawrat is accomplished over a rather narrow rocky path on the side of a ridge emerging on the right. Chains and steel handrails have been built into the rock in places. Here also the first ascent (or descent) should only be attempted under the eye of an experienced guide. The descent (about 400-meters in altitude) takes about an hour. From the foot of the gully, the way becomes easier, that is to say less dangerous. It takes another 45 minutes to get to Czarny Staw Gasienicowy, and 30 minutes more to make Murowaniec on Hala Gasienicowa. After a rest, following the already familiar trail by Kopa Magury and along Skupniowy Uplaz, you can reach Kuznice in about 1½ hours.

While an excursion to Giewont is in the category of "school" trips, the crossing from Kasprowy Wierch, through Swinica, Zawrat and Hala Gasienicowa, is a test of an amateur mountaineer's physical stamina and mental resistance in face of sheer rocky walls, dangerous crossings and precipitous gullies. All of these perils, however, even possible physical complaints caused by the altitude of the mountains, are recompensed by the magnificent views of the Tatras, whose true beauty can only be appreciated from above.

The excursions described in this guidebook, such as the climb to Rysy (see Excursion V), to Swinica and Giewont, along with the hike from Morskie Oko through Swistowka and Opalone to Dolina Pieciu Stawow Polskich and then through Dolina Roztoki to Wodogrzmoty Mickiewicza and the trip from Kasprowy Wierch through Swinica and Zawrat to Hala Gasienicowa, are a large dose of high mountain thrills for the amateur-tourist. All mountains must be treated seriously; those who ignore them sometimes pay with their health or even their lives. Several people perish in the Tatras every year, usually because they are unprepared for the sudden changes in temperature so common in the mountains, because they don't know how to behave in fog, when visibility and orientation are limited, because they ignore the rules, or simply because they overestimate their abilities.

The tourist to Zakopane will not encounter these perils during excursions to the sub-alpine part of the Tatras, which also have a great deal of charm. (Of course, it is possible to twist your ankle even on Krupowki!)What we call Regle are sub-alpine forest-covered mountainsides below the line of the mountain pasture lands, which in turn have only the rocky peaks above them. The Regle region near Zakopane has two tourist trails worthy of your attention: Droga nad Reglami (The Way Over the Regle) and Droga pod Reglami (The Way Under the Regle).

Droga pod Reglami is an old trail over which ore was transported to the blast-furnaces from Dolina Chocholowska and Dolina Koscieliska through Kiry to the ironworks in Kuznice. In the old days, it was also called the iron road, since it was the shortest route connecting excavation sites and the blast furnaces with the "Hamry" (ironworks). It begins on Przewodnikow Tatrzanskich Street, continuing toward the ski-jumping center, which it bypasses and goes on to Dolina Bialego. The name of the valley comes from Bialy Potok, which runs through it; it is also a source of Bialy Dunajec. This valley is one of the most popular tourist destinations. Crowded in between Krokiew and Sarnia Skalka, it is 2½ kilometers long, has two small waterfalls, a lovely growth of beech trees and even some stone pines which are already rare in the Tatras. The next little valley to the left of the Droga is Dolina Spadowiec, also with a stream of the same name—another source of Bialy Dunajec. A little waterfall cascades down from a terrace into this valley. The next valley is called Dolina ku Dziurze (Valley Toward the Hole), taking its name from the cave. The cave has one chamber with two subchambers measuring about 50 meters; you must use a flashlight to see it. The valley is about one kilometer long; walking time round-trip to the Droga about 30 minutes. The Droga then goes on to the outlet of Dolina Strazyska and then after half an hour to Dolina Za Bramka. It is about two kilometers long and rises gently uphill. The slopes of the Dolina are composed of limestone and dolomite, with both desiduous and coniferous tree growth. The stream flowing down the valley (and bearing the same name) creates minor cascades in places. Narrowing of the valley, called *bramki* (gates) by the highlanders, occurs at irregular intervals. Across from the outlet of this valley, on a hill set back from the *droga* (road), stands another relic of highland architecture—Sabala's Cottage—from the XVIII century. This was the family home of the Gasienica clan, who added the surname of Krzeptowski, later officially adopted as their name, from the name of a nearby settlement called Krzeptowki. There is an ethnographic exhibit in the Chata Sabaly (Sabala's Cottage), which is a branch of the Tatra Museum. At the height of the setlement of Krzeptowki, the Droga crosses Malolacki Potok. It flows out of the Dolina Malej Laki, which many consider the prettiest in the Tatras. It is worthwhile to go into it, if only a small distance. The whole valley is 7½ kilometers long, with an altitude difference of more than 1,000 meters. The trail leads alongside the stream, with spruce and fir forests on both sides. After 35 minutes, the valley is blocked off by a post-glacial moraine ridge. When you pass it, you come upon a wonderful view of the central valley. For centuries, it has been pasture land, with permanent shacks and sheds. The trees growing in the valley are young; the ancient trees which once prospered there have fallen victim to Tatra mining and metallurgy in the past century. The final section of the Droga pod Reglami leads to Kiry at the outlet of Dolina Koscieliska. From there, as well as from Krzeptowki, you can travel by bus to Zakopane.

Droga nad Reglami is longer and a bit more difficult, since it has many climbs and descents. A march along the entire length of this road would take close to six hours, a day-long escapade, or it might be divided into two parts: the first from Kuznice, through Kalatowki and then uphill in zigzag fashion to Przelecz Bialego (one hour from Kuznice). Then, after a 200-meter section over the ridge of a hill, the Droga achieves its highest point—1,335 m. asl and goes over to the side of Dolina Bialego. After about one hour, you reach Czerwona Przelecz in the region of Sarnia Skalka. From there, over hairpin bends, with a steep drop in the slope, you go down to Polana Strazyska, which is in the upper part of the valley of the same name. This marks what is considered the end of the first part of the Droga nad Reglami. Krom Kuznice, it takes about 2½ hours to get there. Now, you can either go down over Dolina Strazyska to the Roma bar and to Zakopane via Strazyska Street, or enter the second part of Droga nad Reglami. From Polana Strazyska, it will go on to Przelecz nad Grzybowcem (which is another variation of the trail to Giewont), further over a wooded ridge to Dolina Malej Laki. Here you can enjoy a beautiful view of the precipitous walls of Ciemniak and Krzesanica—two peaks of the Czerwone Wierchy group—descending down the valley. From the ridge, the Droga leads to Przyslop Mietusi and then down to the bottom of Dolina Mietusia. From its outlet, mentioned in Excursion VIII, after crossing Koscieliski Potok and turning left, you come to the meadow called Stare Koscieliska. You can end your excursion there and go by way of the nearby outlet of Dolina Koscieliska to

Kiry, to the bus stop, where you can take a 20-minute bus ride to Zakopane. The time needed for the second section— about three hours. Droga nad Reglami continues further to Dolina Chocholowska, but the three hours needed for the second section or the six hours necessary for the whole length may be too exhausting.

APPENDIX I

Fishing in the Highlands

Highland waters have trout and grayling, although you might also encounter salmon, huchen, migratory and lake bulltrout, along with smaller fish, such as minnows and cottids in the highland rivers and streams. According to old chronicles, eels could also be found on occasion. Today the fish population of highland waters is not great, despite annual stocking activities of the Fishery in Lopuszna and regional fishing circles. There are two reasons for this: dams on the Dunajec in Roznow and Czorsztyn are obstructions for spawning fish such as salmon, bulltrout and eel, despite installations designed to facilitate the passage of fish; the development of towns, industry and the increased use of chemicals in agriculture. From year to year Polish rivers, particularly the Vistula, through which migratory fish once swam to the Dunajec—and even Dunajec itself—have become an increasingly unfriendly habitat for fish.

But, since there are many fishing circles in the highlands, and there is a Regional Fishing Association in the provincial capital, this indicates that there are fishermen-anglers around, and thus fish as well.

The catch limits listed in a later section of this guidebook serve the purpose of at least maintaining the existing fish population. There are severe consequences for breaking these rules. This is how it was before the war as well, which gave birth to the half joking admonition: "telo za pstraga, co i za cleka" (as much for a trout as for a man), since a poacher caught in the act was assured of two years in prison, in effect the same as for killing a man.

There are private fisheries, where, for a fee, you can catch trout with success assured. One such fishery is near Czarny Dunajec (from the side of NowyTarg) on the road turning right before the bridge to Wroblowka (look for sign).

Anglers who belong to the Association have permanent licenses with stamps attesting to the fact that they have paid the necessary fees. These are either annual or seasonal fees. People visiting the highlands temporarily can purchase one-time or short-term angling permits in the following places:

1. Headquarters of the Circle of the Polish Angling Association in Nowy Sacz, 56 Wisniowieckiego Street
2. Circles of the Polish Angling Association in Zakopane, Nowy Targ, Sromowce Wyznie and Szczawnica

Since the circles do not have permanent offices and the permits are arranged by either the circle president or secretary at his residence, you can get the current address of the above-mentioned offices at the local government office.

The fees for permits are not exorbitant. In 1994 in US$, they cost: $2 for a 1-day angling permit, $5 for a 3-day, and $10 for a 7-day.

The effects of fishing with a pole in the mountain rivers and streams cannot be measured by the number and weight of fish caught, even though this is stated reason you come to the river bank. It is much more desirable that you spend a few hours in the fresh air, with the murmur of the stream flowing over rocks. It is also a chance to perfect your techniques, since mountain angling is decidedly different from fishing with a float. The lure has to be manipulated in the water in such a way as to "deceive" an opponent as shrewd as a trout. The masters of this art do not continue to "flog" the river after three unsuccessful tries, but move on to another place. They also claim that if the fish does not attack the lure, this means that it is not there.

Limitations are imposed in accordance with the Rules for Amateur Fishing. Fishing is prohibited from dusk to dawn in all waters containing trout and grayling. This period begins one hour after sunset, and ends one hour before sunrise—according to the calendar. It is also forbidden to fish with more than one pole, regardless of the permitted system of fishing. There must a a distance of at least 50 meters between fishermen in the waters of trout and grayling, unless the angler who came there first agrees to a lesser distance.

Anglers have to conform to the following Protective Measurements, meaning the length of the fish from the top of its head to the longest extension of its tail fin:

- Salmon prohibited
- Huchen: 70 centimeters
- Migratory bulltrout: 40 cm
- Lake bulltrout: 50 cm
- Grayling: 30 cm
- Stream, rainbow, spring trout: 30 cm

Protected Periods include the following:

- Huchen—grayling and rainbow trout from March 1 to May 31
- Stream and spring trout and lake bulltrout from September 1 to January 31
- Salmon and migratory bulltrout fishing completely prohibited:

—in the Vistula River and its tributaries above the dam in Wloclawek, all year.

—from the mouth of the Vistula River (from 935 to 940 kilometers) from 7.1 to 8.31 and from 12.1 to 1.15, and at other times on Fridays, Saturdays and Sundays.

—in the remaining rivers from 10.1 to 12.31.

The angler is permitted to catch and keep the following number of fish of various types:

—migratory and lake bulltrout: 2
—specimen altogether, grayling, trout: 5
—specimen altogether, huchen: 1

If the first or last day of the protected period for a specific kind of fish falls on a holiday, the period is shortened by one day.

Lures allowed for fishing on various sections of rivers and streams are listed in section 6 of the instructions. In accordance with the directive of the Minister of Agriculture, Forestry and the Food Industry regarding lures to be used in the areas where there are trout and the grayling, the only lures permitted are artificial lures and natural lures of various composition.

Lures include the following:

• Natural lures consist of vegetation and their parts (e.g. fruits, seeds) and their various products (baked goods, pastes), and also artificial aromatic substances and dyes.

• Artificial lures cover all products made of materials such as metal, wood, rubber, horse hair, wood, synthetic fabrics, varnish, glue, and are armed with at most two hooks with heads no bigger than the width of the artificial lure at its widest point (tolerance of 2 mm for fishing in the waters of PZW).

• Artificial flies are lures made with a single or double hook with any combination of the materials contained in the composition of the groups named below:

—feathers and horse hair
—thread, wool, metal and plastic lamets, straw, raffia, cork, rubber, varnishes and glues

It is forbidden to fish using a water ball (any round object made of artificial materials, filled with water, serving to eject even the lightest lure) or any object which might take its place, in the waters of trout and grayling.

When fishing in waters where angling is permitted only with an artificial fly or an artificial fly with natural lures, at most, two artificial flies may be used on one fishing pole. If two artificial flies are used, it is forbidden to weigh down the line.

Other restrictions (see section 6 of the instructions) also specifiy what parts of rivers and streams are off limits for fishing. Some need explanation:

• A protected district is a small stream or a portion thereof which is closed to fishing because of its special character (gathering place for fish, spawning spot, etc.).
• An alternate protected district is a place of temporary fish protection to increase the stock of particular breeds of fish. Alternate protected districts are changed about every three years.
• A nursery is a section of a river or stream located in the immediate proximity of a hatchery or stock pond of PZW, where schools of spawners are kept in natural surroundings for breeding purposes—it is an area where fishing is not allowed.
• A spawning district is a small stream or a portion thereof in which fry of the Salmonidae family are bred for stocking purposes—no fishing allowed.

Limits of Sectors is a list by provinces in alphabetical order and within every province according to the catchment area, theoretically in an easterly to westerly direction. In individual catchment areas, rivers and their tributaries are usually mentioned in turn according to the flow of the main river. Generally the borders of individual sections (column 4) are delineated by constant geographic points (bridges, dams, mouths of tributaries). If there are no such guiding points, the border is described as precisely as possible, and the place itself is marked clearly by the Regional Office of PZW. Some descriptions of borders between sections need some clarification, however, such as:

- "Over its whole length" means the whole course of the river or stream from its source to its estuary.
- "All tributaries" means all feeders on both the left and right side on the given section of the river described.
- "From the estuary of the feeder" means all tributaries including this one.
- "To the estuary of the feeder" means all tributaries except this one, unless the description clearly states otherwise.
- "From the dam, weir, floodgate, etc." means that in the rivers (streams) from the edge of the overflow of the water down 200 meters before the above-mentioned structures and 200 meters beyond them fishing is forbidden.
- "From the mill, sawmill, etc." means the river (stream) from the place of all installations banked up below (such as working sluice-gates, no-load flood-gates, dams, etc.) Mill-races and working canals are also considered part of the area of Salmonidae family of fish.
- "To the bridge" means the river (stream) under the bridge is also included in the described section.
- "From the bridge" means that the river (stream) under the bridge is not included.

Marking of "PZW" Waters was the subject of a regulation

passed on June 19, 1976, by the Presidium of the Headquarters of PZW. It was decreed:

- Every body of water (lake, pond, excavation or other), and also every section of river, stream lawfully used by the Association (on the basis of a binding rental agreement or legal water rights) must be marked from January 1, 1977, on.
- The following, uniform signs are to be introduced throughout the country:

a) PZW emblem in blue—with which all PZW waters will be marked.

b) A fish silhouette to be marked in the following colors:

—Blue for waters qualifying as area of Salmonidae family
—Green for special fishery
—Red for waters or their parts where fishing is entirely prohibited
—Yellow for waters or their parts where fishing is partially prohibited

c) Arrow with number indicating direction and distance in kilometers (symbol **KM**) or meters (symbol **m**) supplementing information given by means of colored fish symbol.

Fish mentioned in directory include salmon (Salmo), huchen (Hucho), eel (Anguilla), barbel (Barbus), grayling (Thymallus), stream trout (Salmo Trutta), rainbow trout (Salmo Gardinieri), brook trout (Salmo Fontinalis), bulltrout (Salmo Trutta), cottid (Cottidae—a bottom-feeding fish with no commercial value, 15 centimeters long, with "mini-suma" look, serves as food for predatory fish).

PART FOUR

POLISH HIGHLANDERS IN AMERICA

APPENDIX II

Polish Highlanders of America

Beyond the Great Water

The highlanders call the Atlantic Ocean "the Great Water." There is a lack of detailed information on when the first Tatra highlander crossed the Atlantic and landed on North American soil. But, according to Wlodzimierz Wnuk, "the mass emigration of highlanders to the United States and, to a lesser extent, to Canada began at the end of the XIX century, with the greatest volume coming in the first years of the XX century, until the outbreak of World War I. At the end of the war, emigration revived, but on a smaller scale."

The reason for this mass emigration from the area of Galicia, where the highlands constituted only a small territorial fragment, was the proverbial Galician poverty in the villages, with no prospect for a better future. This poverty made itself felt in the highlands with particular intensity because of the region's poor soil conditions. There was also a lot of recruiting done by people who seduced the peasants with visions of a marvelous life "beyond the Great Water," high pay and magnificent living conditions. These were agents of shipping lines and groups working for American industrialists. When the first money began to flow in from early emigrants, others shook off their fears and succumbed to the risky move. When he decided to leave, the highlander left all his worldly possessions behind, often selling them to pay the agent off for his passage by train to Hamburg and then by ship to New York. In most cases, this was to be a departure "for a while," to earn some *talars* (this is what dollars were called), then come back and buy some land, thus improving the returning emigrant's life in the highlands. Not everyone was successful with this plan. Many did not survive the journey in the steerage-class ships carrying emigrants, or get used to the grueling work in mines and foundries. Upon their return to the highlands, many were no longer able to work on the land. They became chronic invalids. Despite these costs in terms of human existence, the emigration played an important role in the material well-being of many highland families, giving it a big boost; the influx of money from abroad served to enrich the area. Although tourists began to visit the Tatras in the second half of the XIX century, which also brought in money for the highlanders, this was confined to Zakopane and a few neighboring villages. But highlanders from the whole area emigrated "beyond the Great Water."

After arriving in New York, they dispersed to where they could find work. Since they did not know English, and had no professional skills outside of agriculture, they undertook any simple work they could find, which was usually poorly paid. They had practically no opportunity to start their own farms—lack of capital and the long waiting period before seeing monetary rewards from farming led them where they could count on a weekly wage, even if it was 75¢ for a day's work.

The states of Pennsylvania, New Jersey and New York

were closest to the ports of arrival, and they offered opportunities for work in coal mines, foundries and steel-mills, as well as textile factories. Soon, the highest concentrations of highlanders appeared in cities such as Pittsburgh, Uniontown, Johnstown, Altoona, Allentown, Wilkes-Barre, Passaic, Garfield, Wallington, East Patterson, Clifton, Utica, Rome and Buffalo. Smaller groups of highlanders also settled in lesser localities in the above-mentioned states.

With the influx of new emigrants, the region of settlement of the highlanders expanded. After the great fire which consumed nearly the whole city of Chicago in the state of Illinois, this is where the highlanders discovered their "El dorado." There was a lot of work during the rebuilding of residential housing, factories, public buildings and farms springing up on the outskirts of the city. Later, there was work available in the slaughter houses, cast iron foundries and machine factories. Besides newly-arriving emigrants, Chicago also served as a magnet for earlier arrivals who had settled on the east coast, searching for better work and living conditions. As the years went by, Chicago, Illinois, became the city with the largest concentration of Polish emigrants.

In Their Own Circle

At first, the highlanders formed a somewhat closed society. Living and working among Americans, they had difficulties establishing closer contact with them, since they were separated by a language barrier. The first generation of highland emigration did not speak English, outside of the small store of words necessary for making themselves understood in the factory or the shop. This gave birth to a peculiar slang, consisting of adding Polish endings to English words, and adapting them to highland jargon. Having a return to the highlands with their saved dollars constantly in mind, and sending those dollars home, the highlanders lived day to day, often denying themselves the most basic

271

comforts. In this situation, they sought the company of others like themselves, and found them precisely among other highlanders. Neighborhood gatherings, in the tradition of the highland *posiady*, participation in family celebrations such as christenings, weddings and funerals—all this took place in their own circle. It was only the second generation, the children of those who had decided to start their families in the U.S.A., after finishing elementary schools and establishing contact with their American counterparts, that began the process of the highlanders' opening up to the outside. This was and continues to be a difficult process, as is any assimilation in a foreign society. At the same time, there followed the inevitable estrangement of the young generation from its highland roots.

Polish Parishes

The Catholic Church played an important role in the highlanders' integration in Chicago. This was also true of other centers, particularly in Pennsylvania. Missionary-priests sent from Poland celebrated the mass for Poles by preaching and teaching in Polish, at first under very primitive conditions. The oldest Roman-Catholic parish, the Saint Stanislaw Kostka church, was founded in the northern part of Chicago in 1867. The very name of its patron indicates that it was a Polish parish. And in fact, it included 150 Polish families, among them several families from the highlands. The Polish section in this part of town was dubbed Kostkow. Luckily the church, located on the banks of a river, did not burn during the great Chicago fire of October 8, 1871. However, the highlanders arriving in Chicago in the years which followed preferred to settle in the southern part of the city. This is where farms were started, the breeding of cattle and sheep developed, and large meat processing facilities were built. It is also where a second Roman Catholic parish, St. Wojciech's, was founded. The Polish section which grew up around this church was called "Wojciechow." The dynamic nature of the development of the Polish ethnic group in Chicago at the turn of the XIX century is attested to by the fact that by 1910 there existed twenty Roman Catholic parishes in Chicago, most with a decided majority of members of Polish extraction. Records show that highlanders formed a plurality in ten of them, and these ten churches—three in the northern part of the city and seven in the south—counted about 80% of all highlanders in Chicago as their members. The Sunday masses in these highland churches served as an occasion to meet friends and relatives and to exchange information about work and living conditions. After church (as was also true of the highlands) the socializing continued in taverns, an increasing number of which were in highlander hands. Nursery schools were formed by the churches for instruction in the Polish language and Polish history. The situation in other U.S. towns was similar to the one in Chicago—where the generosity of parishoners, among them highlanders, made possible the building of churches and organizing of Polish schools. It was at these parishes that the first highlander circles and clubs in North America took place. It was there that highland musicians gathered and highland singing—expressing longing for the Tatras and the hope for a speedy return—could be heard on the occasion of various celebrations.

Establishing Roots in America

In time, the number of highlanders rooted in American soil began to grow. Many clearly Polish names were noted in the chronicles of the Civil War (1861-1865), among them typically highland names—highlanders who fought on the side of the Union. There was also no shortage of Tatra highlander names among the names of American soldiers fighting on the European front in World War I from 1917 on, when the Americans entered the war on the side of the

Entente. In large numbers, they reinforced General Jozef Haller's Polish army in France after 1918, entering Poland with this army.

In 1898 two important Polish American organizations were formed in the U.S.—the National Polish Association and the Association of Polish Women in America. Conditions were not ripe yet for forming an organization of the increasingly numerous highlanders in the U.S., even though there were people who, besides their deep love for the highlands, also had the ability to organize civic activities, along with the skill and qualifications to contact state authorities. But the idea that regionalism did not constitute a danger for the Polish American community had not yet come to fruition.

The Spark Ignited the Highland Shepherds' Watch-Fire

The chroniclers of the highlands movement in America agree that everything started with Stefan Jarosz. Although he was not a native highlander, he was one of those people who was enchanted with the Tatras and the highlanders. While attending high school in Nowy Sacz, he traveled during his vacation in Beskid Sadecki, Pieniny and finally the Tatras. He learned the highland dialect and highland songs, as well as the intricate highland dances. After completing his studies at Poznan University, he received a scholarship in 1927 from the Foreign Affairs Ministry and went to the U.S.A. to visit and study the Polish-American centers there. He began his peregrinations among Polish clubs and schools, holding lectures and speeches on the subject of post-war Poland and showing slides he had brought with him. Jarosz was a member and activist of the Polish Tatra Society in Zakopane, so that he was aware of the highlanders in the U.S.A. and particularly of the great numbers of them in Chicago. Organizing his first appearance there, he was pictured on posters for the lecture in a highland costume and prepared slides of the Tatras for his lecture. Having already made some contacts with highlanders in Chicago, he invited a highland musical group (led by Karol Stoch, who was well known among the highlanders) to perform after his lecture. The Schoenhofen Hall on the corner of Milwaukee and Ashland Avenues was filled to overflowing. This was the first time in Chicago that highland music was heard from a stage, words in highland dialect were spoken and the whole charm of the Tatras and the highlands unfolded before the audience. As Wlodzimierz Wnuk put it: "This was the spark which ignited the highland Shepherd's Watch-Fire." Jarosz held dozens of such lectures in Pennsylvania, both Virginias and New Jersey. They awakened the realization in the highlanders that they hailed from an unusually beautiful part of Poland, representing an old folk culture whose roots reached back to the Slavic beginnings of the Polish nation, with a colorful folklore was something to be proud of. Of course, these reactions were not universal; they especially touched those who were the co-creators of this regional culture, such as musicians, dancers, singers, and handicraftsmen from father to son. They had brought their talents with them Beyond the Great Water, and continued the highland traditions for their own and their fellow highlanders' needs. These feelings were intensified among those who, hailing from Skalne or some more broadly understood region of Podhale, came to America as educated men, often outstanding specialists in the profession they had studied at home.

Some of were:

Henryk Lokanski, born in 1880 in Zakopane. Even though his parents were not of highlander stock, he felt himself to be a highlander and a half, and always proudly emphasized the place of his birth. After finishing school, he emigrated to the U.S. in 1900, where from the beginning he engaged his journalistic talents in the Polish-American press. He worked in the editorial offices of *Tygodnik Nowojorski* (New York Weekly), *Dziennik Narodowy* (National Daily), *Dziennik Zwiazkowy* (Union Daily ofChicago) and the periodical *Polak w Ameryce* (The Pole in America). He used all his influence to gain backing for the activities of Stefan Jarosz in his quest to form a separate highland organization in America.

Jozef Lopatowski, born in 1885 in Rabka-Zaryte in the northern part of the highlands. He finished the Cracow Commerce Academy and in 1909 emigrated to the U.S. He was Henryk Lokanski's right hand man in his work aimed at uniting the highlanders in America. He is especially remembered as the author and director of plays in the highland dialect—whose locale was the highlands—works which easily reached the highlanders, awakening an awareness of their roots in them.

Antoni Zygmuntowicz, born c. 1885 in Bialka Tatrzanska. From 1911 worked in Pennsylvania coal mines and later in the Pullman car factory in Chicago. He invested the money he had saved to buy his own farm on Marshfield Avenue in Chicago. It soon became an unofficial highlander center, where musicians, dancers, and those who cared about highland affairs used to gather. Zygmuntowicz was the first president of the Jan Sabala Highland Circle formed later, head of a highland group called Polish Roman-Catholic Association, and organizer of the Highland Soccer Club in Chicago. He also arranged the first meeting between Stefan Jarosz and the Chicago highlanders which turned out to be of such importance.

Representatives of original highland folklore, which they brought beyond the Great Water with them right from their homes, found professional backing from the above-mentioned men. Some of these artists were:

Stanislaw Bachleda, born in 1889 in Zakopane, arrived in Chicago in 1913. He married there and brought his energy, spirit and imagination into the highland community, and perhaps most importantly he made people remember how beautiful the highland songs were. He was considered the best highland singer of the time, with records which gained popularity beyond the highland community as well.

Franciszek Chowaniec, born in 1891 in Poronin. He came to Chicago in 1909. He was a soldier in General Jozef Haller's Army. He returned to the U.S. in 1923. He was a musician, organizer of highland choirs, and author of many publications on regional themes and works performed in highland dialect.

Jan Wladyslaw Gromada, born in 1905 in Ostrowsko near Nowy Targ. His father, also Jan, hailed from Suche near Poronin and was known as a lover of highland music and dance. From his early youth, Jan W. Gromada had the makings of an excellent musician, but he chose a very difficult trade for himself—sewing and decorating highland woolen cloth pants and overcoats. He emigrated to the U.S. with his future wife. After various vicissitudes, he settled in Passaic, N.J., started a family and, under the influence of Stefan Jarosz, became the most active organizer of the highland movement on the East Coast.

We should also mention the names of native highlanders such as **Andrzej Rafacz, Karol Stoch, Franciszek Cyrwus, Stanislaw Tatar**, who, after living in Chicago for a dozen years understood the necessity of giving an organized character to the diffuse activities of the highlander groups in the U.S.A.

Organizational Beginnings

In the summer of 1927, the first general meeting of highlanders and their sympathizers was held at the hall of the Polish Women's Association in Chicago through the efforts of Stefan Jarosz. Highlander Dr. Franciszek Lenart chaired the meeting, and besides Stefan Jarosz he was backed by the Polish Consul General in Chicago—Zdzislaw Kurnikowski—also a highlander. Considering it necessary to create a joint highland organization, Jarosz proposed the acceptance of the organizational principles of the Tatra Society which was already in existence in Poland. And here is where the old "parochial" antagonisms long rampant in the highlands, mainly defining the territory of the highlands, came to the fore. Should the expression "The Highlands" mean exclusively the so-called Rocky Highlands, or also neighboring Beskid and Gorce regions? These parochial antagonisms have appeared in the past and continue to appear not only in the highlands—boys from a neighboring village coming a dance were never welcome. Often such "visits" ended in bloody rows. But in the highlands these antagonisms had an additional source in slight differences in dialect, dress, songs, music and customs. The "Rocky" highlanders thought they were better than their neighbors from Pieniny, Spisz or Orawa. They had a similar attitude toward the residents of the southern parts of the Nowy Sacz and Limanowa districts, sweepingly calling them Lachy. In fact, those neighbors paid the "Rocky" highlanders back in kind. The people of Nowy Targ, residents of the capital of the highlands, were not considered highlanders either, but rather "burghers." These antagonisms made the voyage overseas with the highlanders, and they were hard to overcome for the very reason for their irrationality.

And so, although after this first organizational meeting of the Polish-American Tatra Society other smaller meetings took place as well and a Board of Directors was elected in 1928, it was not possible to develop programs of broader interest. Instead, what did develop was Circles of the Society, independently organized in Chicago, as well as in other localities in the U.S. and Canada. It is difficult to establish their chronology today, but we must consider the following organizations to be pioneers in this movement: **Jan Sabala Highlanders Alliance** for the southeastern part of Chicago, Town Lake; **Wladyslaw Orkan Highlanders Circle** in the northwestern part of town; **Highlanders Alliance** in Brighton Park; **Highlanders Alliance** in "Wojciechowo;" **Morskie Oko Circle** in the Kensington district of Chicago; **Morskie Oko Circle** in Detroit, Michigan; **Wladyslaw Zamoyski Circle** in Chicago; **Kazimierz Przerwa-Tetmajer Circle** in Passaic, New Jersey; and the **Highlanders Alliance** in North America.

The numerical force of these circles and the evident progress in recruiting new members resulted in the convocation of a meeting of their representatives, who approved a plan for a constitution of a future joint highland organization in the U.S., to be called the Highlanders Alliance in North America. The first general meeting of this Alliance, at which the proposed constitution was adopted, was held on June 8, 1930, at the Juliusz Slowacki Hall in Chicago. At the same time, the Polish-American Tatra Society ceased to exist. For the record, let us say that the "Wojciechowo" Circle and the Circle from Brighton Park did not send delegates to this meeting.

It would be worthwhile to recall the composition of the first Board of Directors of the Highlanders Alliance elected on June 8, 1930: **Henryk Lokanski**—president; **Franciszek Chowaniec**: vice-president; **Jozef Lopatowski**: secretary general; **Ludwik Kalemba**: treasurer; and the **Rev. Walerian Pach**: Alliance chaplain. Circle directors entering into Board of Directors: Stanislaw Bachleda, Anna Gorz, Jozef Orawiec, Franciszek Polak, Anna Powarzynska, Karol Stoch, Aniela Zych, Antoni Zygmuntowicz.

According to the adopted Constitution, members of the Highlanders Alliance in North America had to be highlanders, of any faith, born in the highlands proper, which is to say in the old Nowy Targ district, in Orawa and Spisz, in the Zywiecki and former Makowski districts, and in the southern part of the Limanowski and Sadecki districts, with an eastern border up to Jaslisko and Dukla and a western border to and including Jablonkow. Also, highlander-Poles born in the Tatra-Carpathian mountain areas in Slovakia and in Czech Silesia could join the Alliance as well. Persons born outside of Poland, but with highlander parents or at least one parent, living in the highlands in the areas described above, could also belong to the Alliance. It is evident that this broad interpretation of what constituted the highlands did not sit well with everyone, and that is why the representatives of some circles failed to attend the first General Meeting.

The goal of the Highlanders Alliance in North America is to organize highlanders scattered throughout the United States and Canada, creating one large organizational highland family in America. The alliance organizes and carries out fraternal help to members in need, works to raise their moral and educational level, awakens in them an awareness of their highland traditions and attachment to the land of their fathers, particularly among the young.

The activities of the Alliance are designed to preserve and expand appreciation of the highland dialect and all forms of highland folk culture, and to propagate and present these values on the American continent. There is also a provision in the Constitution to offer material help to organizations and institutions in Poland in the realization of projects undertaken in the civic interest of highland villages where the Alliance members come from.

The members of the Alliance are organized in circles (or groups) which are autonomous organizations with their own board of directors and finances, drawing funds from membership dues and various types of income-producing endeavors organized by the Circles. Traditionally, the circles of the Higlanders Alliance are organized in keeping with former membership in family parishes in the highlands. It sometimes happens that members hailing from one village, part of which belongs to a neighboring parish, belong to two different Circles. At least 15 persons are needed to form a Circle. The Board of Directors approves the creation of the Circle and enters it on the list under a successive number. Although they are run on an autonomous basis, the Circles are obligated to carry out the decrees and directives of the Board of Directors in organization-wide matters. The Circles retain the right to choose their name, which is either simply the name of the parish, the first and last name of its patron or simply a name connected with the highlands, such as "Morskie Oko," "Pieniny," or "Orawa." A symbol of the Circle and a measure of its organizational maturity is its banner, whose consecration is conducted in a very ceremonial way, with the participation of other Circles. When they hold elections, the Circles choose directors to the Board of Directors, who then serve as liaison between the Circle and the central authorities of the Alliance, whose meetings they are entitled to attend. Besides the "parochial" Circles, the Highlanders Alliance also encompases special groups such as: the Dramatic Circle, the "Tatry" Sports Club and the Highland Women's Division.

The Parliaments of the Highlanders Alliance in North America

The highest organ of the Alliance are Parliaments organized every three years, in which Circle members take part. They elect the Board of Directors and the other principal divisions of the Association, vote on acceptance of accounts presented by the departing management, approve organizational and financial statements and point out in a resolution the tasks and directions the Alliance is to undertake during the next three years. Chicago is the seat of of the Board of Directors, although the Parliament has the power to move it to another city if it wishes. The vice-presidents of the States of New York, New Jersey and Pennsylvania sit on the Board of Directors, and the president of the Highlanders Alliance in Canada, located in Toronto, is also invited.

In the period from 1928, when the Polish-American Tatra Society was formed, to 1993, when the XXII Parliament of the Highlanders Alliance was held—that is, during the 65 years that the Alliance has existed—the Parliaments have noted milestones on the road of the highlanders activities in North America. Nearly every three-year period of the activities of the management elected by the Alliance has been marked by a small but steady rise in the number of Circles. While six Circle delegates took part in the Parliament held on June 8, 1930, the XII Parliament, held on September 4-6, 1993, was attended by delegates from nearly fifty Alliance organizations. It is necesary to explain here the difference between the numeration of the Circles and their actual number. During the past 65 years, some of the Circles ceased to exist for one reason or another. The Circle of the Highlanders Alliance in Detroit, along with New York, Pennsylvania and Wisconsin, died out when their members moved to different parts of the U.S. in search of work. New Circles were still given consecutive numeration, without going back to the past.

The I Parliament of the Alliance honored the memory of the troubadour of the highlands—Wladyslaw Orkan—who died in May of 1930, by passing a resolution obligating the highlanders of North America to raise a statue of Orkan in Nowy Targ at their own expense. This was the first time that a stipulation was made to create a press section of the highlanders Alliance. As an example of the energetic activities of the Board of Directors elected at the I Parliament, we might cite the organization of the first excursion of American highlanders to Poland. It took place in May 1933, with 125 participants. These trips became a tradition as time went on, which greatly contributed to the close cooperation between the highlanders from "Beyond the Great Water" and the highlanders in Poland. In 1934, during the second excursion to Poland, the participants took part in the unveiling of the statue of Wladyslaw Orkan.

Then came the war years. The V Parliament, held September 4-6, 1940, took place in face of Poland's loss of independence. The highlanders decisively backed the Polish government in exile, expressing the conviction that Poland would once again be free. The next Parliament was held after the conclusion of the war, in early September 1945, in an atmosphere of jubilation over the Allies' victory over Germany and Japan; at the same time, there was a great deal of worry over the fact that Poland had been hurled into the sphere of Soviet influence.

The VII Parliament (8/31-9/2/48) undertook the following important tasks:

• Revive the song and dance school for children and young people
• Transform the sporadically appearing *Echa Podhalanskie* (Highland Echoes) into a quarterly
• Build or buy a home for the organization

In January 1949 the Kazimierz Przerwa-Tetmajer Literary-Dramatic Circle began its productive activities. It united all those people whose abilities in the field of music, singing, dance and the spoken word could be presented on stage.

A large group of new immigrants from the highlands, former Polish soldiers from the western front who settled in England after the war and were later granted American visas, took part in the VIII Parliament, held on September 1-3, 1951. There were many pre-war highland activists and sportsmen, particularly skiers. They greatly enlivened the proceedings of the Highlanders Alliance in North America. The Fund for a Highlanders' Home was started during this Parliament to gather funds for realizing the plans made three years earlier.

The IX Parliament, early in September 1954, was marked by the participation of distinguished guests. Among them were: **Alojzy Mazewski**, director of the Polish National Alliance; **Maria Brzezinska**, director of the Alliance of Polish Women; **Arthur Coleman**, the rector of Alliance College.

And the folowing guests spoke at the following X Parliament: **Karol Rozmarek**, president of the Polish-American Congress and also of the Polish National Alliance; **Congressman Edward Derwinski**, of highland descent; and **Congressman Roman Plucinski**.

The participation of these V.I.P's attested to the fact that the highlanders Alliance had become an organization which counted for something in the United States. But it was still "a tenant"—with no home of its own. The highlanders were able to solve this problem as well. In 1951 Andrzej Rafacz, the richest highlands *gazda* (farmer) in the State of Illinois, became president of the Alliance, and under his leadership the fundraising for the home took off at a rapid pace. More than $30,000 was needed to buy the building the Alliance had in mind and further thousands were necessary to adapt this building to the organization's needs. It was therefore decided to make use of bank credit for part of this outlay. The highlanders celebrated the opening of their Home for three days (November 7-9, 1958) in Chicago at 3035 W. 51st. Street. Many highlanders lived in this part of the city, clustered around the Pieciu Braci Meczennikow parish.

The political thaw which occurred in Poland after October 1956, made it possible for the highlanders to resume their excursions back home. There was also renewed cooperation between the management of the Highlanders Alliance in Chicago and in Zakopane.

New Highlanders' Home

The following account is not a chronicle of the Highlanders Alliance in North America, but is designed to remind you of the most important events in its history. Such an important event is undoubtedly the construction of a new home for the

Alliance at 4808 N. Archer Avenue in Chicago. The house on 51st Street became decidedly too small in face of the systematically growing number of Circles. It so happened that the land the Home stood on was urgently needed by an expanding steel mill, so that the highlanders were able to get a good price for it. For the money this brought in, along with increased dues from the growing Circles, the highlanders were able to build a new Highlanders' Home in Zakopane style, with two large banquet-meeting halls (one with a stage), a restaurant, bar, kitchen, first-aid station and space for the Board of Directors, the Circle meetings and rehearsals of regional troupes. The ceremonial opening of this House was held on May 27, 1984.

A significant accomplishment of later Boards of Directors has been the annual organization of festivals of song, dance and music at the highlanders home named "Na goralskom nute" (to the highlanders' tune). November 1993 saw the twelfth such festival. For two days, the stage of the Highlanders Home plays host to children's, young people's and adult troupes which compete in highland dance, song and music, before an audience which is several hundred strong. It is hard to overemphasize the role of this festival in promoting highland folklore in North America, particularly for children and young people. Invited guests have also participated in two festivals—an American dance troupe, a Mexican troupe, the "Cracovia" troupe from Canada and a Bulgarian troupe. Also taking part was Circle #6 Kazimierz Przerwa Tetmayer of Clifton, NJ, Stanislaw Trojaniak, President. It was reactivated after the 1993 Parliament.

The Highlanders on the East Coast

Not to belittle the accomplishments of the Alliance Circles in the State of Illinois, the organization of highlanders on the U.S. East Coast (inaugurated on June 1, 1929, at the Polish Peasants' Home in Passaic, N.J.), deserves special appreciation. Stefan Jarosz was present at this inauguration. The Circle selected Kazimierz Przerwa-Tetmajer as its patron, and its recording-secretary Jan Wladyslaw Gromada became its most vigorous moving force. Sparing no effort, together with his wife Aniela he made sure that highland costumes appeared in Passaic and plays with highland content began to be seen on the stage. But in this circle (as in some others), envious people appeared, putting their interests above the good of the Alliance, and that caused Jan Gromada to separate himself from Circle activities. After Gromada's departure, the organization soon ground to a halt. But Gromada did not give up the highlands cause. Together with other like-minded highlanders, he started a new Circle, which was named Polish Tatra Mountaineers Alliance of America. They applied for membership in the Highlanders Alliance in North America and were registered under Number 11. This Circle is fruitfully active to this day, and its undisputed success—which even the Chicago community cannot boast of—is the publication of a periodical entitled *Tatrzanski Orzel* (Tatra Eagle) which has been coming out since 1947 without interruption. This periodical was preceded by three albums named *The Highlander in America*, which were a form of diary of the activities of the Polish Tatra Mountaineers Alliance of America in Passaic, NJ.

Jan Wladyslaw Gromada, despite his age, had not given up his activities for the highlands cause, although most of the burden in this area had been taken over by his daughter, Janina, and her husband, Henry, as well as Gromada's son, Professor Tadeusz Gromada. Jan Wladyslaw Gromada died in 1996.

Circle number 11 in Passaic is always promoting highland folklore. The highlander column is always impressive as it marches in the Pulaski Parade in New York.

On the Eagle's Mountain Path

When presenting a Board of Directors report at the IV Parliament of the Highlanders Alliance, Jozef Lopatowski said:

> Before the Highlanders Alliance was formed here, people knew nothing or next to nothing about the highlanders, and what is worse there were those who taunted and humiliated the highlanders. But the moment the highlanders awoke from their langor and got organized in their own Highlanders Alliance, when they showed their countrymen from other parts of Poland the beauty of the highland dialect, the originality of its costumes, the lovely melodies and original music and dances that can be encountered only in the highlands, then everyone began to admire, respect and show interest in the highlanders.

This statement is fully justified. Today it is hard to imagine the Pulaski Parade in New York, or the May 3 Parade in Chicago without the distinctive colorful highlanders' column. The Board of Directors of the Polish National Association has given the highlanders diplomas of recognition many times for their performance. Highland music, song and dance are a frequent entertainment at spectacles presented by Americans or at international folklore festivals. The most prestigeous record companies have recorded highland music and songs before the war. These have met with great success in the marketplace because of their originality and unique style. Now these records have been replaced with audio casettes and videos.

A representative of the governor of the State of Illinois always participates in the highland Parliaments. U.S. President George Bush visited the Highlanders' Home on Archer Avenue on March 16, 1992. In turn on June 29 of that year, the President received Secretary for Veterans' Affairs Edward Derwinski (who, as a Pole of highlander parentage, wore a highland costume for the occasion) in the Rose Garden of the White House. A delegation of highlanders came to Washington on the occasion of the ceremonies preceding the removal of Jan Ignacy Paderewski's ashes to Poland. Earlier, the highlanders greeted the Pope in the United States. John Paul II, born in Wadowice, was an enthusiastic mountaineer and skier during all the years he spent in Poland.

And finally, something that may seem trivial: the best pork-butcher's products in Chicago are those made by the highlander firm of Gil and Bobak.

Pulaski at the Highlanders

The end of 1993 was marked by a significant occurrence at the Highlanders Alliance in Chicago. Namely, a bust of General Kazimierz Pulaski, which about 100 years earlier had decorated the facade of the Polish Home built by the Polish-Americans at the end of the XIX century, was found in the garden of property belonging to Mrs. Janiec of Chicago. The Polish Home burned down, but somehow the bust survived. After it was found, there was consternation about what should be done with it. The choice fell to the Highlanders Alliance. On October 21, 1993, there was a solemn ceremony to unveil the bust in front of the Highlanders' House on Archer Avenue in Chicago, with the participation of Polish Consul General Michal Grocholski, representatives of state and city authorties, and many Polonia and combattant delegations. The Board of Directors of the Hhighlanders Alliance bore the cost of placing the bust and holding the ceremony.

Highland Publicity

It is difficult to unequivocally answer the question—why an organization as large as the Highlanders Alliance in North America has not yet come to the point of having its own periodical, which would be its voice throughout its existence or at least from the time of the second or third Parliament.

Attempts were made—in 1937 two issues of the *Highlands Echo* appeared, and later *Echo* was published irregularly, with a last issue in 1963. It is not clear exactly how many issues there were altogether—they did not have sequential numeration. In a certain sense, the publishing activities of Circle number 11 of the Alliance in Passaic, NJ, can be called autonomous. There, besides the three album-style publications called *The Highlander in America*, we have the appearance, more or less regularly on a quarterly basis, of the publication *Tatra Eagle* (first issue named *Tatra Man*) containing a short general-highland chronicle and literary works, some in highland dialect.

Since 1978, the Toronto-based Highlanders Alliance in Canada, headed by Stanislaw Szaflarski, has been bringing out its own periodical entitled *Polana*.

On the initiative of former Alliance president Henryk Janik, *The Highlander in America* was revived in 1993 as an informational bulletin of the Highlanders Alliance. The fifth issue of this periodical appeared in December.

Every three years, "Diaries" of the Alliance's successive Parliaments are published. Outside of the first ones, which could be called a summation of the deliberations of the just-concluded Parliament, later ones appeared in the first days of deliberations, or even before they started. They contain few problem papers, and consist mostly of wishes for "fruitful deliberations" from various firms and private persons, as well as from individual Highlanders Alliance Circles and fraternal organizations. In the case of the "Diaries," as well as other self-financing publications—economics and substantial content have come up against each other. Economics won, since the publication of every item is quite costly. Thus the good wishes offered, usually with a photograph of people doing the offering, are in the nature of paid advertisements. Little room is left for serious presentations of highlands questions or even problems of the Alliance itself. Nevertheless, the "Diaries" fulfill an important role, perhaps not the one intended; they are a peculiar informational document on Alliance Circles and their management, since every Circle is anxious to find a place in "The Diaries."

Since December 1992, highland dialect, song and music are reaching radio listeners in Chicago and surrounding areas. highland programs are broadcast by station WPNA, 1490AM for 90 minutes each week (on Sundays); the first half hour is devoted to information on the life of the highlander community in Chicago and news from the highlands (direct broadcast from Ludzmierz), and the second full hour covers the history of the highlands, its various regions, poems and stories told in dialect, reminding people of the old ceremonies and highland customs. The ads, which are a must for financial reasons, do not overwhelm the meritorious quality of the two programs.

Summary

Instead of summing up the presented fragments concerning the more than 65-year activities of the Highlanders Alliance in North America, it might be better to cite the words of President Henryk Lokanski, delivered during the second Parliament of the Alliance, which still hold true today:

> First of all, the Highlanders Alliance in North America, through its bold presentation of the highland regional type and the promotion of all of its customs and cultural values, has preserved for Poland in general, and particularly for the Polish cause in America, thousands of highland families which, forgotten in the past, were quickly heading toward the precipice of denationalization. Today not only older folk, but also the young, have a lively interest in their Polishness, awakened in them by their highland pride, and these young people must be considered as saved for the Polish cause in America. This is the first great civic and patriotic achievement of the Highlanders Alliance in America.

APPENDIX III

Presidents of the Polish Highlanders Alliance in North America

1928—1937	Henryk LOKANSKI
1937—1944	Antoni DABROWSKI
1944—1951	Stanislaw JANIK
1951—1959	Andrzej RAFACZ
1959—1972	Andrzej WROBEL
1972—1978	Jozef F. KROZEL
1978—1984	Jozef GIL
1984—1987	Andrzej CZYSZCZON
1987—1990	Jozef KROZEL
1990—1992	Stanislaw DZIERZEGA-GUBALA
1992—1993	Henryk JANIK
1993—1996	Andrej PITON
1996—	Edward WILCZEK

Circles (Associations) of Polish Highlanders Alliance in North America

(as of December 31, 1993)

Registration Number	Name of Circle
1	Jan Sabala
2	Wladyslaw Orkan
2	(bis)Brighton Park
3	Morskie Oko
5	Wladyslaw Zamoyski
8	General Andrzej Galica

11	Polish Tatra Mountaineers Alliance of America
14	"Tatry" in Uniontown, Pennsylvania
19	Andrzej Duch Knapczyk
20	Dramatic Circle
21	Czarny Dunajec
22	Maniowy
59	Morawczyna
23	Odrowaz-Podhalanski
60	Male Ciche
24	Szaflary
25	Harklowa
27	Witow
28	Nowy Targ
29	Gronkow
30	Ciche
31	"Wierchy"
32	Spytkowice
33	Dzianisz
34	Zakopane
35	Maruszyna
37	Gron-Lesnica
38	Ludzmierz
40	Bialy Dunajec
41	Wroblowka
42	Bialka Tatrzanska
43	Chocholow
44	"Sleboda"
45	Zofia Graca—Poronin
46	Stare Bystre
47	Sports Club "Tatry"
48	"Babia Gora"
49	Kluszkowice
50	"Pieniny"
51	Ostrowsko
52	Czerwienne
53	Klikuszowa
54	Koscielisko

55	Ratulow
56	"Royal Wawel"
57	Bukowina Tatrzanska
58	Zab
60	Kazimierz Przerwa-Tetmajer
61	Lopuszna
62	Lowieckie
63	Waksmund
64	Czarna Gora
65	Ciche Dolne (parusg Mietustwo)
66	Debno
67	Pieniazkowice

Index

Index

Index

Index

Index

Index

Index

Highlander Polish-English / English-Highlander Polish Dictionary

by Jan Gutt-Mustowy
translated by Miroslaw Lipinski

"As a proud American of Polish *góral* descent, I am delighted that Jan Gutt-Mostowy from Poronin in Podhale prepared a Polish-Góral-English dictionary. It is obviously a labor of love that will elicit appreciation and recognition and allow the richness and beauty of the *gwara góralska* to become more available to the English speaking world."

—*Dr. Thaddeus V. Gromada*
Vice President & Executive Director
Polish Institute of Arts and Sciences

111 *pages   4 x 6   2000 entries   0-7818-0303-9 $9.95pb   (297)*

Also of interest from Hippocrene Books . . .

POLISH HISTORY

OLD POLISH LEGENDS
As retold by F. C. Anstruther with wood engravings by J. Sekalski
Now available in a new gift edition! This fine collection of eleven fairy tales, with an introduction by Zygmunt Nowakowski, was first published in Scotland during World War II, when the long night of German occupation was at its darkest.
66 pages • 7¼ x 9 • 11 woodcuts • 0-7818-0521-X • $11.95hc • (653)

THE POLISH WAY
A Thousand-Year History of the Poles and Their Culture
by Adam Zamoyski
"Zamoyski strives to place Polish history more squarely in its European context, and he pays special attention to developments that had repercussions beyond the boundaries of the country. For example, he emphasizes the phenomenon of the Polish parliamentary state in Central Europe, its spectacular 16th century success and its equally spectacular disintegration two centuries later.... This is popular history at its best, neither shallow nor simplistic ... lavish illustrations, good maps and intriguing charts and genealogical tables make this book particularly attractive." —*New York Times Book Review*
422 pages • 170 illustrations • $19.95pb • 0-7818-0200-8 • (176)

THE FORGOTTEN HOLOCAUST
The Poles Under German Occupation, 1939-1945, Revised Edition
by Richard C. Lukas with a Foreword by Norman Davies
This new edition includes the story of Zegota and the list of 700 Poles executed for helping Jews.
"Dr. Richard C. Lukas has rendered a valuable service by showing that no one can properly analyze the fate of one ethnic community in occupied Poland without referring to the fates of others. In this sense, *The Forgotten Holocaust* is a powerful corrective." —*from the foreword by Norman Davies*
"Carefully researched—a timely contribution." —*Prof. Piotr Wandycz, Yale Univ.*
"Contains excellent analyses of the relationship of Poland's Jewish and Gentile communities, the development of the resistance, the exile leadership, and the Warsaw uprisings. A superior work." —*Library Journal*
300 pages • 6 x 9 • illustrations • 0-7818-0528-7 • $24.95hc • (639)

DID THE CHILDREN CRY?
Hitler's War Against Jewish and Polish Children
by Richard C. Lukas
Winner of the 1996 Janusz Korczak Literary Competition for books about children.
"... [Lukas] intersperses the endless numbers, dates, locations and losses with personal accounts of tragedy and triumph.... A well-researched book."
—Catalyst
263 pages • 15 b/w photos, index • 0-7818-0242-3 • $24.95hc • (145)

JEWS IN POLAND: A Documentary History
by Iwo Cyprian Pogonowski with a Foreword by Richard Pipes
Originally published in 1993, this classic historical work is now available in paperback! Jews in Poland describes the rise of Jews as a nation and the crucial role that the Polish-Jewish community played in this development. The volume includes a new translation of the Charter of Jewish Liberties known as the Statute of Kalisz of 1264; 114 historical maps; as well as 172 illustrations including reproductions of works of outstanding painters, photographs of official posters, newspaper headlines and cartoons.

"This pioneering attempt, as well as the sheer volume of documentation gathered in this volume, make Pogonowski's opus remarkable and unusual."
—Professor M.K. Dziewanowski, The Sarmatian Review
402 pages • maps, illus, index • 8½ x 11½ • 0-7818-0604-6 • $19.95pb • (677)

THE LAST KING OF POLAND
by Adam Zamoyski
One night in December, 1755 Stanislaw Poniatowski, the twenty-three year old secretary to the British Ambassador in St. Petersburg, was introduced to the Grand Duchess Catherine Alekseyevna. This marked the beginning of an affair which led to Stanislaw being crowned King of Poland in 1764. The dashing, young king was a great believer in art, education, and cultural projects. He transformed the mood and outlook of his country and brought it to a new phase of reform and independence, culminating in the passing of the Constitution in 1791, hailed in Britain, France and the United States as one of the greatest events of the century. Best-selling author Adam Zamoyski relates this rich and enthralling story of a personal dream with all the elements of grand tragedy. It is also an important chronicle of the birth and death of liberalism in Poland and the establishment of Russian power in Europe.
560 pages • 16 pages, b/w illustrations • 0-7818-0603-8 • $39.95hc • (676)

THE FORGOTTEN FEW: The Polish Air Force in the Second World War
by Adam Zamoyski
This is the story of the few who are rarely remembered today. Some 17,000 men and women passed through the ranks of the Polish Air Force while it was stationed on British soil in World War II. They not only played a crucial role in the Battle of Britain in 1940, but they also contributed significantly to the Allied war effort.
272 pages • 30 illus, 30 maps • 6 x 9 • 0-7818-0421-3 • $24.95hc • (493)

Your Life is Worth Mine
by Ewa Kurek with an Introduction by Jan Karski
First published in Poland in 1992 as *Gdy Klasztor Znaczyl Zycie*, this is the story of how Polish nuns saved hundreds of Jewish lives while risking their own during World War II. This long awaited American edition includes a section of interviews with nuns and Jewish survivors which did not appear in the Polish edition.
"A welcome addition to Holocaust literature... deserves a wide readership."
—*Zgoda*
250 pages • 5 1/2 x 8 1/2 • 0-7818-0409-4 • $22.50hc • (240)

POLISH-ENGLISH UNABRIDGED DICTIONARY
by Iwo Cyprian Pogonowski
Years in the making, this three-volume set is the definitive Polish-English dictionary. It is the most up-to-date, comprehensive, and scientific Polish-English dictionary available. Slang and colloquialisms take their places alongside the general vocabulary to give a truly vivid picture of Polish as it is spoken today. Pogonowski's unique phonetic system is employed to full advantage, thus the non-Polish speaker can more easily grasp the unfamiliar.
3800 pages • 5½ x8½ • 250,000 entries • 3-vol set • 0-7818-0441-8 • $200hc (526)

The Polish-English Dictionary of Slang and Colloquialism
by Maciej Widawski, Ph.D.
To be able to use colloquialisms appropriately is what separates the fluent speaker from the student. Here Professor Maciej Widawski of Poznan University provides definitions and usage examples for 5,000 of the most common Polish colloquial expressions.
361 pages • 6 x 9 • 5,000 entries • 0-7818-0570-8 • $19.95pb • (692)

POLISH LITERATURE

A TREASURE OF POLISH APHORISMS A Bilingual Edition
Compiled and translated by Jacek Galazka
With an Intorduction by Jerzy R. Krzyzanowski
This collection comprises 225 aphorisms by eighty Polish writers, many of them
well known in their native land. Sixteen pen and ink drawings by talented Polish
illustrator Barbara Swidzinska complete this remarkable exploration of true
Polish wit and wisdom.
140 pages • 5 ½ x 8 ½ • 20 illus • 0-7818-0549-X • $14.95hc • (647)

POLISH FABLES A Bilingual Edition
by Ignacy Krasicki and translated by Gerard T. Kapolka
Sixty-five fables by eminent Polish poet Bishop Ignacy Krasicki are translated
into English by Gerard Kapolka. With great artistry, the author used
contemporary events and human relations to show a course to guide human
conduct. For over two centuries, Krasicki's fables have entertained and
instructed his delighted readers. This bilingual gift edition contains twenty
illustrations by Barbara Swidzinska, well known Polish artist.
250 pages • 6 x 9 • 0-7818-0548-1 • $19.95hc • (646)

TREASURY OF POLISH LOVE POEMS, QUOTATIONS & PROVERBS
Miroslaw Lipinski, editor and translator
Works by Krasinski, Sienkiewicz and Mickiewicz are included among 100
selections by 44 authors.
128 pages • 0-7818-0297-0 • $11.95 • (185)
Audiobook: 0-7818-0361-6 • $12.95 • (576)

**TREASURY OF CLASSIC POLISH LOVE SHORT STORIES IN
POLISH AND ENGLISH**
Edited by Miroslaw Lipinski
This charming gift volume delves into Poland's rich literary tradition to bring
you classic love stories from six renowned authors, including Sienkiewicz,
Irzykowski, Rittner, Nalkowska, Dygat, and Poswiatowska. These stories
explore love's many romantic, joyous, as well as melancholic facets.
128 pages • 0-7818-0513-9 • $11.95 • (603)

DICTIONARY OF 1000 POLISH PROVERBS
Edited by Miroslaw Lipinski
In this bilingual volume, the proverbs are arranged side-by-side with their
English translations. The collection is organized alphabetically by key word,
with an index listing the proverbs by English subject
141 pages • 5 x 7 • 0-7818-0482-5 • $11.95pb • (568)

THE DARK DOMAIN
by Stefan Grabinski and translated by Miroslaw Lipinski
The greatest author of fantasy fiction in Polish, Stefan Grabinski (1877-1936) explores the extreme in human behavior.
153 pages • 4½ x 7 • 1-873982-25-9 • $10.95pb • (408)

GLASS MOUNTAIN
Twenty-Eight Ancient Polish Folktales and Fables
As retold by W.S. Kuniczak and illustrated by Pat Bargielski
"It is an heirloom book to pass on to children and grandchildren. A timeless book, with delightful illustrations, it will make a handsome addition to any library and will be a most treasured gift." —*Polish American Cultural Network*
171 pages • 6 x 9 • 8 illus • 0-7818-0552-X • $16.95hc • (645)

PAN TADEUSZ
by Adam Mickiewicz and translated by Kenneth R. MacKenzie
On the 200th anniversary of Mickiewicz's birth comes a reprint of Poland's greatest epic poem in its finest English translation. For English students of Polish and for Polish students of English, this classic poem in simultaneous translation is a special joy to read.
553 pages • Polish and English side by side • 0-7818-0033-1 • $19.95pb • (237)

THE DEDALUS BOOK OF POLISH FANTASY
Edited and translated by Wiesiek Powaga
Most of these stories from Polish fantastic literature appear in English for the first time.
320 pages • 5½ x 8¼ • 1-873982-90-9 • $18.95pb • (267)

All prices subject to change. **TO PURCHASE HIPPOCRENE BOOKS** contact your local bookstore, call (718) 454-2366, or write to: HIPPOCRENE BOOKS, 171 Madison Avenue, New York, NY 10016. Please enclose check or money order, adding $5.00 shipping (UPS) for the first book and $.50 for each additional book.

THE WORKS OF HENRYK SIENKIEWICZ

QUO VADIS New paperback edition!
by Henryk Sienkiewicz and Translated by W.S. Kuniczak
Written nearly a century ago and translated into over 40 languages, *Quo Vadis* has been a monumental work in the history of literature. W.S. Kuniczak, the foremost Polish American novelist and master translator of Sienkiewicz in this century, presents a modern translation of the world's greatest bestseller since 1905. An epic story of love and devotion in Nero's time, *Quo Vadis* remains without equal a sweeping saga set during the degenerate days leading to the fall of the Roman empire and the glory and agony of early Christianity.
589 pages • 6 x 9 • 0-7818-0550-3 • $19.95pb • (648)

IN DESERT AND WILDERNESS
by Henryk Sienkiewicz and edited by Miroslaw Lipinski
In traditional Sienkiewicz Style, Stas and the little Nell and their mastiff Saba brave the desert and wilderness of Africa. This powerful coming-of-age tale has captivated readers young and old for a century.
278 pages • 0-7818-0235-0 • $19.95hc • (9)

FIRE IN THE STEPPE
by Henryk Sienkiewicz, in modern translation by W.S.Kuniczak
"The Sienkiewicz Trilogy stands with that handful of novels which not only depict but also help to determine the soul and character of the nation they describe." —*James A. Michnener*
750 pages • 0-7818-0025-0 • $24.95hc • (16)

THE LITTLE TRILOGY
by Henryk Sienkiewicz in a new tranlation by Miroslaw Lipinski
Comprised of three novellas, *The Old Servant*, *Hania*, and *Selim Mirza*, this collection will be enjoyed by the thousands of admirers of the greatest storyteller in Polish literature and the winner of the Nobel Prize for Literature in 1905.
267 pages • 0-7818-0293-8 • $19.95hc • (235)

TEUTONIC KNIGHTS Illustrated Edition
by Henryk Sienkiewicz in a translation edited by Alicia Tyszkiewicz and Miroslaw Lipinski
"Swashbuckling action, colorful characters and a touching love story..."
—*Publishers Weekly*
"...one of the most splendid achievements of Polish literature."
—*Zgoda*
"...a memorable, massive, breathtaking and compulsive read."
—*New Horizon*
800 pages • illus • 0-7818-0433-7 • $30.00hc • (533)

POLISH ARTS, CRAFTS & FOLKLORE

POLISH FOLK DANCES & SONGS: A Step-by-Step Guide
by Ada Dziewanowska
The most comprehensive and definitive book on Polish dance in the English language, with in-depth descriptions of over 80 of Poland's most characteristic and interesting dances. The author provides step-by-step instruction on positions, basic steps and patterns for each dance. Includes over 400 illustrations depicting steps and movements and over 90 appropriate musical selections.

"Not just a general overview, but an in-depth study which will be useful to folklore scholars and enthusiasts. Background information gives an excellent understanding of each region presented... and of the Polish character and people." —*Stas Kmiec, professional Broadway ballet dancer and founder/ director of the Lubliniacy Polish Song and Dance Ensemble of Haverhill-Boston*

Ada Dziewanowska is the artistic director and choreographer of the Syrena Polish Folk Dance Ensemble of Milwaukee, Wisconsin.
800 pages • 0-7818-0420-5 • $39.50hc • (508)

POLISH WEDDINGS: Customs & Traditions
by Sophie Hodorowicz Knab
A unique planning guide for Americans who want to organize and celebrate a Polish-style wedding. Sections titled Engagement, Bridal Flowers,Wedding Clothes, Ceremony, Reception and even Baby Names, will assist the bride- and groom-to-be through every step of the wedding process. Special tips on "How to Draw from the Past" at the end of each chapter provide helpful suggestions on how to incorporate Polish tradition into the modern wedding, to make it a truly distinctive and unforgettable event.
250 pages • 0-7818-0530-9 • $19.95hc • (641)

THE POLISH HERITAGE SONGBOOK
Compiled by Marek Sart and annotated by Stanislaw Werner
Illustrated by Szymon Kobylinski
This unique collection of 80 songs is a treasury of nostalgia, capturing echoes of a long struggle for freedom carried out by generations fo Polish men and women. The annotations are in English, the songs in Polish.
166 pages • 65 illus • 74 songs • 6 x 9 • 0-7818-0425-6 • $14.95pb • (496)

POLISH CUSTOMS, TRADITIONS & FOLKLORE Revised Edition
With an introduciton by Rev. Czeslaw Krysa
Now in its fourth printing!
This unique reference is arranged by month, showing the various occasions, feasts and holidays prominent in Polish culture—beginning with December it continues through Holy Week customs, superstitions, beliefs and rituals associated with farming, Pentecost, Corpus Christi, midsummer, harvest festival, wedding rites, namedays, birth and death. Line illustrations complete this rich and varied treasury of folklore. Now updated with a new chapter on "Customs for Kids"!
340 pages • 0-7818-0515-5 • $19.95hc • (500)

POLISH HERBS, FLOWERS & FOLK MEDICINE
by Sophie Hodorowicz Knab
Besides taking the reader on a guided tour through monastery, castle and cottage gardens, this book provides details on over one hundred herbs and flowers and how they were used in folk medicine as well as in everyday life, traditions, and customs.
207 pages • illus, woodcuts • 0-7818-0319-5 • $19.95hc • (573)

SONG, DANCE & CUSTOMS OF PEASANT POLAND
by Sula Benet with a Preface from Margaret Mead
"This charming fable-like book is one long remembrance of rural, peasant Poland which almost does not exist anymore... but it is worthwhile to safeguard the memeory of what once was... because what [Benet] writes is a piece of all of us, now in the past but very much a part of our cultural background."
—Przeglad Polski
247 pages • illus • 0-7818-0447-7 • $24.95hc • (209)

POLISH HERITAGE ART CALENDAR 1998

A Celebration of Wilno/Vilnius
Compiled by Jacek Galazka
with an Introduction by Jerzy R. Krzyznowski

The town of Wilno—now Vilnius—has played a prominent role in the history of Poles, Lithuanians, Jews, Byelorussians, Tartars, Germans, and Russians. Multi-ethnic, open to many cultural influences from the fifteenth century, home to many writers and scholars, Wilno has always attracted painters. In this unique tribute to a remarkable town and its enchanting setting, this, the twelfth edition of the popular calendar series, is dedicated to Wilno. The fourteen reproductions in full color celebrate the beauty of the town, its churches, castles, its summers and its winters, its sons and daughters, its rivers and surrounding countryside.

24 pages • 12 x 12 • 14 color illustrations
0-7818-0551-1 • $10.95 • (640)

COOKBOOKS

OLD POLISH TRADITIONS IN THE KITCHEN AND AT THE TABLE
A cookbook and history of Polish culinary customs. Short essays cover subjects like Polish hospitality, holiday traditions, even the exalted status of the mushroom. The recipes are traditional family fare.
304 pages • 0-7818-0488-4 • $11.95pb • (546)

POLISH HERITAGE COOKERY, Illlustrated Edition
by Robert & Maria Strybel
New illustrated edition of a bestseller with 20 color photographs! Over 2,200 recipes in 29 categories, written especially for Americans!
"An encyclopedia of Polish Cookery and a wonderful thing to have!"
—*Julia Child, Good Morning America*
"Polish Heritage Cookery is the best [Polish] cookcook printed on the English market!" —*Polish American Cultural Network*
915 pages • color photos • 0-7818-0558-9 • $39.95hc • (658)

OLD WARSAW COOKBOOK
by Rysia
Includes 850 authentic and easy to prepare Polish recipes.
300 pages • 0-87052-932-3 • $12.95pb • (536)

THE BEST OF POLISH COOKING, Revised Edition
by Karen West
"A charming offering of Polish cuisine with lovely woodcuts throughout."
—*Publishers Weekly*
219 pages • 0-7818-0123-3 • $8.95pb • (391)

All prices subject to change. **TO PURCHASE HIPPOCRENE BOOKS** contact your local bookstore, call (718) 454-2366, or write to: HIPPOCRENE BOOKS, 171 Madison Avenue, New York, NY 10016. Please enclose check or money order, adding $5.00 shipping (UPS) for the first book and $.50 for each additional book.